ARTANDFILM

BRITISH FILM INSTITUTE

bfi

BFI PUBLISHING

Hayward Gallery

First published in 1996 by the
Hayward Gallery, London, and the
British Film Institute, 21 Stephen Street,
London W1P 2LN, on the occasion of
the exhibition *Spellbound: Art and Film*,
organised by the Hayward Gallery in
collaboration with the British Film Institute

Exhibition curated by
Ian Christie and Philip Dodd

Exhibition organised by
Greg Hilty and Fiona Griffith

Cover: Douglas Gordon, *24 Hour Psycho*,
1993 (detail), installation shot,
photograph by Mike Fear

Catalogue edited by
Philip Dodd with Ian Christie
Sub-edited by Joanna Skipwith
Picture edited by Millie Simpson
Designed by Esterson Lackersteen
with Adam Brown and Stephen Coates
Printed by The Beacon Press, UK

British Library Cataloguing
in Publication Data
A catalogue record for this book
is available from the British Library

ISBN 0 85170 610 X

*Spellbound: Art and Film* is distributed
by Plymbridge Distributors Limited in
the UK on behalf of BFI Publishing
Tel: 01752 202301; fax: 01752 202331

Hayward Gallery, National Touring
Exhibitions and Arts Council Collection
publications are distributed by
Cornerhouse Publications
70 Oxford Street, Manchester M1 5NH
Tel: 0161 237 9662; fax: 0161 237 9664

*Spellbound: Art and Film*

The Centenary of Cinema is celebrated in Britain in 1996, one hundred years after the Lumière Brothers' first public film screenings in London. The Centenary offers a wonderful opportunity to celebrate the twentieth century's great art form, but it also calls for an appreciation of how widely, and how profoundly, film as a medium and cinema as an industry have influenced, and been influenced by, the other contemporary arts.

The Hayward Gallery and the British Film Institute are delighted to combine forces to present *Spellbound: Art and Film*. This innovative exhibition emerged out of a desire to explore, and to encourage, the close links that have always existed between film and the 'fine arts', as they are still known, including the media of painting, drawing, sculpture, printmaking, photography, performance and installation. By pooling the knowledge, skills, contacts and resources of our two institutions we have sought to create an event that is cross-disciplinary in the fullest and most creative sense of the phrase.

The exhibition is accompanied by a range of jointly organised educational activities, by this exhibition catalogue co-published by the Hayward Gallery and the British Film Institute, and by a special supplement to the April issue of *Sight and Sound* magazine.

Complementing *Spellbound* at the Hayward Gallery is a season of events at the Royal Festival Hall and the National Film Theatre, designed to highlight the dynamic interplay between film and music, film and literature, film and fashion.

The link between the British Film Institute, particularly its public venues, the National Film Theatre and Museum of the Moving Image, and the SBC, the Hayward Gallery and the Royal Festival Hall, is a natural one. We are next door neighbours on London's South Bank, and share a mission to bring new art to a wide audience. Although we have often collaborated before, it has never been on such an ambitious scale.

Our collaboration on *Spellbound*, however, is not a matter of simple institutional convenience; it has arisen as testimony to the vibrant interaction between the art forms themselves, to the close and often direct response that artists and film-makers have to each other's work, and, above all, to the capacity of ever-increasing audiences to enjoy a wide view of what constitutes the visual culture of our age.

*Nicholas Snowman*
Chief Executive,
SBC

*Wilf Stevenson*
Director,
British Film Institute

*Spellbound* brings together ten highly original visual imaginations to show the complex relationship between film and art in contemporary Britain. In exploring the pervasiveness and power of the cinematic image, the exhibition also deliberately attempts to undercut familiar distinctions between 'high' and 'low' art, between notions of the 'popular' and the 'avant-garde', and between the institutions of 'art' and 'film'.

Around the world, many film exhibitions have been prepared to mark the centenary of the invention of cinema in 1895-6. These projects can be divided roughly into two types: those that examine the history of cinema itself and those that bear witness to the current widespread tendency for contemporary artists to use film and video, and to draw upon the history of the moving image as much as on the history of more traditional art. Of the former type, there have been ambitious examples over the past 12 months in Berlin, Paris, and Zürich. Among the latter, notable examples have been *Wild Walls* in Amsterdam and the *Biennale de Lyon*, both devoted to the moving image, and indeed our own National Touring Exhibition, *The British Art Show 4* (travelling from Manchester to Edinburgh and Cardiff), which demonstrates through its selection of artists and works just how strong this tendency is. A major exhibition at the Museum of Contemporary Art in Los Angeles, examining in depth the historical links between post-war art and film, also opens this Spring.

Our own priorities were established early on: that any project we undertook should involve the creative collaboration of practising artists and film-makers, in roughly equal numbers and working on equal terms; and that its narrative should be driven by the memories, imaginings, and personal and generational histories of the participants themselves. The final defining criterion for the exhibition that has become

*Spellbound* was that all its participants should have been born in Britain or have lived here for a substantial period. What could have seemed a parochial restriction has in fact proved remarkably liberating, as it has allowed us to look in depth at a single, though many-faceted, national culture: Britain today has been shaped by dialogues with so many other cultures. There are also many outstanding artists and film-makers working here.

The exhibition has been curated by Ian Christie and Philip Dodd. Ian Christie, jointly responsible for the Hayward exhibitions *Film as Film* in 1977 and *Eisenstein* in 1988, is known as a distinguished film historian and author, most notably on Powell and Pressburger and Martin Scorsese; formerly Head of Special Projects at the British Film Institute, he is now a Fellow at Magdalen College, Oxford, where he is bringing film studies into the University curriculum. Philip Dodd, formerly an academic, is currently Editor of *Sight and Sound* and Deputy Head of Research and Education, British Film Institute. In his dual career he has written widely on both art and film and has, from the early 1980s, been at the forefront of redefining thinking about British national identity, most recently with the political think-tank DEMOS. We are enormously grateful to both curators, and to the British Film Institute's Director Wilf Stevenson, who has actively supported their engagement with this project. Ian Christie and Philip Dodd have applied their distinct sensibilities to devise a complex and innovative exhibition over a relatively short period of time. The word 'curate' scarcely does justice to their close liaison with artists and the nurturing of ideas that have underpinned the development of this show, or to their involvement in the details of fundraising and production for a number of ambitious new works.

At the outset, we received valuable advice

towards defining the scope of this project from Dave Curtis, Lutz Becker, Simon Field, and John Wyver.

To the participating artists (for which, read artists and film-makers throughout) – Fiona Banner, Terry Gilliam, Douglas Gordon, Peter Greenaway, Damien Hirst, Steve McQueen, Eduardo Paolozzi, Paula Rego, Ridley Scott and Boyd Webb – we owe a profound debt of gratitude. Most striking have been the faith and enthusiasm with which they embraced the idea and format of this exhibition and recognised its ambition to go beyond standard practices so as to reach the heart of its subject. Early discussions were based on a deliberately open brief. Each artist's response has led to works in a wide variety of media which, we believe, both achieve internal coherence and match the overall range we originally sought.

On behalf of the Hayward Gallery and the British Film Institute, together with the artists themselves, we should like to thank the many people who have made this exhibition possible, including all those mentioned by name in the Artists' Credits section. For their key roles in co-ordinating the participation of individual artists and production of specific works, we thank in particular Glyn Williams, for Terry Gilliam; Eliza Poklewski Koziel and Renier van Brummelen, for Peter Greenaway; Nira Park, for Damien Hirst; Polly Nash, for Steve McQueen; Nick Gorse, for Eduardo Paolozzi; Julie Payne, for Ridley Scott; and Pamela Asbury, for Boyd Webb.

The exhibition has been designed by architect Tony Fretton, whose probing sensibility and energy have contributed greatly to the form and therefore the meaning of the show. We warmly thank him and his assistant, S. Kari Karason.

Sincere thanks are due to Tony Jones of Cityscreen and the Clapham Picture House for help with obtaining cinema seating; to Blitz Vision for their audio-visual expertise; and to David Bouchier of Olswang for legal advice.

We are most grateful to all those involved in the writing and production of this catalogue, particularly the authors, who were often working to tight deadlines and writing about work they could not yet see in a finished form; Vicky Allan, Arts Council Trainee with *Sight and Sound*, for compiling the chronology and much else; picture editors Millie Simpson and Hannah Tyson; sub-editors Joanna Skipwith and Vicky Wilson; proof-reader Clio Whittaker; Neus Miro; the designers at Esterson Lackersteen; Caroline Moore for her valuable work, especially on the catalogue; and the staff of *Sight and Sound* particularly Collette O'Reilly and Rebecca Russell.

We greatly appreciate the contribution of the Artists' Film and Video Distribution Fund of the Arts Council of England in supporting the production of new works in film by Damien Hirst and Boyd Webb.

Finally, we should like to record here our thanks to all those members of staff, too numerous to mention individually, from the British Film Institute, from the Hayward Gallery and more widely across the SBC, who have worked on this project with great dedication and skill.

*Henry Meyric Hughes*
Director,
Hayward Gallery

*Greg Hilty*
Senior Curator,
Hayward Gallery

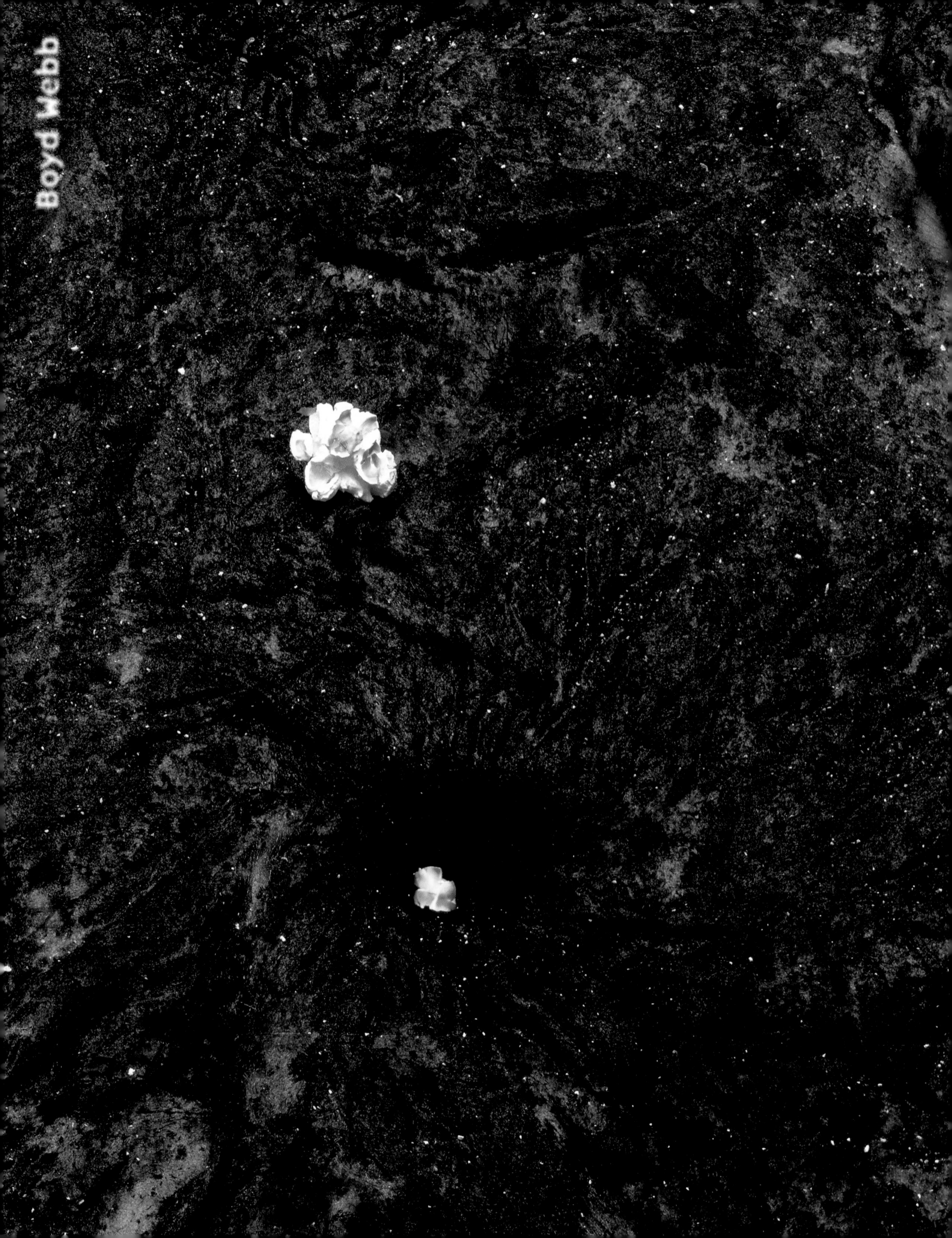
Boyd Webb

17

Douglas Gordon

5 YEAR DRIVE-BY  :   proposal for public art project


To reconstitute the narrative of
John Ford's film 'The Searchers'
in such a way as to stretch the
cinema duration (113 minutes) back
to what was the original, literal
narrative (5 years).

So, if 113 minutes is to become
extended to 5 years...


|   |              |   |                    |
|---|--------------|---|--------------------|
|   | 113 minutes  | : | 5 years,           |
| = | 113 minutes  | : | 1826 days,         |
| = | 113 minutes  | : | 43824 hours,       |
| = | 113 minutes  | : | 2629440 minutes,   |
| = | 1 minute     | : | 23269.38 minutes,  |
| = | 1 second     | : | 23269.38 seconds,  |
| = | 24 frames    | : | 23269.38 seconds,  |
| = | 1 frame      | : | 969.5575 seconds,  |
| = | 1 frame      | : | 16.159291 minutes  |

Damien Hirst

# TEXT

Cinema is text-driven. Despite those who would argue that cinema is a visual medium, the origin of practically every one of its products — like 90 per cent ... manufactur... ... as paint... and most of the history of painting ...

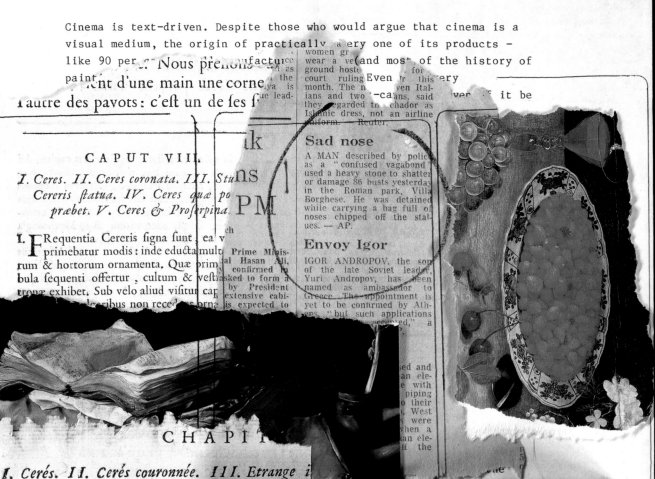

Nous prenons ...
...nt d'une main une corne...
l'autre des pavots : c'est un de ses f...

**CAPUT VIII.**

I. Ceres. II. Ceres coronata. III. Stu...
Cereris ſtatua. IV. Ceres quæ po...
præbet. V. Ceres & Proſerpina...

I. FRequentia Cereris ſigna ſunt, ea v...
primebatur modis : inde educta mult...
rum & hortorum ornamenta. Quæ prim...
bula ſequenti offertur, cultum & veſti...
tronæ exhibet. Sub velo aliud viſitur cap...
...eribus non rece...t orna...is expected to

**Sad nose**

A MAN described by polic... as a "confused vagabond" used a heavy stone to shatter or damage 86 busts yesterday in the Roman park, Villa Borghese. He was detained while carrying a bag full of noses chipped off the statues. — AP.

**Envoy Igor**

IGOR ANDROPOV, the son of the late Soviet leader, Yuri Andropov, has been named as ambassador to Greece. The appointment is yet to be confirmed by Ath... "but such applications ... a

**CHAPIT...**

I. Cerés. II. Cerés couronnée. III. Etrange i...
...donne à boire. V. C...

I. L Es mon...
rentes n...
de la planche f...
laiſſe voir un orn...
gulier : elle tien...
de l'autre main...
d'épis, tient en...
failles, copiée...
core³ pour C...
une gerbe & ...
Baccante, ou...
nitez qui alloient ſouvent enſemble. L'a...
figure eſt peu reconnoiſſable, eſt un tigre q...

## Panel 1 (top-left)

Cinema is text-driven. Despite those who would argue that cinema is a
visual medium, the origin of practically every one of its products -
like 90 per cent of all manufactured images (and most of the history of
painting till the mid 1850s) - is text-based. Even now every
post-illusionist painting invariably has a text-caption - even if it be
"untitled". One could say the industry of the constructed image is
primarily a history of illustration - a second-hand industry.

Curiously, cinema's spin-off technologies are - though televisual in
name - seriously text-driven in nature and practice. Literacy is a
high-demand necessity with E-mail, the Internet, the CD-ROM, not to
mention 50 per cent of broadcast TV, and Teletext and Fax. But then
from high-street to designer-label clothes we are text-obsessed. The
manipulation of information is the manipulation of text. Derrida's wry
"The image has the last word" is equivocal, if not null and void, since
the word itself is an image. "In the beginning was the word" - all
faiths are text-substantiated, none more so than the secular faiths.
And cinema? I am not so sure we have seen any cinema yet - even after
a hundred years. Perhaps all we have seen is illustrated text -
cinema's prologue.

All of which ..... implies we must find a text, many texts. What better
than the daily newspaper? Build a long table - same length as the
props-table - marked off in dates in the same way - and place, day by
day, 100 copies of the day's newspaper - the text of the day
(information with attitude) - news, gossip, trials, crime and
punishment, accident, misfortune, scandal - the raw material of the
stuff of cinema - from its self-reflexive subject-use of Citizen Kane -
newspaper-hero-villain ....
We might well exhibit a broadsheet and a tabloid - opened out to
present page one. The Guardian and the Independent's front page, laid
flat, measure approximately 15x22 inches. The Sun and Mirror measure
12x15. Make a fixed space on the table of 24x30 inches (with an
overlap) for each day's news.
The newspapers are to be delivered to the Gallery each morning. The
string that wraps the newspaper (do they still use string?) to be
kept.

## Panel 2 (top-right)

## Panel 3 (bottom-left)

IN THE DARK

ACTORS

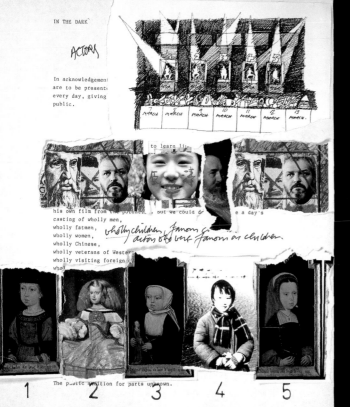

In acknowledgement
are to be presented
every day, giving
public.

to learn li

his own film from the potential ... but we could do ... a day's
casting of wholly men,
wholly fatmen,            wholly children, famous g
wholly women,                actors who were famous as children.
wholly Chinese,
wholly veterans of Wester
wholly visiting foreign
who

The public ambition for parts unknown.

1    2    3    4    5

## Panel 4 (bottom-right)

ILLUSION

On the wall/screen above
projection-white - are 10
longest-lasting cinema-sc
lighting-effect familiar
water, fire, fog, rain, f

We might expand this - po
same screen, and include
the Scottish moor, the ai
... erior, the lift-sha ...
...

HYDROBIOLOGIE

Paula Rego

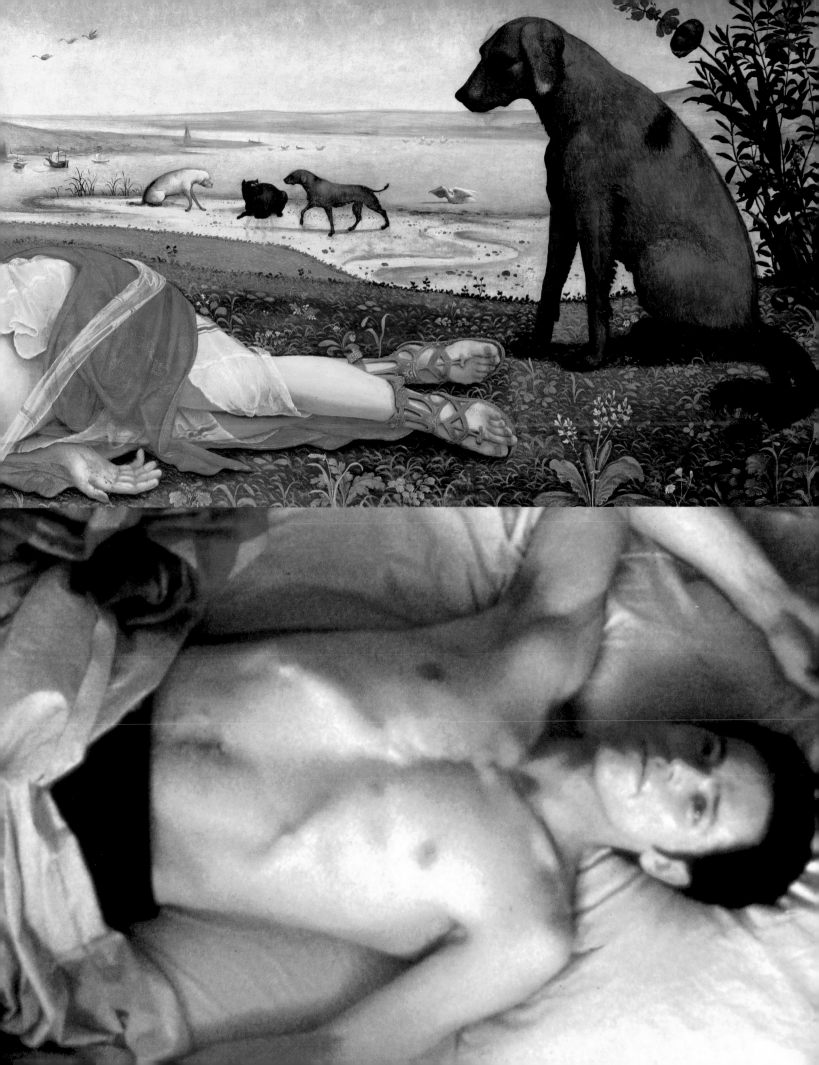

Opposite:
*Colour Box* (1935),
an abstract film
made by Len Lye,
who considered
himself part of
the art community.

# Modern Stories

## By Philip Dodd

1. See the catalogues of the two most recent surveys of new British art, *The British Art Show 4*, South Bank Centre, 1995, and *Brilliant!: New Art From London*, Walker Art Center, Minneapolis, 1995.
2. The male protagonist of *sex, lies and videotape*, who is emotionally impotent, satisfies himself by making do with a camcorder; the protagonist of Michael Haneke's *Benny's Video* (1992) is an alienated 15-year-old who videos various brutal events, including his murder of a girl.
3. See Thomas Elsaesser, 'Rivette and the End of Cinema' in *Sight and Sound*, vol. 1, issue 12, 1991–2, pp. 20–3.
4. The shorthand term for summarising, if not explaining, these changes is post-modernism. The literature is legion: for an early example, see Hal Foster, ed., *Postmodern Culture*, Bay Press, Port Townsend, 1983; for a recent example, which makes very interesting connections between post-modernism and that seedbed of both artists and film-makers, the art school, see, Alex Seago, *Burning the Box of Beautiful Things: The Development of a Post-Modern Sensibility*, Oxford University Press, Oxford, 1995.

These are the best of times and the worst of times to mount a show such as *Spellbound*, with its ambition of revealing the extraordinary richness of the relationship between art and film in contemporary Britain. For the Jeremiahs of the art world, this miscegenation is no cause for celebration, more a confirmation that these are the worst of times. The 1990s for them has been a continuing nightmare, reminiscent of some scene from *Invasion of the Body Snatchers*, with film as the alien force supplanting painting and sculpture in the hearts of the good men and women of the art world. It is not that high profile names such as Robert Longo, David Salle and Julian Schnabel have moved into feature films, with, respectively, *Johnny Mnemonic*, *Search and Destroy* and a biopic about the artist Basquiat (these artists could be dismissed as also-rans). It is not even that these artists have chosen to make Hollywood feature films rather than artists' films, which at least have a genteel pedigree. Most disheartening is the fact that the new generation of artists working in Britain, and enjoying recognition here and abroad, have taken to film and video not as light relief from their 'real' work but as a central and absorbing activity. It is the air they breathe. This is as true of Jane and Louise Wilson and Sam Taylor-Wood (not in the show) as of Fiona Banner, Steve McQueen and Damien Hirst.[1]

Matters are not much better for the paranoid among the film world. Here the fight to have cinema established as a high art may have been won, at long last. But as it reaches its 100th birthday film, as understood by the cinephiles, now seems to be threatened by new technology. Sometimes the threat to cinema is said to come from computer and digital technology, which promises to make the photographic image entirely redundant. Sometimes the threat comes from cheap technology such as the camcorder, which offers to make everyone an auteur, at least in principle. This is something viewed with such horror by the cinephile community that the camcorder has become a sign of corruption, whether in Hollywood independents such as *sex, lies and videotape*, or auteur European art cinema such as *Benny's Video*.[2] Is it any wonder that beleaguered European directors are making films about the lives of painters, such as *La Belle Noiseuse* and *The Quince Tree Sun*, as a way of reflecting on their own melancholy fate, in the way that painters once made paintings about the Old Masters when threatened by the rise of photography and film?[3]

For others, on the other hand, these are the best of times to mount the exhibition *Spellbound*. The art/film interpenetration is stronger than it has been for some time. And this is no accident; it is a matter of historical change. Much of the way we have traditionally thought about art and film, their relationship with one another and with the wider culture no longer holds sway. The relationship between such apparently opposed terms as experimental and mainstream, high and low, popular and avant-garde – as well as perhaps the most tricky of them all, British and modern – can now be reassessed, together with the history from which they sprang.[4] With the collapse of these binary oppositions, it is easier to mount such a promiscuous exhibition as *Spellbound*, which opts for a principled eclecticism, mixing popular and art film-makers together with artists from several generations and cultural backgrounds, staging films made by artists and film-makers' installations, and stirring together cinema as memory (Rego and Paolozzi) and cinema-as-society-of-the-spectacle (Banner). *Spellbound* has committed itself to working with artists and film-makers who work in Britain, not on some misguided 'Little Englander' principle (the identities of the exhibitors put paid to that) but precisely because the art/film relationship has been very strong in Britain. Indeed, the underlying argument of the show is that by grasping the relationship of art and film in Britain, we are forced not only to revise the orthodox histories of British art and film but also to recognise (and admire) British culture's wider ambitions.

This is not to say that the old paradigms did not produce good work. It is simply that the terms used to describe that work initially no longer seem appropriate or illuminating. In the 1970s, during the heyday of structuralist film-making, an

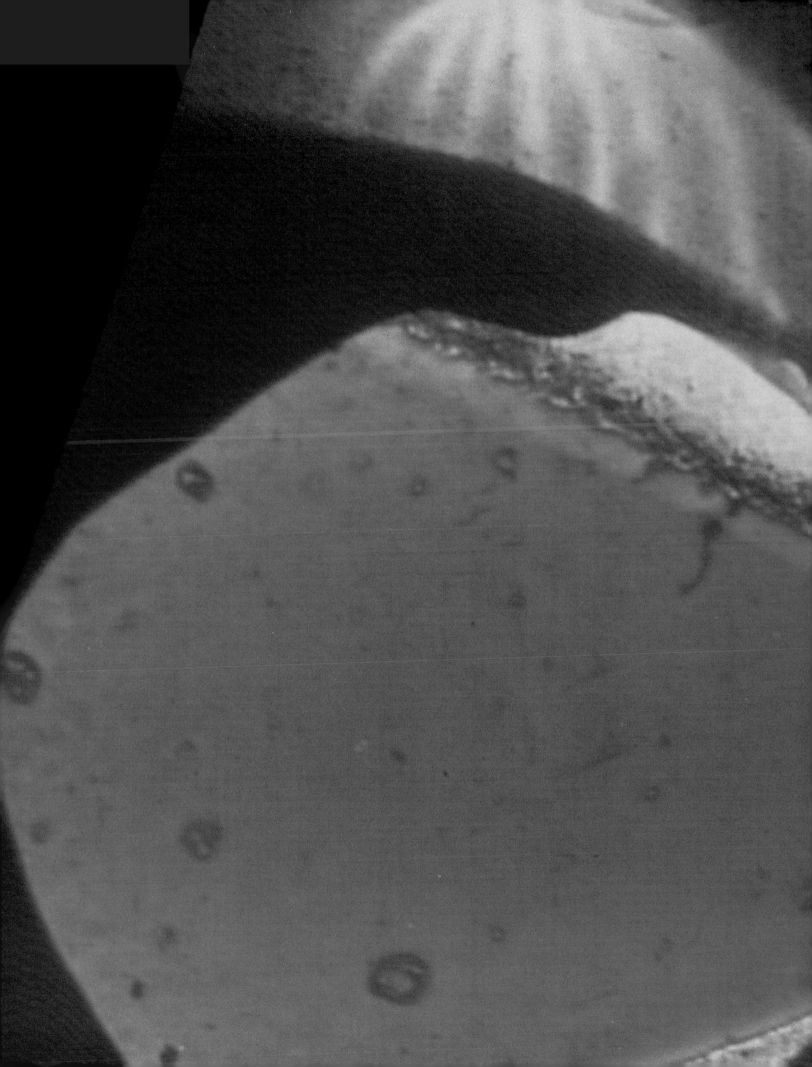

5. See *Undercut*, 7/8, Spring 1983, a special issue devoted to 'Landscape in Film, Photography and Video'.

6. Raymond Williams's strenuous account of the avante-garde as a cultural formation is the best antidote for those who wish to claim that a work's formal self-reflexiveness is a sufficient condition of its avant-garde status. See Williams, *The Politics of Modernism: Against the New Conformists*, Verso, London, 1989.

7. See David Mellor's 'Situation; 1960–3' in *The Sixties Art Scene in London* , Phaidon Press, London, 1993, pp. 75–92 (the catalogue for the Barbican show of the same name).

8. Charles Harrison, *English Art and Modernism 1900–1939*, Allen Lane, London, 1981.

9. *Sickert Paintings*, Wendy Baron and Richard Shone, eds. ,Yale University Press, New Haven and London, 1992, p. 344.

10. Virginia Woolf, 'The Cinema' reprinted in *The Captain's Death Bed*. On Bloomsbury as the heart of English painting, see Harrison, *op. cit.*; also Philip Dodd, 'How Ben Nicholson proved that you can be British and Modern' in *Tate: The art magazine*, 1, Winter 1993, pp. 30–6.

11. Roger Horrocks, 'Len Lye: The Career of an Independent FilmMaker' in *Film Library Quarterly*, 14, 1981, pp. 4–22.

Top:
Alfred Wallis,
*Wreck of the Alba*
(c. 1939).
Above:
John Grierson's
*Drifters* (1929).

important series of screenings of *Avant-Garde British Landscape Films* was held at the Tate Gallery.[5] But from the standpoint of the 1990s, these films look avant-garde only at a formal level and only when seen in relationship to a certain notion of commercial cinema; within a more adequate historical understanding of what counts as the avant-garde they would not even pass first base.[6] But more interesting is the fact that if looked at in terms of the history of art, these films seem to add little to Monet's concern with time and landscape painting: hardly an avant-garde strategy by the 1970s.

The tragedy is that there have been no major intellectual spaces in which to explore the rich and complex relationship between art and film in Britain. A debate might start with the obvious, painters using feature-film imagery in their work, but it would also have to consider the way that the work of British abstract painters such as Robyn Denny has been shaped by a cinematic language.[7] In the same way, discussion of the importance of art to film-makers working in Britain might well begin with that most overused term, 'painterly films', but would need to go on to address the specific character of the art worlds from which film-makers such as Ridley Scott or Peter Greenaway have emerged.

If there is a failure to grasp the importance of the relationship between art and film in Britain, then perhaps the finger should be pointed initially at the custodians of art and film, the scholars. But here it is not a matter of some moral failing on the part of individuals, more a matter of the power of the disciplinary boundaries that exist, whether within the academy or the newspaper. It has also been damaging that film studies, at least since the 1960s, have been dominated by people with literary backgrounds, unable to make the necessary art connections. But even among people who can, the connections are not often made (and this includes art as well as film historians). Charles Harrison's study *English Art and Modernism 1900–1939*,[8] for example, an exemplary account in many ways, pays no attention to cinema, even though the period he covers was precisely the time when art had to come to terms with cinema. After all, the most cursory glance at such an important figure as Sickert shows him moving from painting a cinema as early as 1912 to re-examining his whole approach to painting in the 1930s, in relation to the dominance of photography and cinema (consider the painting *Jack and Jill*[9]). For further anecdotal evidence about the visibility of film in art circles, one need look no further than Virginia Woolf's 1926 troubled essay 'The Cinema' – written from Bloomsbury, then the heart of the English art world – which proclaims 'that some residue of visual emotion which is of no use either to painter or to poet may still await the cinema'.[10]

Even when Charles Harrison does refer to film it is only to William Coldstream's engagement with film (and presumably only then because he was principally a painter). This means that there is no reference to the extraordinary films of Len Lye, even though Lye saw himself as a fine artist and even though he was one of the members of the *Seven & Five Society* (which Harrison discusses at length and whose membership he prints in an appendix). But the connection of Lye with art is not a matter of formal membership of a Society. There are real connections between apparently unrelated figures such as Len Lye and, for example, Ben Nicholson: their common passion for 'primitives' (Nicholson's for Alfred Wallis, Lye for aboriginal art), their common desire to work more 'directly' with their materials (Lye by scratching or painting directly on to film, Nicholson by turning his canvases into 'the carver's block').[11] It is not simply admiration for Lye that makes me lament the fact that he falls between the orthodox histories of the two art forms and into the ghetto of 'experimental film' (a catch-all term, if ever there was one); it is a sense that to condemn Nicholson and Lye to separate histories is to relinquish the opportunity of weighing up the rich complexities of British visual culture between the two World Wars. In the same vein, while it may be useful to see the connections between Nicholson's 'adoption' of Alfred Wallis and that of Henri Rousseau by avant-garde artists such as Delaunay and Picasso, it is more useful to reflect on the connection between the discovery of the Cornish artist-fisherman and John

12. See Kathryn Dodd and Philip Dodd, 'Engendering the Nation: Documentary Film 1930–39' in Andrew Higson, ed., *Dissolving Views: Key Writings on British Cinema*, Cassell, London, 1996, pp. 38–50.

13. See Alan Lovell and Jim Hillier, 'Free Cinema' in *Studies in Documentary*, Secker and Warburg, 1972, pp. 133–75.

14. David Curtis, *Experimental Cinema: A Fifty-Year Evolution*, Studio Vista, London, 1971.

15. The author in conversation with the Alien Effects Designers of *Alien³*, 'Kaleidoscope', Radio 4, 15 July 1992.

16. Whistler, 'The Red Rag' (1878) reproduced in J.M. Whistler, *The Gentle Art of Making Enemies*, 1892, p. 128.

17. Greenaway saw Kitaj's paintings at the Marlborough Gallery in the 1960s. Author in conversation with Peter Greenaway, 'Kaleidoscope', Radio 4, 22 June 1991.

18. In R.S. Lambert, *Art in England* (1938), quoted in Harrison, *op. cit.*, p. 338.

Dialogue:
The nurse from Eisenstein's *Battleship Potemkin* (top). Francis Bacon's *Study for the Nurse in the Film* Battleship Potemkin, (Bottom) 1957.

connection between the discovery of the Cornish artist-fisherman and John Grierson's contemporaneous 'discovery' of his fishermen heroes in his first documentary, *Drifters*. What drew such metropolitan men, committed to the visual arts, to the peripheries of Britain in search of these new icons?[12]

Not that film historians have been more alert to the art/film connections than art historians. Read an account of *Free Cinema*, the 1950s movement that provided the personnel for feature films such as *Saturday Night and Sunday Morning* and *This Sporting Life*, and you would hardly know that *Together*, a film made by Lorenza Mazzetti in collaboration with the artists Eduardo Paolozzi and Michael Andrews, was part of the first *Free Cinema* programme at the National Film Theatre. Yet attention to *Together* – which plays with the 'realist' language of British documentary, by charging it, through the score and through Paolozzi's and Andrews's 'dumb' performances, with a surrealist idiom – calls into doubt the wearisome critical conviction that *Free Cinema* was realist. Equally it should make us alert to the surrealist elements in other *Free Cinema* films, Lindsay Anderson's *O Dreamland*, for example.[13]

There have been histories of and screening programmes based on the intersection of art and film in Britain, but they shelter under the umbrella of experimental film (which at one time tied itself in with performance art, at another with a particular film movement). There are two problems with this. Firstly, even the best of these histories, David Curtis's *Experimental Cinema: A Fifty-Year Evolution*,[14] for example, tend, as the title of Curtis's book suggests, to see experimental film as some self-contained evolutionary creature, passing on the gene of 'experiment' from one generation to the next. They rarely show how these films connect with other art or film histories, particularly within national cultures. Secondly, to shunt the art/film connection into the 'experimental' siding – or to focus on the 'video art' that emerged in the late 1960s – is to underestimate its centrality to that most hybrid of creatures, British culture, and to fail to see how it has insinuated itself into its heart during the century. After all, Britain is a place where a well-established English painter could set up his own film studio in the early part of the century; where Lázló Moholy-Nagy, a Hungarian émigré artist, could work on *Things to Come*, a major British feature film, as early as 1935; where the artist Francis Bacon could make a painting from the film *Battleship Potemkin*, and where one of his own paintings, *Three Studies for Figures at the Base of a Crucifixion* (1944), could in turn provide the inspiration for the 'look' of the creature in the popular film series *Alien*;[15] and where Ken Russell and Derek Jarman, two former art-school students, could come together in the early 1970s as, respectively, film director and designer to make a number of commercial films including *The Devils* and *Savage Messiah*.

The richness of the relationship between art and film in Britain obviously includes their historical rivalry, which was foreshadowed when still photography took hold in the late nineteenth century, prompting Whistler to claim that art now had to do something else: 'in portrait painting to put on canvas something more than the face the model wears for that day, to paint the man, in short, as well as his features'.[16] In this sense art and film each define what the other is not. Equally the relationship has included envy for what the other can do, which in Peter Greenaway's case led him to turn his 'envy' into ambition by deciding to make films of the density that he found in R.B. Kitaj's paintings.[17] In the case of William Coldstream, his envy for the popularity of film led him to abandon painting temporarily in the 1930s 'to work in some medium which is by its nature more essentially of the present age, more easily accessible to a large number of people.'[18] It is reasonable to claim that Coldstream's view sums up the dominant view of the art/film relationship, with its *Animal Farm*-like bleat: Film/Popular/Good, Art/Elite/Bad. (There is of course a variant of this: Film/Popular/Bad, Art/Elite/Good.) This has blighted thinking about art and film for several reasons. First, it tends to equate the cinema with film, without being aware that cinema may be popular, but film not; and second, by emphasising the popularity of film, its aesthetic potential is

Opposite:
memories of a
fine art. Ridley
Scott's *Alien*
(1979), the look
of whose
creature was
partly inspired
by Bacon's
paintings.

Echoes and
Premonitions:
Francis Bacon,
*Three Studies for
Figures at the
Base of a
Crucifixion* (1944).

19. The writing on Britishness and Englishness continues to grow: see Tom Nairn, *The Break-up of Britain*, Verso, London; Robert Colls and Philip Dodd, *Englishness: Politics and Culture 1880–1920*, Croom Helm, London, 1986; Alison Light, *Forever England: Femininity, Literature and Conservatism Between the Wars*, Routledge, London, 1991; Philip Dodd, *The Battle over Britain*, Demos, London, 1995.

20. Michael Powell, *Million-Dollar Movie*, William Heinemann, London, 1992, pp. 166–7; on modernism and whiteness see Mark Wigley, 'White-Out: Fashioning the Modern', *Assemblage* 22, 1993, pp. 6–49.

21. See Philip Dodd, 'Englishness and the National Culture' in *Englishness: Politics and Culture 1880–1920, op. cit.*, pp. 1–28.

22. Sidney Lee, 'The Place of English Literature in the Modern University', *Elizabethan and Other Essays by Sir Sidney Lee*, Frederick Boas, ed., Clarendon Press, Oxford, 1929, p. 4.

23. Terry Eagleton, 'A Suitable Case for Treatment', *The Guardian.*. 18 March 1993.

Derek Jarman:
One of the
*Caravaggio*-
related works
exhibited during
his Turner Prize
nomination.

ignored. In the case of Coldstream this was a tragedy; if he could have brought back to his painting some of the formal inventiveness of the film he made with Benjamin Britten and the Brazilian Alberto Cavalcanti, the Euston Road School might have been remembered for something other than solemn glumness. Of course not all artists have moved into film to court popularity – what aesthetic possibilities, for instance, did the sculptor Phillip King believe the medium offered him when he made his only film, and why did he not try to repeat the experiment?

Indeed if 'popular' were the touchstone of value (which it is not) then it might well be argued that the early 1950s print-work of some of The Independent Group – which made use of imagery from popular culture, not least cinema – showed more respect for the popular than a film of the same period such as Lindsay Anderson's *O Dreamland*, which patronised popular culture in the same 'candy floss' terms that Richard Hoggart used a few years later in *The Uses of Literacy*.

The variety of conjunctions between film and art in Britain inevitably confirms one's bewilderment that the relationship has been rendered so marginal, even invisible. But it would be foolish to point the finger exclusively, or even primarily, at the 'blindness' of art history and film history. Perhaps at least one powerful explanation is to be found in the fact that the art/film connection cannot be easily accommodated within the terms that have structured cultural debate in Britain for too long, where one has been forced to choose between being modern (and modernist) or being British.[19]

The difficulty for art and film is that it falls between the two camps. Since the modernist position was that all art aspires to the condition of music, then art aspiring to film looked like some illegitimate family member, insufficiently pure to be seen in modernist terms. Or rather it has been possible to subsume certain kinds of art films under this rubric (the experimental) but not others. What would modernist tenets have to say about set design, a crucial but undervalued component of film: the projected Michael Powell collaboration with Graham Sutherland, for example, or the Russell/Jarman *The Devils*, where the modernist white city of Loudon looks like some analogue for the authoritarianism of its ruler? The truth is that modernism cannot easily find a place for such an 'impure art'.[20]

But if the conjunction art/film is not principally modernist, it is still no easier to fit within received notions of what it is to be 'British', which, over the century, has come to mean anti-modern. (The connection between art and film is, whatever else, undeniably modern.) In these circumstances it is more than a coincidence that the first stirrings of film in Britain were at a moment when what it was to be British was being redefined in ways that still bear down on us today. Around 1896, for example, the year when film was first shown commercially in Britain, the National Portrait Gallery moved into its own building, the Tate Gallery was about to open, English Literature had just begun to be taught as a subject at Oxford University, and the *Dictionary of National Biography* and *The New (Oxford) English Dictionary* were in the process of being established.[21] This 'nationalisation' was couched in distinctly non-modern (and perhaps anti-modern) terms. What it was to be British was always a matter of precedent, perhaps nowhere more clearly expressed than in the opening lecture given by Sidney Lee, editor of the *DNB* and Professor of English at University College, London, who believed that contemporary literature ought to be kept out of the universities until it could match up to its predecessors.[22]

Centred on the universities and public schools this new national identity began to celebrate the importance to that identity of the national literature. Traces of this assumption of the superiority of writing can be found in the words of Terry Eagleton, a current Professor of English Literature at Oxford University, who recently said of his collaboration with the late Derek Jarman on the film *Wittgenstein* that all the ideas were the scriptwriter's since it was impossible to think in visual terms.[23]

Beginnings and endings: *The Devils,* the story of the destruction of Loudon, directed by Ken Russell; Derek Jarman was the design consultant.

24 See *Beyond the Crisis in Art*, Writers and Readers, London, 1980, passim.
25 The only sustained account of the importance of art schools is Simon Frith and Howard Horne, *Art into Pop*, Methuen, London, 1987; see also John A Walker, *Cross Overs: Art into Pop; Pop into Art*, Comedia, London and New York, 1987.
26 Raphael Samuel, *Patriotism: The Making and Unmaking of British National Identity*, Routledge, London, 1989, I, xxii.
27 Paul Gilroy, *The Black Atlantic: Modernity and Double Consciousness*, Verso, London, 1993.

Sur-real:
Eduardo Paolozzi as
one of the dumb men
in Lorenza
Mazzetti's *Together*.

Of course there have been other, very different, accounts of Britain and British culture in this century, but the idea of Britain as anti-modern continued into the 1980s, not least in the work of Peter Fuller – who championed an indigenous, provincial, non-modernist British art in opposition to what he saw as a bogus international modernism. The very logic of such principled provincialism was to resist what Fuller called the mega-visual world (by which he meant film, advertising etc.).[24] Fuller was swimming with a tide that brought with it a renewed fascination with the national/pastoral in British art. The 1980s, after all, was the decade when Turner was finally given his own home and the decade when a number of interesting shows about a certain strain of British art (or rather *mostly* English art) took place, not least *Landscape and British art 1850–1950* and *A Paradise Lost: The Neo-Romantic Imagination in Britain, 1935–55*.

But the fact that British visual culture has not been predominantly modernist does not mean (*pace* Peter Fuller) that it is necessarily provincial and insular. One of the claims that *Spellbound* makes is that, seen through the prism of art and film, British visual culture is promiscuous, outgoing and, to quote that former art-school student Mary Quant, 'looking, listening and ready to try anything new'. Modernist it may not have often been but modernising it has been, at least from the art schools' point of view (and why should we not claim that the art schools have been at least as central to British cultural life this century as the universities?).[25] Just add to the number of artists who have been produced by the art schools in the last 30 years, not only the fashion designers, musicians (John Lennon, David Bowie) and writers (Len Deighton, David Mercer, David Storey) but also the wide variety of film-makers (Ridley Scott, Sally Potter, Peter Greenaway, Ken Russell, Derek Jarman and Isaac Julien) and the argument about the centrality of art schools to British cultural life becomes axiomatic. And those art schools, and their products, have been nothing if not outward looking, heavily involved in the British import/export culture.

Yet, even though no one challenges the claim that the modern visual arts have tended towards the international (for cultural and industrial reasons), it still goes against the grain to agree that part of the distinctiveness of modern British visual culture is that it has been involved in the import/export business throughout this century. The historian Raphael Samuel, for example, has written recently that 'British Society between the two World Wars was peculiarly inward looking'.[26] But where would the evidence be in the visual arts? Not in the work of those two icons of Englishness, Henry Moore and John Piper, both involved with European Surrealism; nor in the work of Len Lye with its soundtracks of Caribbean music; nor in the epics of that Central-European exile living in England, Alexander Korda, whose films included the imperial *Four Feathers*; nor in the movement to Hollywood of such British talent as Alfred Hitchcock and Cary Grant; nor in the central role played by English fashion designers in Parisian *haute couture*?

To note the variety of artists in *Spellbound* alone is to have the import/export thesis confirmed in the most obvious sense. It is not merely a question of biographical histories, although there is that: Boyd Webb is from New Zealand, Paula Rego from Portugal; Eduardo Paolozzi is Scottish-Italian and Steve McQueen British-Caribbean. It is much more the fact that for complex historical reasons British culture has stood at the crossroads of a number of cultures – and has given liberally and taken (sometimes ruthlessly) from them, whether they be European, American or from the former 'Empire'. The catalogue essays testify to the range of resources used by the artists in this show, but it may, nevertheless, be worth adding to these, since they are all ones that overturn orthodox assumptions. Martha Gever's essay on Steve McQueen, for example, quite rightly refers to Robert Mapplethorpe and Isaac Julien, but might also have talked in more detail about the resonance in McQueen's work of European art cinema, from Dreyer to Bresson, a connection that is not at all exceptional, according to Paul Gilroy's recent study of the relationship

28. On the emergence of the gothic and its place in British culture, see David Pirie, *A Heritage of Horror: The English Gothic Cinema 1946–72*, Gordon Fraser, London, 1973.

29. In conversation with the author, 3 March 1995.

30. On Wales and modernity, see Dai Smith, *Aneurin Bevin and the World of South Wales*, University of Cardiff Press, Cardiff, 1993.

The prestige of whiteness: Odeon, Leicester Square, 1937 (top). The Saatchi Gallery (bottom).

between black and European cultures.[27] If the traffic between the US and Britain is mostly seen as one way, then people need to be reminded not only that, with *Thelma and Louise*, Ridley Scott helped reinvigorate Hollywood cinema (not to mention the American landscape in films); but also that with *Blade Runner* and *Alien* he helped infuse American genre cinema with gothic imaginings, something that has a long provenance in British culture.[28] On the other hand, when asked recently why in 1964 he had alighted on Wittgenstein as a subject for his series of prints *As Is When*, Paolozzi responded that he was weary of everyone's lust after America and wanted to work on a 'serious' European intellectual.[29] (It is one of the hand-me-down clichés that Eduardo Paolozzi is in love with all things American.) Indeed, it might well be worth arguing that Paolozzi's memory of cinemas rather than films, particularly those of his youth, with their exotic oriental decorations and leopard-skin seats, served to inoculate him against the orthodoxies of the pure white (American) modernist gallery space.

The sad fact is that British art and film have suffered for too long from seeming like the Bates's Motel of their respective fields – somewhere off the main road and unable to shake off a traumatic past. Whatever else this show does, it takes a knife to that hoary old tale, by showing how omnivorous the artists and film-makers working here are, how mongrel a world Britain is. By doing this it also makes it possible to break up the unitary category 'British', which may be due for an overhaul in art and film as well as in the political arena. For although it would be reductive to isolate the fact that Douglas Gordon is Scottish and ignore his education at the Slade, or his generational affiliations and his position among a number of European artists, it may be equally reductive to ignore his Scottish identity – or to ignore the Calvinism that has shaped Scottish culture to such an extent. Calvinism, after all, is primarily concerned with what is at the core of *24 Hour Psycho*: unredeemable time and punishment. Or consider Peter Greenaway. While Thomas Elsaessar, in his illuminating essay, draws some persuasive comparisons between Greenaway and English landscape artists such as Richard Long, Greenaway's self-confessed absorption in 'excess' suggests less the minimalism of Richard Long and more his affiliation to a larger cultural Anglo-Welsh tradition (Greenaway has Welsh roots) that has – from the poet Gerard Manley Hopkins to the poet and artist David Jones – exploited excess to set itself apart from the dreary realism of the dominant English tradition – whether the Euston Road School or television naturalism.[30]

There is, then, no single narrative weaving together all the exhibitors in *Spellbound* because the show has taken a stand against narrow explanations attempting to define what is or is not quintessentially British or suggesting that enlightenment about the art/film connection lies in only one particular direction. This is not to abstain from argument, however. This show's argument is precisely that there are a number of important stories to be told and that they make us revalue British culture. To paraphrase Ezra Pound, art in Britain has sometimes been able to make film new, as is the case with Douglas Gordon's riffing on *Psycho*. Sometimes film has allowed artists to draw on art traditions beyond that of Greenbergian modernism, as is the case with Paula Rego whose Disney-inspired paintings renew her intimacy with certain kinds of European painting. Sometimes the camera and the resources of film have provided artists with an aesthetic language that paint cannot always match, as is the case with Steve McQueen's work. And at other times, a particular film is unimaginable outside its relationship with the long history of the fine arts, as is the case with Ridley Scott's *Blade Runner*. What all of the exhibits show in their diverse and rich ways, is that film and art have been, are and inevitably will be spellbound by the ambitions and possibilities that each continues to offer the other. With the Bankside Tate Gallery now more than a dream, there is the real possibility of re-imagining the relationship between modernity and the visual arts in Britain. There could not be a better place to start than with the dialogue between art and film.

# The Odd Couple

## By Ian Christie

It may or may not be part of the English nature – I carefully avoid calling it the British – that its contacts with reality should always be disguised as something else.
John Grierson

Since painting is not film – and not simply because one moves and the other doesn't – I wanted to explore their connections and differences.
Peter Greenaway

*Spellbound* is not a retrospective. It has been created, now, to address the barriers of taste and tradition that have kept art and film apart in Britain, perhaps more resolutely than in any other country, and subjected both to a long-standing inferiority complex. Other cultures, we feel instinctively, do it better; and we are constantly surprised, even disbelieving, when we learn how much these cultures value our art and our film.

Behind the inferiority complex there is of course a history, and this essay (to be read with Vicky Allan's chronology), is a contribution to charting Britain's troubled relations between modernity and the visual – snapshots of a strange relationship.

*A Modern Art Mystery*

A psychiatrist falls in love with her new boss only to discover that he is an impostor who believes he is a murderer. But she is able to prove his innocence by analysing his dreams, and the asylum's previous director is revealed as the real murderer. Alfred Hitchcock's first post-war thriller, *Spellbound*, has more in common with Europe's first great 'art film', *The Cabinet of Dr Caligari*, than a play with madness and authority – all the characters in *Caligari* turn out to be patients in an asylum and the supposed villain is their benevolent director. In 1919 German Expressionism supplied *Caligari* with its sensational 'mad' settings and launched two decades of modernism popularised on screen. Twenty-five years later Surrealism had become an international style, so who better to create the traumatic dream sequences for *Spellbound* than the most celebrated Surrealist of all, Salvador Dalí?

But was it anything more than a publicity stunt? Neither Hitchcock nor Dalí connoisseurs have ever been enthusiastic about *Spellbound*; and François Truffaut clearly had this collaboration in mind when he set out to restore the reputation of the 'master of suspense' in his marathon interview: 'Hitchcock, whose genius for publicity was equalled only by Dalí, had been victimised in American intellectual circles because of his facetious response to interviewers'.[1] Hitchcock had indeed learnt to act the sardonic showman rather than the artist during his English apprenticeship.

Despite Hitchcock's dismissal of *Spellbound* to Truffaut as 'just another manhunt story wrapped up in pseudo-psychoanalysis', we might interpret his wish to work with Dalí as a bid to raise his artistic sights, to escape from the limitations of being a British film-maker, which he had recently re-experienced after a brief return visit to London in 1944. Hitchcock had encountered psychoanalysis in America, and he wanted Dalí to help him create 'dreams with great visual sharpness and clarity, sharper than the film itself'. But there were problems: the producers vetoed shooting the dreams as sunlit exteriors, and he, in turn, rejected Dalí's idea of encasing Ingrid Bergman in a statue that would crack open to reveal her covered in ants.[2]

*Spellbound* may not show either Dalí or Hitchcock at their individual best. Like Hans Richter's *Dreams That Money Can Buy* (1947), with Alexander Calder, Marcel Duchamp, Max Ernst and Man Ray, it underlines the difficulty of inserting 'art' into narrative cinema without neutralising it. It also recalls how cinema's power has tempted artists, and shows Hitchcock's constant willingness to take artistic risks, despite his bluff publicity manner. From *Rear Window* to *The Birds* his films show a deepening development of dream-like structures, which undermine the whole reality/fantasy distinction. Indeed the extraordinary repetition of *Vertigo* now stands as a modern symbol of the uncanny and is quoted as such in Terry Gilliam's time-shift fantasmagoria *Twelve Monkeys*.

1. François Truffaut, *Hitchcock*, London, 1968. Quotation from the preface to the 1978 revised edition.
2. *Ibid.*, pp. 192–5.

3. O. Winter, 'The Cinematograph' in *New Review*, May 1896 (reprinted in *Sight and Sound*, Autumn 1982, with an introduction by Stephen Bottomore).

4. Fry's catalogue essay is reprinted in his *Vision and Design*, London, 1920 (reprinted Oxford, 1981) and quoted in Frances Spalding, *British Art Since 1900*, London, 1986 (reprinted 1994), p. 39.

5. *Bioscope* review of 17 October 1912, quoted in Rachel Low, *The History of the British Film*, vol. 2, 1906–14, London, 1948 (reprinted 1973), p. 262.

6. *Ibid.*

7. Harry Furniss, *Our Lady Cinema*, Bristol, 1914, p. 26.

8. Hugh Kenner, *A Sinking Island. The Modern English Writers*, London, 1988, p. 139.

9. The reassessment of Vorticism began with Richard Cork's 1974 Hayward exhibition *Vorticism and its Allies* and the Royal Academy's *British Art in the Twentieth Century* in 1987, and continues with Bridget Peppin's *Helen Saunders* retrospective at the Ashmolean Museum, Oxford, in 1996.

10. On *Le Ballet mécanique*, see Standish Lawder, *The Cubist Cinema*, New York, 1975.

11. On British trick films, see Rachel Low, *The History of The British Film*, vol. 1, 1896–1906, London, 1948, pp. 78–85; and Ian Christie, *The Last Machine. Early Cinema and the Birth of the Modern World*, London, 1994, pp. 2off.

12. Yuri Tsivian, *Early Cinema in Russia and its Cultural Reception*, London, 1994, pp. 150–1.

13. Luke McKernan and Olwen Terris, eds., *Walking Shadows: Shakespeare in the National Film and Television Archive*, London, 1994, p .6.

Hitchcock not only lends this exhibition its title, he is also present in Douglas Gordon's elegant deconstruction of the devastating film with which he reinvented himself as a director of the 1960s and godfather to the stalker/serial-killer genre. Gordon's *24 Hour Psycho* invites us to 'visit' *Psycho* as we might a 'classic' in a museum, and see it according to our contemporary codes of video viewing and surveillance monitors. Truffaut placed Hitchcock among 'such artists of anxiety as Kafka, Dostoevsky and Poe', but the intertextual homages of Gordon and Gilliam are surely a more vital way of acknowledging his status as a modern Old Master.

*Better than Nature*

The potential of film as a new visual art was raised in Britain as early as May 1896, less than three months after the first public Lumière and Paul screenings.[3] The writer 'O. Winter' (possibly a pseudonym) compared Pre-Raphaelite painters and cinematographers, equally 'incapable of choice', with the 'true impressionist' who is the 'Cinematograph's antithesis', by virtue of his creative selectivity. 'Has the Cinematograph a future?', asked Winter, and his answer anticipated a complaint that will echo down the decades: 'Artistically no; statistically, a thousand times, yes'.

The cinematograph had arrived at the beginning of a watershed period in British art, which would see Impressionism extolled over the prevailing naturalism of late Victorian painting, only to be challenged almost immediately by the Post-Impressionism of Cézanne, Gauguin and Van Gogh, and later by Cubism and Futurism. Behind the skirmishing of modernists and traditionalists, Little Englanders and cosmopolitans, what was basically at stake during the two decades after 1896 was the autonomy of the image. As Roger Fry claimed in the catalogue of his second Post-Impressionist exhibition in 1912, the new artists 'do not seek to imitate form, but to create form; not to imitate life but to find an equivalent for life'.[4]

If painting was abandoning imitation, might cinema take up its mantle as the medium of naturalistic narrative? This idea was certainly in the air in about 1911–16, when film-makers like Elwin Neame and Cecil Hepworth developed a short-lived school of English pictorialism. Neame's *The Lady of Shalott* (1912) was praised in terms that would have gladdened a turn-of-the-century pictorial photographer: 'the artistry of the photography and arrangement generally is so admirable as to move one to avow that it is "better than nature".'[5]

A year later, cinema's 'low' cultural status received a welcome boost when the veteran painter Sir Hubert von Herkomer R.A. announced that he was taking up professional film production. 'I see the greatest possibility of art in the film', he declared, 'I should think the black-and-white artist never had such a chance as now, with the cinema by his side.'[6] Unfortunately Herkomer died before he could prove his point, but there were others ready to push the same case further. The cartoonist turned film-maker, Harry Furniss, wrote in 1914: 'I have seen better pictures of composition ... and effects in one evening at an ordinary cinematograph show than I have seen in a year at the Royal Academy and the Salon'.[7]

Clearly Furniss and Herkomer were not thinking of Post-Impressionism but of the exhausted tradition of English naturalism. However, few of the new kinds of film attracting record audiences at the cinemas were produced in Britain. Historical epics from Italy, slapstick and Shakespeare from America, art films and comedies from France, detective thrillers from Denmark – all these contributed to a golden age of innovation and internationalism. But a vicious circle of low ambition and low investment had driven British production to the margins of the world's cinema trade. Would Britain be the first nation to lose its own reflection on its screens, as if the victim of a vampire, in the new twilight era of the movies?

*The Avant-Garde That Wasn't*

Film history, like art history, is ultimately a story believed by enough people to support its re-telling and research. So we learn of British art reacting to foreign modernism, rather than producing its own, and of the absence of any avant-garde cinema until the 1930s. But these are as much matters of definition as of history.

Hugh Kenner has identified both the victim and the culprit.[8] 'Vorticism' was a 'vertiginous ... island in the placid and respectable archipelago of English art', named by Ezra Pound and led by the combative artist and writer Wyndham Lewis. It had a manifesto as 'modern' as any Italian or Russian Futurist tract, with a distinctive ideology of England as a nation formed by the sea, by 'northernness' and by industry. And visually it had 'an idiom for northern starkness: lines savagely straight, an energy of the diagonal, human figures ... suppressed, an urban subtext of grids, traffic, blocks, steel frames'.

If the movement had little reputation other than as 'a provincial ripple' until recently,[9] Kenner believed that 'the opposition all along had stemmed from Bloomsbury – from Roger Fry and Clive Bell'. Since Vorticism has been consistently marginalised, it is hardly surprising that few have connected Alvin Langdon Coburn's prismatic, abstracted photographs of 1916–17, which Pound christened 'Vortographs', with Pound's later project to attach the Vortoscope mirrors to a film camera. This occurred in 1923, when Pound was moving from London to Paris and when his film adviser was the young American Dudley Murphy, who would shortly help Léger use similar prismatic techniques in his film, *Le Ballet mécanique* (1924), for which Pound's friend George Antheil wrote a notable percussive score.[10]

Might there have been other unrealised Vorticist film projects? And why are the personal films of artists such as Dora Carrington and the patrons of modernism classified as home-movies when many French and American avant-garde films of the inter-war years are equally 'amateur'? The idea that Britain had no avant-garde has been insidiously self-confirming.

*Primitives and Parodies*

In a culture deeply suspicious of both modernist art and of cinema's 'trade' status, a film vanguard was always likely to pass unremarked at home. Arguably this is what happened to the British 'trick film' producers who gained an international reputation between 1898 and 1906, with such anarchic masterpieces as Cecil Hepworth's *How It Feels to be Run Over* and *The Explosion of a Motor Car*, Smith's *Grandma's Reading Glass* and Paul's *The Haunted Curiosity Shop* and *The ? Motorist*. Once considered merely primitive, these can now be seen as a kind of naïve avant-garde, owing more to the traditions of nursery nonsense, the Wellsian scientific romance and graphic satire, than to the contemporary art world.[11] Although it was the French Surrealists who canonised Méliès's trick films, no British Surrealists seem to have recognised an equally promising native source of the bizarre and subversive. Indeed, while it is hard to find any cultural response to these in Britain, the Russian Symbolist Andrei Bely incorporated memories of both *The ? Motorist* and Fitzhamon's *That Fatal Sneeze* into his apocalyptic vision of modern city life.[12]

But film is as fragile as it is international, and a tantalising British film of the 1910s is known only through accounts by those who worked on it.[13] *The Real Thing At Last* was a satire on Shakespearean production, written and largely directed by J.M. Barrie in 1916, which sounds like an anticipation of Monty Python's iconoclastic parodies. Barrie gleefully contrasted a brash American version of Macbeth with a genteel English production, including a contemporary Shakespeare worrying about his contracts.

Made in the same year that Beerbohm Tree played Macbeth for D.W. Griffith in Hollywood, Barrie's satire on Bardolatry strikes a welcome note of irreverence and shows that at least one major British artist grasped the subversive comic potential of cinema. In fact, parody has proved a durable genre, and it was Adrian Brunel's spoof newsreels of the mid-1920s, *The Pathetic Gazette* and *The Typical Budget*, that eventually attracted H.G. Wells to write three inventive comedies for Brunel and Ivor Montagu in 1928.

A 'Vortograph' (1917) by Alvin Langdon Coburn.

14. Woolf's essay appeared first in the New York journal *Arts*, then in the London *Nation and Athenaeum* and again as 'The Movies and Reality' in the New York *New Republic*, all in 1926. It is collected in Rachel Bowlby, ed., Virginia Woolf, *The Crowded Dance of Modern Life. Selected Essays*, vol. 2, London, 1993.

15. Rosalind Krauss, *The Optical Unconscious*, Cambridge, Massachusetts, 1993.

16. *C.O.D. – A Mellow Drama* (c. 1928), made by Desmond Dickenson, Gerald Gibbs and Lloyd T. Richards (all technicians at the Stoll studios) and preserved in the National Film and Television Archive, was shown at the Pordenone Giornate del Cinema Muto in 1995.

17. Barbara Guest, *Herself Defined. The Poet H.D. and Her World*, London, 1985, p. 184.

18. On Pool Productions and *Borderline*, see Roland Cosandey, 'On *Borderline*' in *Afterimage* 12, Autumn 1985, pp. 66–84.

19. Anne Friedberg, 'Approaching Borderline' in *Millennium Film Journal*, nos. 7, 8, 9, Fall/Winter 1980–1.

20. Charles Davy, ed., *Footnotes to the Film*, London, 1938, pp. 116–34.

21. Mary-Lou Jennings, ed., *Humphrey Jennings: Film-Maker, Painter, Poet*, London, 1982.

22. Paul Nash, 'The Colour Film' in Davy, ed., *Footnotes to the Film, op cit.*, p. 124.

### Manifesto for a New Cinema

If Bloomsbury played down the significance of Vorticism's assault on English gentility, was it also hostile to cinema? Once again, received history is largely silent on this issue – as it is on what should be considered a key text, Virginia Woolf's 1926 essay on cinema.[14] After recalling how moving pictures revealed 'life as it is when we have no part in it' and noting ironically how this phenomenon puzzled 'the English unaesthetic eye', Woolf deplored the dominance of literary adaptation before speculating on 'what the cinema might do if left to its own devices'.

Appropriately, as Freud's English publisher, Woolf found a clue to cinema's potential in a mishap during a screening of *Caligari*: 'a shadow shaped like a tadpole suddenly appeared at one corner of the screen. It swelled to an immense size, quivered, bulged, and sank back again into nonentity.' The unintended drama of dirt in the projector gate – a kind of paraphraxis of the cinema apparatus – suggests to her:

if a shadow ... so much more than the actual gestures and words of men and women in a state of fear, it seems plain that cinema has within its grasp innumerable symbols for emotions that have so far failed to find expression. Terror has, besides its ordinary forms, the shape of a tadpole ... Anger is not merely rant and rhetoric ... it is perhaps a black line wriggling on a white sheet.

Ignoring the Expressionism of *Caligari*, Woolf finds in this accidental animation a pointer towards 'some secret language which we feel and see, but never speak' and wonders 'could this be made visible to the eye?'

Writing midway between her two great stream-of-consciousness experimental novels, *Mrs Dalloway* and *To the Lighthouse*, Woolf's concern with expressing the hitherto unexpressed is understandable. Woolf imagines a cinema freed from literary adaptation to explore a predicative 'residue of visual emotion which is of no use either to painter or to poet', which we might term, following Rosalind Krauss, the 'optical unconscious'.[15] It could be a new way of grasping the flux of modern life: 'in the chaos of the streets ... when some momentary assembly of colour, sound, movement suggests that here is a scene awaiting a new art to be transfixed'.

Woolf's remarkable essay touches on many of the ideas that would put cinema at the centre of aesthetic debate in the 1920s and 1930s. It also recalls the importance of The Film Society, where she saw *Caligari*, as Bloomsbury's main contribution to British film culture, bringing together artists, intellectuals and the film industry.

The Society was formed to circumvent Britain's highly restrictive censorship – which rejected *Caligari* as incomprehensible and, therefore, potentially objectionable – but it soon developed a distinctive pattern of programming innovative German, French and eventually Soviet feature films alongside scientific films, animation, American slapstick and British shorts (such as Brunel's comedies and the recently discovered Expressionist parody *C.O.D.*).[16] In 1929 – three years after its Berlin release – the Film Society finally managed to show Sergei Eisenstein's already celebrated *Battleship Potemkin* in a typically challenging programme that included animation and Grierson's manifesto for a new documentary cinema, *Drifters*. Woolf's essay offers an oblique insight into The Film Society's influence, but the full extent of its impact remains uncharted.

### An Avant-Garde in Exile

In 1927 the novelist and heiress Winifred Ellerman, known as Bryher, bought a film camera for her fiancé Kenneth Macpherson on the advice of a family friend, Marc Allegrét, the nephew of André Gide and later a leading film director.[17] The gift bore unexpected fruit. During the next three years Macpherson made a full-scale experimental feature film and several short films; and between 1927 and 1933 this unusual couple – rich, cosmopolitan and bisexual – ran the first magazine devoted to film as an art, *Close-Up*.[18]

Macpherson and Bryher, based in Switzerland, formed the nucleus of a British avant-garde in exile. Among their close associates in Pool Productions, working both on the films and the magazine, were the feminist writers Dorothy Richardson and H.D. (Hilda Doolittle, Pound's former 'imagist' protégé), and the film-makers Oswald Blakeston and Robert Herring. Macpherson maintained that 'the hope of the cinema lies with the amateur'; and in this spirit they set out to learn at first hand about the most advanced film-making of the period in Berlin.

Their first mentor was Pabst, whose bold treatment of sexuality and interest in psychoanalysis appealed to the group, especially to H.D. But within a year the new Soviet films of Eisenstein, Lev Kuleshov and Abram Room appeared, and *Close-Up* became a passionate advocate of Soviet montage cinema – seen as a last defence against the commercial banality of the new Talkies.

In 1929 Bryher published *Film Problems of Soviet Russia*, and Macpherson wrote and directed Pool's most ambitious film, *Borderline*, with Paul and Eslanda Robeson and H.D. playing the main parts. Both book and film are original, 'amateur' in style, yet highly sophisticated in their themes. Marginality and borders to be crossed – psychological, sexual, racial, political – are their common themes. Predictably, *Borderline* met with puzzlement and hostility in Britain and soon disappeared; *Close-Up* ceased publication in 1933. Pool was forgotten until a new interest in marginality and in combining theory with practice – among groups like Sankofa and the partnership of Laura Mulvey and Peter Wollen – stimulated research into the activities of this prescient avant-garde.[19]

*Surrealism/Realism*

In 1938 the painter and critic Paul Nash contributed an essay on 'The Colour Film' to an anthology, which included contributions from Alfred Hitchcock, Alexander Korda and John Grierson, as well as from Graham Greene, John Betjeman and Alistair Cooke, all then actively interested in movies.[20] Nash wrote as an amateur, disclaiming any expertise on colour film and admitting that his sympathies lay with black-and-white films – not surprisingly, since colour was still a novelty and the first British Technicolor, *Wings of the Morning*, had only just been released. He is scornful of naïve attempts to privilege the 'colourful' in these early efforts, comparing a landscape sequence with 'upsetting the local-views kiosk in the village shop', while preferring the 'clean, bright, cool colours' of colour postcards that would 'do credit to any painter'. But beyond mocking the solemn rhetoric that accompanied early Technicolor, Nash identified the aesthetic problems – a misconceived obsession with 'harmony' and the tendency of saturated colour to obliterate form – which he believed would eventually need artists who understood film technique to solve.

Nash quoted 'Humphrey Jennings, the Surrealist' on the issue of colour and form; they were both among the organisers of the 1936 International Surrealist Exhibition in London. For many British artists this would begin a process of liberation and self-discovery, a redefinition of 'Englishness' amid the internationalism of Surrealism. Nash had already moved from his early visionary landscapes to the relatively abstract Dymchurch beach images of the early 1920s; now Surrealism would lead him to a more complex Romanticism. Jennings described himself in 1936 as having 'survived the Theatre and English Literature at Cambridge [and] connected with colour film direction' and argued that 'to settle Surrealism down as Romanticism is only is to deny this newest *promise*'.[21] But as he moved from Surrealism into the poetic anthropology of the Mass Observation movement, delving into the reality of individuals' lives in modern society, Jennings continued to work across the traditional and new media. He was a prototype of that new kind of artist envisaged by Nash, although the British documentary movement gave him few opportunities to work in colour. Another was the New Zealander, Len Lye, whom Nash had first noticed exhibiting at the Seven & Five Society and whose original painted-on-celluloid films, *Colour Box* and *Rainbow Dance*, he hailed, in terms reminiscent of Woolf, as 'a new form of enjoyment quite independent of literary reference; the simple, direct visual-aural contact of sound and colour through eye and ear'.[22]

Expressionist settings: *The Cabinet of Dr. Caligari* (1919) designed by Hermann Warm, Walter Reimann and Walter Röhrig.

Expressionism and
Surrealism:
Hein Heckroth's
designs for Powell
and Pressburger's
*The Red Shoes*
(1948).

Lye's radical technique would also influence another pioneer of graphic cinema, Norman McLaren, along with Surrealism, communism and a frustrated love of dance. While still a Glasgow art student, McLaren's amateur work attracted the attention of John Grierson, who declared that his first abstract film 'brought a new contribution to the cinema' and encouraged him to take up film professionally.[23]

Jennings, Lye and McLaren all worked for different periods under John Grierson at the G.P.O. Film Unit, which served as a focus for such avant-garde work. The paradoxes of this unusual arrangement were numerous: a government department was sponsoring the most radical experiments in film technique being undertaken anywhere, yet most of the films were advertisements, and Grierson himself was a leading advocate of realism. In practice, Grierson's realism spanned a 'truth to materials' exploration of film's basic structures as well as the more conventional photographic and thematic realisms. But he was frustrated that the 'documentary' group he had so successfully promoted was destined to remain outside the mainstream of cinema, 'tight, tidy and removed in its own separate finances, and too wisely removed from the commercial scramble to join hands with it'.[24]

As the most successful impresario of artists' cinema that Britain has known, as well as the arch-exponent of realism, Grierson remains an enigmatic, contradictory figure. Among recent commentators, Brian Winston condemns Grierson's willingness to subordinate both art and truth to the demands of sponsorship;[25] while the French philosopher and visual historian Paul Virilio challenges the British to make explicit the buried connections between power and vision, and provocatively links Anthony Blunt's 'betrayal' of modern art with Grierson's promotion of the British documentary movement as 'a vast anti-aesthetic movement ... and a reaction against the art world'.[26]

But while Grierson's confusing legacy remains all too firmly on our agenda, little attention has been paid to the contemporary development of the Expressionist/Surrealist idiom that would erupt within mainstream British commercial cinema after the Second World War. The key figure in this was the painter and designer Hein Heckroth, who came to Britain as a refugee from Nazi Germany in the 1930s, and who first made his name in expressionist stage design, before teaching at Dartington Hall, which had become a bastion of Surrealism.[27]

In 1944 Heckroth entered the film industry, initially as a costume designer. After working with Michael Powell and Emeric Pressburger on *A Matter of Life and Death* and *Black Narcissus* he became production designer of *The Red Shoes* in 1948. It was, Powell claimed, the first time a painter had been put in charge of designing a whole film, and Heckroth made the most of his opportunity with an eclectic range of painterly references built up into an extraordinary cocktail of neo-Romanticism. Powell and Pressburger's *The Tales of Hoffmann* (1951), shot entirely in the studio, allowed him to go further towards a wholly stylised non-naturalistic cinema, influenced as much by Disney as by Surrealism. Here, finally, was a painter, as imagined by Nash, using Technicolor to compose true colour films.

The Powell/Pressburger films of 1947–55, designed by Heckroth, are the antithesis of Griersonian realism or Woolf/Nash purism; and to many schooled in modernism or in the new post-war realism, they seemed reactionary. But we can now see that they both anticipated a neo-Romantic shift in British culture and were also part of a great international movement in cinema, embracing such diverse figures as Eisenstein, Hitchcock, Vincente Minnelli and Jean Renoir, which sought to realise its potential as a synthesis of the arts.

### Return to the Forbidden Planet

Eduardo Paolozzi grew up in Edinburgh in the 1930s, belonging to three cultures, all saturated with film. One was the everyday Scottish-Italian world of a confectionery shop, where people bought ice cream, sweets and cigarettes on their way to the cinema. Another was the highly organised culture of the Italian diaspora, which provided weekly propaganda film shows and summer camps in Italy, and

23. *Norman McLaren* , catalogue of a Scottish Arts Council touring exhibition, Edinburgh, 1977.
24. John Grierson, 'The Course of Realism' in *Footnotes to the Film*, p. 158.
25. Brian Winston, *Claiming the Real*, London, 1995.
26. Paul Virilio, *The Vision Machine*, London, 1994.
27. 'Hein Heckroth: Film-Designer', special edition of *Kinematograph*, Deutsches Filmmuseum, Frankfurt, 1991.
28. Lawrence Alloway, 'The Iconography of the Movies in *Movie* no. 7, February-March 1963, pp. 4–6.
29. Derek Jarman, *Dancing Ledge*, London, 1984, p. 105.
30. *Ibid*,. p. 110–11.
31. Tony Rayns, 'Submitting to Sodomy' in *Afterimage* 12, pp. 60–64.

introduced the young Paolozzi to Fascism's peculiar blend of Futurist-inspired modernism and Cinecittá-style imperialism. Alongside this was the Hollywood fantasy world on offer in Edinburgh's many and varied cinemas, supported by fan magazines, comics and cigarette cards.

When Paolozzi applied to enter Edinburgh College of Art he was advised to replace his tracings of film stars with more appropriate artistic subjects. Not until he reached post-war Paris, after the Slade, did he discover how Surrealism had kept faith with popular culture, and how its influence guided the Cinématheque Française in showing equal enthusiasm for popular and art cinema. Léger showed him *Le Ballet mécanique* and 15 years later, in 1963, he, too, would use everyday ephemera as the material for his collage film *History of Nothing*.

In that same year one of Paolozzi's fellow founders of the Institute of Contemporary Arts, the critic Lawrence Alloway, wrote on 'The Iconography of the Movies' for the new film magazine *Movie*.[28] This had been started by a group of young critics at Oxford University to attack the complacency of British film culture, as exemplified by *Sight and Sound*, and it defiantly championed Hollywood professionals over most British film-makers. But Alloway argued that insistence on 'treating movies as personal expression' ignored their greater potency as bearers of a pervasive iconography. Movies, he insisted, 'are the index of a Baudelairean art of modern life ... ephemeral, fugitive, contingent upon the occasion'.

Alloway challenged the new definition of film's status as art in the same terms that Pop Art challenged prevailing notions of gallery art's proper subjects. Film, he observed, 'is continually dissolving into its connections with environment, politics, personalities, fashion'. His call for a descriptive non-auteurist film criticism was eventually taken up by semiological analysis. Meanwhile the new wave of artists' films signalled by such isolated works as *History of Nothing* and Jeff Keen's contemporaneous 8mm film-making, led in 1966, at the climax of London's reign as the capital of a new Baudelairean culture, to the formation of the London Filmmakers' Co-operative. Artists' film had achieved its own vertical integration.

*Another England*

In 1970 a chance encounter led to the young painter and stage designer Derek Jarman designing Ken Russell's *The Devils*. For Jarman it was a turning point: 'When I began in January, I had no idea that a film of this size completely usurps your life. And by the time I emerged from Pinewood in December, the easy life of the sixties – designing and painting – had gone for ever.'[29]

In fact, art-making returned almost immediately, albeit ironically, through Jarman's involvement in Russell's next project, *Savage Messiah*, a biopic about the short, intense life of the Vorticist sculptor Henri Gaudier-Brzeska. Jarman recalled scenes of high comedy, with a team of fellow-artists busily faking Gaudier sculptures and drawings ('they're very easy to forge') and Omega workshop pottery.[30] Vorticism and Bloomsbury had been revived at Lee Studios; *Steptoe and Son* was being filmed next door.

Jarman would eventually make his own artist's biopic in 1986, *Caravaggio*, indirectly influenced by Russell's psycho-biographies. Working with Russell had given him a taste for full-scale cinema and he would continue to oscillate between the lure of feature-scale production, however poverty-stricken, and the direct personal expression of 8mm films. As a result his feature films took on many of the informal qualities of amateur film, with personalities, locations and costumes as important as conventional dramatic elements, while his personal films became more shaped and purposeful, like notebooks intended for eventual publication. The crossover came in *Imagining October* in 1984, when Jarman combined 8mm material, filmed clandestinely in the Soviet Union, with studio scenes of an artist painting, a paradoxically underground film about the public/political role of art.[31]

Painting also returned powerfully in his 'GBH' exhibition in that same year: a passionate protest against Britain's decline, and a tortured declaration of love, on a par with his films *Jubilee*, *The Angelic Conversation* and *The Last of England* – all celebrating the marginal and the despised that constituted Jarman's defiantly queer, libertarian and magical England.[32]

### Landscapes of the Mind

Is landscape the condition to which all British cinema aspires as it struggles to escape the confines of the studio or of the film-maker's inner world? During the 1970s several British artists/film-makers developed a distinctive variation on the international 'structural film' model, which took the form of a meditation on landscape in relation to time.[33]

Time, of course, has always been a vector of landscape art, but in the films of Chris Welsby, William Raban and others it became a central concern. From an art-historical point of view, these could be regarded as a continuation of the English pastoral or visionary tradition, following in the footsteps of Constable, Turner and Nash by novel means. But landscape was also undergoing radically new treatment in Richard Long's 'land art' and Victor Burgin's subversion of the images and texts of advertising; and film-makers like John Smith, Tina Keane, Sally Potter and Patrick Keillor took an increasingly ironic, historical and literary view of landscape/cityscape.[34]

Peter Greenaway's early work belongs to this ironic phase of British landscape film, moving from the mock-pastoral of *Windows* (1974) and *H is for House* (1976) to the mock-structural of *Dear Phone* (1976). But in 1978 Greenaway revealed a new scale of ambition. *Vertical Features Remake* uses a conceptual science-fiction framework to draw a parallel between structural and land preoccupations within the stunted 'landscape' of British cinema and its institutions. In the same year *A Walk Through H* also opened a new door on to the fantastic: collage landscapes of an imaginary quest, approached through an art gallery. Like Calvino's *Invisible Cities* these landscapes are states of mind.

Landscape has always challenged British artists to reveal its historical or ideological meaning. Just as Rudyard Kipling unearthed a history of 'Englishness' from the Sussex landscape in *Puck of Pook's Hill* and William Morris conjured a revolutionary landscape in *News From Nowhere*, so Greenaway shows the English country house as 'property' in *The Draughtsman's Contract* (1982), an arena for financial and sexual conflict, and ultimately a setting for murder, as it has so often been in English fiction. And in Patrick Keillor's *London* (1994), the contemporary city is haunted by the ghosts of its past inhabitants and stories, experienced like a waking dream.

The central paradox of cinema is that we leave the visible world to enter the darkness, in a ritual like falling asleep or returning to the womb, and see that world transfigured. In an era of 'heritage cinema', do we need to adjust our films in order to see the landscape better?

### History of the Future

Perhaps the most important lesson we can learn from looking back at the history of film, and film as art, in Britain is to appreciate the depth and duration of the crisis provoked by the new visual media at the turn of the century. 'When men think pictorially', wrote Holbrook Jackson in 1903, reacting to the appearance of the illustrated *Daily Mirror* (aimed mainly at women) 'they unsex themselves'.[35] However absurd this may sound, it reveals a profound fear of the seductiveness of new visual forms in a conservative literary culture. Photography, 'objective' and technological, was also dangerously democratic and voyeuristic. Cinema amplified and, literally, animated these qualities, threatening to unleash a tide of fantasy that could submerge established values beneath the 'femininity' of popular taste.

The traditional arts were soon implicated in this disturbing new trend, first through the profusion of 'lightning sketch' films, which mechanised the process of drawing, then through the animation of objects and bodies in early trick films.

Homoerotic dreamscapes: Derek Jarman's *The Angelic Conversation* (1985).

32. John Roberts, 'Painting the Apocalypse', in *Afterimage* 12, pp. 36–9.

33. On the 'structural' phase of landscape film, see Deke Dusinberre, 'St George in the Forest: The English Avant-Garde' in *Afterimage* 6, Summer 1976, pp. 4–18.

34. See notes on these film-makers in David Curtis, ed., *The Elusive Sign*: Catalogue for British Film and Video Retrospective 1977–87, British Council, London, 1987.

35. Quoted in John Carey, *The Intellectuals and the Masses*, London, 1992, p. 8.

36. Erwin Panofsky, 'Style and Medium in the Motion Picture' (first published in 1934, revised in 1947) in Daniel Talbot, ed., *Film: An Anthology*, Berkeley, 1966, p. 17.

Colour representation was also being automated through Urban and Smith's successful development of 'Kinemacolor'. These are not normally considered relevant to the well-documented British reaction against 'foreign' modernism in painting and sculpture in 1910–14. But the critic who detected in Post-Impressionism 'a widespread plot to destroy the whole fabric of European painting' was surely voicing a fear similar to Holbrook Jackson's, and one related to the recurrent moral panics over cinema, which led to the introduction of film censorship in 1913.

If we think of this fabric of painting as a map confirming position, identity and a whole network of social and political relations, then the Fauves, Cubists and Futurists (not to mention the Imagists and Vorticists, and the film producers and exhibitors supposedly corrupting the nation's youth) were indeed dangerous. The revolutionaries in the salons and the sensationalists in the film business might join forces with the miners and the suffragettes who were already demonstrating in the streets. After the Great War an uneasy truce left the institutions of art and film in essentially separate compartments, which is how they have remained despite the largely hidden network of relations traced in the Chronology and in this essay.

The essays on individual contributors to the exhibition tease out the implications of artists invoking and working in film, and of film-makers moving from screen to gallery space. They have been commissioned from a spectrum of different positions, intended to broaden the thrust of *Spellbound* beyond the professional discourses of art and film into a wider public sphere, where the claims of the visual and the importance of Britain's stake in an increasingly global culture founded on the moving image need to be registered.

One of the most obvious lessons to emerge from *Spellbound* is that the internationalism and pervasiveness of cinema – often considered threatening by those wedded to ideas of national culture and to defending 'high' art against low entertainment – can generate a wide range of personal and critical responses. Thus when Paul Rego takes familiar Disney icons as her starting point for an exploration of childhood and memory, when Fiona Banner scans the more recent mythology of Vietnam movies and when Eduardo Paolozzi creates a 'memory theatre' of his lifetime's viewing – all of these are mediating between cinema's omnipresence as the folklore of the twentieth century and their precise location as, by different definitions, 'British' artists. Similarly, Terry Gilliam, Peter Greenaway and Ridley Scott are British film-makers – in the same tradition as Hitchcock, albeit very different from one another – and also international virtuosi of contemporary cinema's machinery of spectacle. *Spellbound* is finally about taking risks, attempting what is normally impossible within the art or film world. Damien Hirst and Boyd Webb have added to that exciting, unpredictable line of artists making films as a direct extension of their concerns in other media, while Douglas Gordon and Steve McQueen have extended their previous, highly acclaimed use of video and film within a gallery context.

Perhaps the only truly effective way to mark the centenary of cinema would be to declare a moratorium on all film viewing. Even a day totally without films – in cinemas, aeroplanes, on television and video – would underline, dramatically, how much our whole fabric of daily life depends on film. The art historian Erwin Panofsky had no doubts about its importance when he wrote in 1934:

If all the serious lyrical poets, composers, painters and sculptors were forced by law to stop their activities, a rather small fraction of the general public would become aware of the fact and a still smaller fraction would seriously regret it. If the same thing were to happen with the movies the social consequences would be catastrophic.[36]

Sixty years later our dependence is, if anything, greater. But we also stand on the threshold of a new age, the age of the infinitely malleable electronic image, which is no more predictable than the age of cinema was 100 years ago. *Spellbound* offers a chance to take stock and to imagine the second century of the moving image.

# Fiona
# Banner

By Linda Ruth
Williams

The Vietnam war was a crucial landmark in our increasingly suspicious relationship with the image. When the war's visual icons – photographs, newsfootage, the whole genre of fiction films spawned by the conflict – begin to usurp the historical event itself, the relationship between the reality and the fiction of its representation blurs. The anxiety created by this moment when history and representation bleed into each other lies at the heart of Fiona Banner's Vietnam pieces. For those of us growing up after the event, struggling with the fact that our sense of its history is intimately bound up with its filmic and fictional rendition, Banner's project has particular relevance.

Banner's formal mode of working also occupies a unique place in this exhibition, which connects two distinct but related ways of viewing art and cinema and allows them to overlap and spark off each other. Her extraordinary artistic engagement with film, with visual narratives and with words as images, poses the question of how history can be subsumed by its representations in a very specific way. Viewed through the interdisciplinary context of 'art and cinema', art read as cinema and cinema read through visual art, Banner's works necessarily inject a third term: writing. What, then, is the interconnection between language, cinema and the image here? Why are the films about Vietnam crucial to the way these elements are mixed?

The age-old question that painting has posed and re-posed, of how to address movement in a still image, is rephrased in Banner's work with an uncompromising emphasis, yet at the heart of this work is a paradox. By starting with the movies, moving pictures, the movement-image itself (and thus, in a sense, posing the question the other way round), Banner challenges the stillness of paint, ink or text on paper. For her, works such as the monolithic *Apocalypse Now* (1996, pencil on paper), are still films rather than film stills. Gregor Muir has described Banner's previous works, constructed in this mode – *Top Gun* (1993, pencil on paper), *The Hunt for Red October* (1993, pencil on paper) and *The desert* (1994, black and white poster) – as 'not so much landscapes as wordscapes', but that implies an absence of motion, which is belied by the cinematic concern at the heart of Banner's project. The compendium text comprising *Apocalypse Now, Hamburger Hill, Born on the Fourth of July, Platoon, Full Metal Jacket* and *The Deer Hunter* might be read as a flick-book, a device which, as an ancestor of cinema, plays with the phenomenon of 'the persistence of

*Kurtz* (1995),
pencil on paper,
9'6 ins × 11 ft,
installed in
the Medici
Shipyard, Pisa.

*Top Gun* (1993),
pencil on paper,
7 × 15 ft.

vision'. Banner's images never sit still, and not just because they are prescribed by the movies. 'Inspired by' some of the blockbuster cornerstones of contemporary film history (*inspired?* – yes, although the relationship between filmic starting-point and Banner's response is hardly an easy one), Banner writes out her image, which hovers between categories and between conventional interpretations: is this a novel, a drawing or a picture? It is certainly not a film. Or is it?

Take *The desert*, for example, a wide linear narrative, retelling *Lawrence of Arabia* in toto. Like *Apocalypse Now*, exhibited here, *The desert* is a double epic, an epic of space as well as time. Offering a still version of the impact of Lean's engulfing 70mm Super Panavision, *The desert* covers such a huge visual expanse that it can only be experienced in bits, with the eye acting as secondary editor, necessarily panning and scanning between the different elements within the frame – clearly one of the key experiences of the film too. The fact that you cannot possibly take it all in, so crucial to Lean's vision from *Lawrence of Arabia* right through to his death, also marks Banner's sensibility. Lean's characteristically sumptuous adventure-spectacles marry classic literary adaptation with a romantic boy's own drive – this is true not just of *Lawrence of Arabia*, but of *Doctor Zhivago*, *Ryan's Daughter* and *A Passage to India*. These films have also bound history into an excessive and seductive web of fictionality: film fictions built on and derived from literary fictions, distorting, behind a layering of mythic representation, not just the texts of E.M. Forster or Lawrence's *The Seven Pillars of Wisdom*, but also the reality of the Russian Revolution, the Irish struggle or the Raj. Like 'Vietnam cinema', Lean's cinematic fables have, in part, become our histories. Executed on an epic scale, each is marked by a curious lack of closure, by questions that remain unanswered and by a sense of disappointment.

By mythologising both action and defeat, *Lawrence of Arabia* provided perfect Banner material and set an agenda that would bear fruit in the Vietnam works. Certain issues strike one immediately when observing her work. That she is a woman artist working on boys' material will for some be an obvious point of entry, but is not, I think, the most interesting issue at stake. That she has focused on perhaps the most significant development in film of the past decade or so, the action-adventure spectacle, might be seen as crucial to the critique of action-heroism implicit

in her choice of material. This would impose a moral definition on Banner's project, however, which the works themselves subtly evade. Strange, because another thing that strikes you about these images is their immediate lack of subtlety. *The desert,* for example, is a huge block of material asserting a vast sense of scale, but it is underpinned or undermined by voices of frustration woven into the detail. And – to put it crudely – it is long as well as huge, an epic narrative as well as an epic screen space. It is here that Banner's use of time, and the reader's or viewer's experience of time through the work, becomes crucial. The whole is presented in one image; all 222 minutes of the director's cut is run through this picture as its text, offering in a flash the whole story as the whole picture.

Francis Ford Coppola's 1979 *Apocalypse Now*, arguably exemplifying the next stage of cinema's experiment with the epic, is the starting-point for the work of the same name included in this exhibition. At least it is *one* starting-point, for (as with Lean) Coppola's film also needs to be read as one element in a web of intertextuality, spinning off from Conrad's *Heart of Darkness* and then wrapping itself in the lustre of its own legendary status as a film born of trauma. Rising from the ferment of publicity tales and, later, the self-conscious mythologising of the film's excesses in *Heart of Darkness*, *Apocalypse Now* layers on to the fiction of imperialism (Conrad's) its own fiction of war. Coppola's supremely arrogant statement that the film was not *about* Vietnam, it *was* Vietnam, only reinforces its position as prime example of a genre that has displaced the war itself as an historical event.

The anxiety about representations of representations certainly haunts Banner's work, but in her narrative replay she also engages with the genre's curious compulsion to repeat. Films in this genre have often been read as therapeutic works of national catharsis, expelling from the American body politic the traumatic past. But it seems that this exorcism is unsuccessful: the trauma sticks and film-makers must keep returning to the event and replaying it, excessively and endlessly, not least in Coppola's recycling of *Apocalypse Now*.

Banner's written account of the film needs to be read, however, not just as a companion to this cluster of Vietnam pieces but as a further engagement with scale, text and narrative. As with the earlier works, Banner has striven to keep her narrative retellings as plain as possible (letting the films speak for themselves, perhaps, through the gaps in their scripts as well as

Lawrence intervenes in a loud clear voice, "A friend of Prince Faisal's." Auda swings round to face him, then Ali. He is lost for words, pauses for some moments, then he turns to Sherif Ali, "So you desire... "Your will!" The man rides off furiously, firing a bullet up into the sheer blue sky. On the sand. "Son, they are stealing our water. Tell them we are coming!" Ali retorts, "That flatters me!" "You are easily flattered, Lawrence looks small, standing alone on the sand. The man laughs... Lawrence looks small, standing alone on the sand. "No, there is no resemblance... Alas, you resemble your father. Sheik Ali adds, knowingly, "Gasim's time has come Lawrence, it is written." Again he's visible from behind. Lawrence and spurs his camel even faster forwards. He curves his palm around his hand and yells out "Daoud!... Daoud!...

As Sherif Ali answers, Lawrence glances round to look at him, "We do it for Faisal of Mecca. The Harif do not work for profit... The Howeitats that are already on horseback charge over to greet their master, wailing and firing. The crowd yells "No", again in unison. Rounds of bullets crack through the sky. He turns to the men proudly, "Who told you that?" "I have long ears... "One hundred and fifty Auda!" He turns shocked to Lawrence. Auda passes through the cheering army, still with one arm raised, saying, "God be with you... "One hundred golden guineas!" Lawrence interrupts, The red flags held upright by the two men who flank him bluster in the wind. black sky. It sheds light on a deep

The red flags held upright by the two men who flank him as it passes beneath. The picture dissolves, it's night time. A half moon lingers in the blue, black sky. It sheds light on a deep purple sky, the mountain peaks jutting up into it behind him. Then Lawrence too dashes down towards the camp. Men form a circle round a man, who lies motion. The huge rocks dwarf the army as it passes beneath. "It is the law Lawrence." "The law says the man must die." "Hummm." "If he dies will it content the Howeitat?" "There is. He looks at Lawrence, and seeing his expression says, He fires one shot, grits his teeth and fires another. His body jolts slightly from the kickback as he fires shots thrown himself and looks down the barrel of his gun at Gasim squirming beneath him. As Lawrence watches this scenario unfold his expression is one of terror and loathing. His eyes narrow as he gazes. The man who finds it holds his prize above his head. The others gather round, screaming and cheering. One of the horses jumps a high wall inside the village, landing with full force on a soldier. The soldiers lunge forwards, swords and guns in front of them as they charge the camp. A camel lopes along the beach silhouetted in the distance.

Trees, like palm trees in the distance fill up the foreground. They hardly m[...]
-copter flies in from the left, then another from the right, they criss-cr[...]
shouting out turns into the cabin your bit of helicopter blades. A h[...]
keeps schtum - doesn't know how to respond. All the time looking down a[...]
Captain, "This operation never did ... nor will it ever ... exist." He b[...]
ky, its a helicopter, its blades beat out the air ... wpwpwp ... The green below [...]
did ... shit, charging a man for murder in this place was like handing out [...]
too tight for Vietnam ... shit he was probably wrapped too tight for New [...]
er side ... "Arc light ..." He says, like hes seen it all a hundred times befo[...]
[...]wn. Three of them jump out of a chopper behind, its blades are still whiz[...]
it up. He's striding through the debris and carnage like it isn't even there.[...]
badly injured. He's flailing around on the ground. He grabs onto Kilgores trou[...]
-ance, "Lance Johnston the surfer?" "Yes sir" Kilgore looks well pleased a[...]
its appearing. He drags on his cigarette. Without moving his feet he [...]
[...]ly sky. Its all orange and yellow apart from the smoke, either from [...]
[...] this shits going on behind. Copter after copter flying out of there. A hug[...]
[...]ught doing something wrong. "What is this?!" he demands, pointing j[...]
[...]ades. The camp looks dark and inky apart from a few bright patches of [...]
[...] "What do you mean hairy?" "I've lost a few recon ships on there new a[...]
[...]npathetically. "Why didn't you tell me its a good peak ... there aren't any [...]
[...]ridy right over to it. Another huey starts up their on the sand, betwee[...]
[...]wo khaki blurs streak across the foreground, then one more heading[...]
[...] light shines down from infront of the helicopter. It bores its way thro[...]
[...]ng his dark glasses. His expression doesn't say much except that hes [...]
[...]leaning out of the side of the copter, chewing gum and getting buffeted by t[...]
[...]s mouth moves to say, "Holy shit!" but you cant hear him, the sound [...]
sync. Then one chopper picks up more speed and skims across the top of [...]
[...]-up but they keep firing down at it, Three men are flicking out bulle[...]
[...] the cockpit looks a kinda bluish-green, like its underwater. The gr[...]
[...]achine gun. Its like he's gone mad, lost all control. Then he's visible[...]
[...]mence sound, explosions all the time. The deathly racket of the m[...]
[...]ward looks down. All he can see is the smoke billowing in gusts and [...]
[...]iolently left, then right, the guys in the back ducking way down. Th[...]
[...]em to cool it, he really needs to shout hard to be heard, "What is that [...]
[...]ar and his voice is hoarse with shouting, he so stuck in the riff they [...]
[...]e lined up in neat rows. He curves up behind them. Hes only visib[...]
[...]ray "err ... groups of a ... weve gone wounded here" Getting closer in [...]
[...]d debris scatter to the left, leaving a clear patch on the stones. [...]
[...]e a bonfire. Everything shakey from the vibrations. Then Kilgor[...]

through the text itself; what she leaves out is thus as crucial as what she includes). She gives the 'bare bones' story, starting at the beginning and ending at the end, as all good stories should. What commentary takes place here is enacted through an active re-presentation of the narrative.

What does it mean, then, to 'read' these pictures as stories? What does it mean to judge Banner as a writer, a re-presenter of these filmic representations? How do her words affect or infect their filmic 'origin'? For Banner, *Apocalypse Now* or *Lawrence of Arabia* (films of heroic absurdity and compulsively confessed failures) incorporate and engage in their own self-critique. Working through these narratives reiterates this, posing that self-critique again, or activating it in a new form. A literary response to this would be that there is no such thing as an 'innocent' re-presentation – presenting involves distortion, editing, twisting the tale. Perhaps, then, Banner's work has responded to a contemporary suspicion of the image by producing images paradoxically composed from a relatively non-suspicious use of language. Certainly there is an excited involvement here, a passion that emerges through the handwriting itself as well as through the breathless need to tell the narrative in the present, keeping pace with the moment and the moving action of the images spooling before Banner as cinematic viewer. Still, her narratives have a kind of literary innocence, which her images can never have, yet word and image are intimately bound together in the life of her work, plain tales and deceitful images continuing to play off each other. In the light of this it would be interesting to see how Banner's own literary style has altered in the writing of these works, how 'plain' these renderings are, and how that 'plainness' develops through its engagement with the film in question. Does the seductiveness of these narratives prevent us from approaching the words as suspiciously as we approach the images? Does Banner, perhaps, present a kind of *cinéma vérité* (or *littérature vérité*) account of these fantasy action extravaganzas?

These questions arise from the strange kind of accessibility that haunts these epic works. Despite their exotic *mise-en-scène*, when they are 'translated' into artworks they are actually quite readable. *Apocalypse Now* or *Lawrence of Arabia* – films you might know, films invested with a cult glamour – are here laid out for you with similar titles in unpretentious, unchallenging sentences. Yet, with this simple device, Banner has constructed something that resonates between

story, film and still image, but is none of these. This is coherent prose, certainly; it is even formally conventional. The style is fluid and peculiarly unremarkable. Punctuation is in its place – something Banner plays with in another 1995 work, *Un\*\*\*\*\*\*\*believable* (pen on formica), which is all punctuation and no words. Formica sheets are dotted with punctuation marks, scattered in humorous little groups as if keeping each other company, or conspiring together having banished the words. Unlike *Apocalypse Now*, a text with perhaps too many words, *Un\*\*\*\*\*\*\*believable* is a text with no words: only the situating signs of emphasis or pace are there, with nothing of what they refer to. It is as if a monumental act of deletion has taken place, leaving only the presence of an absence, although the final effect is funnier than that: more of a child's join-the-dots than a philosophical fill-in-the-gaps. By contrast, Banner's pieces for this exhibition are brimful of coherent, 'proper' prose. Yet coherent prose can become quite incoherent, quite unreadable, without a single word being changed, when framed and presented in this way. For these are words loaded, primarily, not with linguistic significance but with the seduction of imagery. These are words that *look* more than they *mean*.

First impressions are deceptive. Apparently accessible, Banner's works can look quite neat, at least when the text is printed as with *The desert*. *Apocalypse Now*, however, is rendered crazier by virtue of the uneasy intimacy in the style and dash of Banner's own hand. The handwriting brings with it not just a self-consciously declared subjectivism but various forms of cracked obsessiveness. The text can begin to look like 'lines': a school punishment – a ritual of empty repetition (like Vietnam cinema itself, perhaps) – or the insane outpouring of a captive. Then, when compared against handwritten scribble, the sheer neatness of the print in other works begins to take on a pristine weirdness all of its own. Look closely or stand back, the words do not stay still; they melt into a dizzying forest, through which rivers of white space (between the lines, as it were), offer a path, or seduce you into reading, reading on, only to lose you. Letters and words melt into the grey-on-white minute patterning of the whole. Sentences fuse and dissolve; your eye will wander. But then again you may find a moment you recognise, a scene you remember and dialogue you recall – your favourite moment, perhaps – and something will make sense, just briefly. Your eye will rewind or fast forward, it will freeze-frame those moments it recognises like a seasoned video user: moments of cult cinema, of dialogue bites remembered, repeated and shared, that seal a film in its own mythology. Then you will think that this is not a picture but a book, a book without its binding (a diary perhaps) and just as you do, the words will be lost again in the frenzy of letter-patterns you are also looking at. If a book, it is a book that exceeds its limits – unbound, the words have bled through the margins. If a diary, it is a diary as monologue, or free association, but this is no exciting confessional: we are merely witnessing the banal tedium of someone else's fascination with the plot. Bored, perhaps, you will stand back, and then significance will melt again into image, and you will slip, and fall, somewhere between reader and viewer, viewer and spectator. Book becomes picture, and back again. Banner presents her viewers with the impossibility as well as the possibility of reading.

Scale is not just a question of mass in these works. There is always an oscillation between the too-big and the minuscule, and here, I think, lies the works' absurdity and humour. Read Banner's *Apocalypse Now* alongside her pencil drawing of Brando as Kurtz (*Kurtz*,1996, pencil on paper) or Kurtz as Brando. Kurtz, icon of terror, is nothing

but a construct of tiny grey lines. The image is merely the effect of diminutive mark-making, yet in long-shot, standing back, it is difficult to tell if they are lines or words (what's the difference?). The closer you look the faster the horror of his vast image dissolves into its component parts. The colossal plays off the minute throughout these Vietnam pieces, and is always dependent upon it. Brando's gesture towards the tragic or grandiose is the film's – and the drawing's – final, ridiculous, disappointment.

Proximity is all, a truth borne out by Vietnam on film when perspective is entirely an effect of distance, of how far or how near your subject is. So much of the power of 'Vietnam cinema' emerges because of a problem of translation, or because the transmission of motifs, images, music even, from one culture to another makes a difference. The global view, or the view from across the Pacific, is quite different from that taken up close. The transplanted subject is a key motif: *Full Metal Jacket, The Deer Hunter, Born on the Fourth of July, Heaven & Earth* – films pitched between 'here' and 'there' – lay out the agonised dislocation of psyches and bodies no longer at home at home, subjects suspended between U.S. pre-Nam training or post-Nam hospitalisation, and the war zone itself. The significance of these

A variety of helicopters from Fiona Banner's collection of Vietnam film stills.

films is, finally, the significance of *not* being there, of never really *arriving* in Vietnam – its reality only becomes real when reviewed from America itself. Even *Apocalypse Now* is essentially a journey, with an absence at the end of it. These are films in which nothing is in its place: home has become something other whilst the other takes on a macabre familiarity (the irony at the heart of *Coming Home*). The Doors never sounded so good as when they were transplanted across the Pacific. Perspective makes the difference.

Distance and translation also mark Banner's works, which are themselves pitched between (at least) two cultures: the language, grunts, inarticulacies and non-linguistic spectacles of American action cinema and the translations and transliterations of a woman artist working in Britain in the 1990s. Thus Banner builds on to the films' own sense of displacement another dimension of foreignness.

So how does all this affect Banner's viewers or readers? If the works themselves hover between different artistic identities, then what of those who experience them? If, at a distance, the written pieces are wall-to-wall texts, in close-up they are also collages of minutiae. In close-up *Apocalypse Now* is readable; in long-shot it is not. Like Molly Bloom's soliloquy in Joyce's *Ulysses*, the whole block image is unravelled the closer you get to the bits. The comparison with Banner's word-works and literary modernism takes place on other levels too. I am reminded of Ezra Pound playing with Chinese ideographs for an English-speaking audience in *The Cantos*, using the form of a word or a phrase solely for its graphic qualities, its pictorial shape on the page. Literary or linguistic meaning is subordinated to image, yet the image is language, a language one is not expected to 'read'. An earlier work by Pound also used the *shape* of the haiku, as well as its fresh literary minimalism, as a way of making striking graphic patterns formed simply with ink surrounded by white on the page. Words then become, briefly, *nothing but* an arrangement of ink on the page. Banner, too, makes words into things, components of an uneasy linguistically patterned image.

Here, then, is another exchange, a double movement, between how you engage with the work and how it then engages you. Here, too, is another unsettling or ambiguous aspect of the whole experience: the oscillation of Banner's audience between different points of view, between different ways of reading and different visualisations. Thus the works emerge at their most paradoxical. The flow of the filmic mobile frames is fixed in text, the visual is drawn into and as the verbal. But the narrative also moves along, as it were, through reading. All that is there is there *at once*, yet all that is there – were one to read it – would involve the reader in a narrative unfolding that would, quite simply, take a good deal of time. *Reading* Banner's *Apocalypse Now* sequentially allows it to unfold as a work of truly epic length – an act itself insane, perhaps impossible – but one that necessarily submerges it in time. Yet *viewing* it as a whole captures the frozen quality of all narrative moments, the narrative being paradoxically present simultaneously. The effect is of a snapshot, which is both moving and still, fixed and continuous, and which negotiates an uneasy line between giving you everything and nothing. Obsessively trawling through the twists of some of cinema's most epic plots, Banner's larger works subject these grandiose projects to an eye for minutiae that renders all events, all speeches, equal to each other. Nothing, except everything, is privileged.

I began by asking what happens when Banner brings moving pictures into still frames. In fact, she keeps the pictures moving, rolling her narratives on to their inevitable conclusion, *and* manages to make the whole picture absolutely fixed. The story moves on, without the loss of earlier passages. Finally, then, the question is not how she makes the still move or the image word, but how her viewers or readers take in this simultaneously moving and fixed image, this image which is text and text which is image, as one piece. *Can* the eye do both simultaneously? *Is* it possible to read a text and see it as a picture at the same time? Is it then possible to see through the image to another text, one that occludes history? And if that history was one of defeat and disappointment, does this influence the tone of Banner's works? These questions are at the heart of the challenge she sets, dancing between these different ways of seeing or reading. Film image becomes word, so that word can become image again.

*Chinook* (1995), pencil on paper, 4 ft × 5'6 ins.

# Terry Gilliam

By Peter Wollen

Soon after VJ day Henry Kaiser, the great Californian industrialist, launched Kaiser Homes as part of his effort to reorganise the Kaiser war machine – shipyards, dams, mines, power, steel, aluminium, airplanes, armaments – in readiness for the coming peace. He announced a new plan to manufacture mass-produced prefabricated dwellings for the millions of new immigrants he predicted would soon be flooding into the Los Angeles area. Panorama City, a new suburb in the San Fernando Valley, was a showpiece for Kaiser's dream – 3,000 uniform Kaiser-designed and Kaiser-built tract homes. It was here that Terry Gilliam grew up. It is not surprising that when he left the Southland for New York City, in the mid-1960s, it was to work for an anarchic humour magazine called *Help!* Later he recalled his first impressions of the great vertical metropolis:

I remember my first view of New York was getting out of the subway at 42nd Street, coming from the airport and that was just Whooah! There you are at the bottom of these monoliths ... When I lived there, I had no money at all. You feel you're at the bottom of all those great towers the whole time and everyone else is up there having a good time except you.

These two experiences of urban life echo throughout Terry Gilliam's extraordinary *oeuvre*. On the one hand there is the horror of standardisation, regimentation, instrumental reason, and, on the other, the feeling of being lost in a nightmarish chaos in which you are excluded from all power, pleasure and enjoyment. *Brazil*, *The Fisher King* and *Twelve Monkeys* form a trilogy of urban blight and dystopian horror unequalled in contemporary art. Gilliam's vision of the contemporary city, moreover, is one in which progress consists purely of perfecting the *modus operandi* of a society that is essentially medieval in its squalor, violence and barbarism. History is collapsed into an overlay of different epochs, all of which are marked by hierarchy, arbitrary rule, civil strife, unpredictable threat and terrifying insanity, whose model, in many ways, is that of the Middle Ages. At the same time, the Middle Ages, through myths like that of the Holy Grail, also proffer the hope of escape into an idealised freedom of bliss. Thus fatality and Utopia go hand in hand as Gilliam's heroes struggle to find the flaw in the paranoid order that besets them and to make their way through into a fantasy world of primal euphoria – to bask in the 'oceanic feeling', which Freud named but never himself experienced.

Gilliam's universe combines the grotesque vision of Bosch and Bruegel, a monstrous world teetering between tragedy and comedy, with the

Terry Gilliam's extravagant and elegiac vision, *The Adventures of Baron Munchausen.*

Overleaf: lost men among the machines in *Brazil*.

Jonathan Pryce as Sam Lowry, the protagonist in Terry Gilliam's *Brazil.*

MINISTRY OF INFORMA
DEPT OF INFORMATION RETRIEVAL

Reg. No.

Classification

Surname
(BLOCK LETTERS)

Christian Names

Sentence

EXPEDIT

anxiety-laden predicament of being trapped and persecuted by an inscrutable and anonymous authority, more in the vein of Kafka: 'the cold grotesque', as Wolfgang Kaysar calls it in his classic study of the mode, *The Grotesque in Art and Literature*. Gilliam's world is one in which the little man – K. or Walter Mitty or Charlie Chaplin, so to speak – is struggling doggedly but helplessly against an implacable system, release from which can only be magical. It is a world similar to that of *Waiting for Godot*, blessed with a Chaucerian exuberance. Only in Gilliam's masterpiece, *The Adventures of Baron Munchausen*, is this exuberance given free rein and is fantasy permitted to triumph in wish fulfilment. In the real world of film production, sadly, this was not to be and Gilliam soon found himself locked in a struggle with the implacable bureaucracy of Universal Pictures, much like one of his own characters.

Like Kafka, Gilliam depicts a world inhabited by white-collar rather than blue-collar workers, a world of office clerks and minor functionaries, well-meaning but utterly confused underlings. In this sense, he is indeed a child of the fifties, the decade of C. Wright Mills's *White Collar* and *The Power Elite* (1951 and 1956) and William H. Whyte's *The Organization Man* (1956, Gilliam was

then 16). It was also the period, of course, of the great counterpart to these studies, Nicholas Ray's film *Rebel Without a Cause*, based on a book by Robert Linder, himself the author of *Must You Conform?* Gilliam's father was a skilled craftsman who worked for Johns-Manville, a large corporation. Gilliam later commented, 'The sad thing is that he was a very good carpenter, and he ended up making nothing else but office partitions.' However, there is a paradoxical sense in which Gilliam's 1950s fixation on white-collar work actually stood him in good stead when the world of bureaucracy was overturned by the computer in the 1970s and 1980s, the world foreseen by Daniel Bell in *The Coming of Post-Industrial Society* (1973) and described more accurately by Manuel Castello in *The Informational City* (1989) – a path-breaking book, which actually post-dated *Brazil*.

In the 1980s the world entered a cataclysmic new phase of information-driven industry, associated, of course, with the development of the computer network as an administrative system, which generated, stored, filed and distributed information. Gilliam responded to these developments more directly and more incisively than any other film-maker. He did this by introducing enigmatic and disturbing elements of the new order into a society still dominated, at its lower levels, by antiquated technologies and work-styles. Gilliam's world was a world of lags and leads in which, once again, the pathetically out-of-date tried to coexist with the disruptively new. The Dickensian office became a kind of pastoral haven, whose beleaguered inhabitants tried by whatever means they could to resist the onslaught of the new system that their smooth-talking and utterly ruthless superiors wanted to impose on them. Gilliam lovingly depicted a tragi-comic world of muddled bureaucratic Luddism.

In 1983 Gilliam was assigned the job of heading a special production unit on *Monty Python's The Meaning of Life*. Gilliam was to direct just one section of the film, and it was originally envisaged that his section would somehow be incorporated later on into the rest of the film. Not surprisingly, this notion did not work out in practice and consequently Gilliam's section ended up as an independent short film, which was then screened before the main feature, directed by Terry Jones. Gilliam's film tells the story of the elderly employees of an old-fashioned insurance company, which is taken over by a dynamic new multinational. The old fogies unexpectedly resist their yuppie masters,

Where dreams come true: Terry Gilliam's *The Adventures of Baron Munchausen*.

White collar
revolt: Terry
Gilliam's short
film *The Crimson
Insurance
Company.*

and, after an unexpected victory, set themselves
up as piratical freebooters, using their fans as
cutlasses, their hatstands as grappling hooks
and their filing cabinets as cannon. In their
antiquated Edwardian office-building they cast
off and set sail between the towering cliffs of
modern office-blocks to storm the citadels of
finance capital. A similar scenario is repeated
in *Brazil*, the plot of which hinges on a filing
error and a doomed battle against the ruthless
power of Information Retrieval. A lone clerk,
who has doggedly resisted transfer from his
administrative backwater, a kind of folk museum
of antiquated office equipment and eccentric
bureaucratic procedures, sets out on an
impossible quest to outwit the system, fulfil
his vision and find true happiness.

The filing cabinet, of course, was the mainstay
of all bureaucratic organisations until it was
superseded by the computer, which incorporates
its own digital filing system. The traditional
cabinet is now little more than a hard-copy back-
up system, already on the slippery slope of
obsolescence. In many ways it was a peculiarly
English article, which flourished during
the heyday of London as an administrative and
financial capital. As it declines it takes on a new
aura of memory-laden desuetude. No longer

a practical system of information storage and
retrieval, it can now be viewed, not as a rational
instrument of order, but as quite the contrary,
an irrational accomplice of chaos. The filing
cabinet is fated to become a kind of treasure-
trove of the uncanny and the irrelevant, an eerie
remnant of Victoriana, a resting place on the
descent to deep nostalgia, a shrine for secret
communion with magnificent obsession,
a tempting grab-bag of delirious miscellanea,
a depository of dust, a columbarium. The filing
cabinet, in Susan Buck-Morss's taxonomy, can
become a fossil, a fetish, a wish image or a ruin.
As historical objects become outmoded they
become part of a nostalgic world, a world in
which obscure images can throw the present
into a garish new light. This refunctioning of the
filing cabinet might suggest Walter Benjamin's
fascination with the dream-world of nineteenth-
century Paris, but Benjamin's interest fell
only on scenes and objects of leisure, not those
of work. The filing cabinet conjures up a world
of bureaucracy, reverie and futility in the
citadel of order and purpose.

Stephen Bann, in an essay on John Bargrave's
baroque cabinet of curiosities, has pointed out
that such a cabinet was not simply the site for the
collection of curious objects – a transitional site

between theology and science, between the shrine and the encyclopaedia – it was an act of mourning. Bargrave, 'deprived of the splendid surroundings of youth,' sought 'to reinvest his spiritual and emotional self in new objects, which could perhaps achieve a limited form of transcendence'. In this sense, much of Gilliam's work (not only his studio, revealed on television as itself a kind of *Wunderkammer*) can also be seen as an act of mourning – the lost object being, ultimately, the Holy Grail, which structures so much of his work. Bargrave's world was destroyed by the Reformation, which ended the role of Canterbury as a site of pilgrimage. His wanderings served as opportunities to collect wonders that other virtuosi would travel to Canterbury to see. Gilliam's master metaphor is not so much the pilgrimage as the quest, but, as Bargrave was, he is compelled to recognise that it can now serve only as a metaphor. At the same time he is repelled by modernity, seen as Max Weber saw it, as the 'disenchantment of the world'. There are two paths to re-enchantment: one is to keep alive the myth of the Grail, the vision of transcendence; the other is to construct and display a kind of meta-cabinet of curiosities, itself filled with the detritus of bureaucracy, an act of

mourning that is also a ritual of resistance.

Terry Gilliam sees the cinema as falling on the side of magic rather than that of instrumental reason: 'When I was a kid I used to do magic shows, which is why I've always admired Georges Méliès.' For Gilliam the dream of cinema has been betrayed all too often, served simply as 'the emperor's new clothes'. Its magic powers, of course, have been destroyed by its banality. There is no quest involved in going to the cinema. The cinema is simply the glittering trinket of the Waste Land. The only way to restore its power is to restore the sense of mystery it once enjoyed. To regain its primal power, the cinema, like the Grail, must disappear. What better place could there be for it to hide than behind a screen of filing cabinets? Like Shangri-La or Oz (to which Salman Rushdie compared Gilliam's *Brazil*) it must be inaccessible a magical shrine that we can visit only as Baron Munchausen visited the moon. Gilliam's over-riding vision, however, is temporal, rather than spatial – as *Twelve Monkeys* and *Time Bandits* have shown, it is only through the magic of time travel that we can hope to free ourselves. The image that reveals the pilgrim's path is always the image of the hidden, the repressed, the detritus of history.

Where magic and cinema meet: Georges Méliès' *L'Armoire des frères Davenport* (1902).

Space and time: Gilliam's new film, *Twelve Monkeys*, with its questor.

# Douglas
# Gordon

## By Amy Taubin

Cinema is truth 24 times a second.
Jean-Luc Godard

There is truth, absolute in its relativity.
Lenin

Slow motion actually brings a new range to dramaturgy. Its power of laying bare the emotions of dramatic engagements, its infallibility in the designation of the sincere movements of the soul are such that it obviously outclasses all the known tragic modes at this time. I'm sure ... that if a high-speed film were made of an accused person during his interrogation [and it were then projected in slow motion], then from beyond his words, the truth would appear, unique, evident, written out. There would no longer be need of indictment or of lawyers' speeches, or of any other proof other than that provided by the profound images.
Jean Epstein, in an interview published in Paris, 1928.

Men do kill nude women you know.
Alfred Hitchcock, 1960 (to a Variety reporter about potential censorship problems with Psycho, cited in Stephen Rebello, *Alfred Hitchcock and the Making of Psycho*, Harper Perennial, 1991.

Regardless of your age or cultural orientation you are likely to know something about Alfred Hitchcock's *Psycho*, even if it is only that a woman is slashed to death in a shower by a maniac whose sexual identity is somewhat confused. Douglas Gordon's *24 Hour Psycho* traffics in the film's uncanny familiarity, which has to do with both the reputation it has acquired in the 35 years since its release and the way, whether you are seeing it for the first or the 100th time, it taps into primal anxieties about sex, castration and death.

*Psycho* is an inescapable film. By slowing down the projection so that it takes 24 hours to run its course, Gordon's piece suggests not only that the film is ever present, but also that its narrative is inexorable. Shown at approximately two frames per second, the film retains just enough motion for us to feel how each image is pulled towards the next. No matter how slowly the wheels grind, the end *will* come. And at the end lies nullification, which is worse than death.

In 1980 Jean-Luc Godard went to the Cannes Film Festival to première his recently completed *Sauve Quit Peut (La Vie)*, later released in Britain under the title *Slow Motion*. The death of Alfred Hitchcock, just days before, coloured the remarks Godard made about the film, his first 35mm theatrical release in nearly a decade. Claiming that Hitchcock's death marked the passage from one era of cinema to another, Godard characterised the coming era as 'the ebbing of

Janet Leigh as Marion Crane in *Psycho,* in a studio portrait.

Jean Luc Godard's *Sauve Quit Peut (La Vie),* titled *Slow Motion* in Britain.

the visual', and went on to say that he doubted whether film-makers would have the strength to continue. Although Godard has continued, there is a way in which his post-1980 work can be seen as an extended elegy for the cinema he both loved and hated: the narrative cinema of *auteurs*, amongst whom Hitchcock was supreme.

Godard had incorporated the experiments made during the 1970s with video slow motion into *Sauve Quit Peut (La Vie)*, hence the British title. Slow-motion effects, which were expensive and labour-intensive to achieve on film, had become available instantly and irresistibly with just a twist of the search mechanism on professional video-editing equipment. Here is Godard writing in 1980 in *Cahiers du cinéma* about his use of slow motion in *France/tour/detour/deux/enfants*, the television series in which he interviews a young girl and boy as they go about their daily routines:

I concluded that when one changes the rhythms ... there were so many different worlds inside the women's movements. Whereas slowing down the little boy's movements was a lot less interesting – every time the image was stopped the same thing was always going on, but with the little girl, even when she was doing something completely banal, one could suddenly see a look of extreme sadness

and then a third of a second later, a look of joy ...

Although Godard then tries to cover his tracks by referring to his 'scientific' orientation, one's response to his remarks is that these were hardly controlled experiments, and that the differences he discovered between the girl and the boy reveal more about his own projections (what he allowed himself to observe about the little girl, and conversely did not allow himself to notice about the little boy) than about difference (natural or cultural) between female and male ten-year-olds. (For the first slow-motion image of the girl, Godard chooses a shot of her undressing to go to bed, while the first slow-motion image of the boy shows him flinging on his jacket as he leaves for school – not a very scientific basis for comparison.) Nevertheless, what is striking is his intent to use slow motion as a way of providing and fetishising sexual difference.

Here is Douglas Gordon explaining the genesis of *24 Hour Psycho*:

In 1992 I had gone home to see my family for Christmas and I was looking at a video of the TV transmission of *Psycho*. And in the part where Norman (Anthony Perkins) lifts up the painting of *Suzanna and the Elders* and you see the close-up of his eye looking through the peep-hole at Marion (Janet Leigh) undressing, I thought I saw her unhooking her bra. I didn't remember seeing that in the VCR version and thought it was strange, in terms of censorship, that more would be shown on TV than in the video, so I looked at that bit with the freeze-frame button, to see if it was really there.

In spite of Gordon's interest in the various perimeters of censorship (like Godard's protestations of scientific analysis), it was his fascination with the illicit image (seen from his vantage point of Norman Bates's peep-hole) of a woman's body and his need to verify whether or not something was there (that something, a woman's hand unhooking her bra, being a sign of sexual difference) that set *24 Hour Psycho* in motion.

Gordon says that as he continued to fool around with the freeze-frame button, he discovered that drastically slowing down the image had an unexpected effect. Rather than making the film clearer, the slow motion made it more chaotic.

There were these beautiful details that Hitchcock couldn't have been conscious of and couldn't have controlled. It was as if the slow motion revealed the unconscious of the film. In the sequence of Norman watching as the car sinks into the swamp, there's this incredible tension between him and the car, but it has

Janet Leigh in the famous white bra in Hitchcock's film *Psycho*.

nothing to do with what came before or what comes after. The micro-narrative takes over.

In the voluminous history of slow motion in the movies, two not entirely separate purposes emerge. One is analytical, one expressive. Claiming the camera as truth machine, the film-makers of the French and Soviet avant-garde rejected transparent modes of realism. They used the camera to reveal physical aspects of gesture and movement unavailable to the naked eye and also to represent the elasticity of time as subjective experience. Slow motion was part of an arsenal of techniques, which also included fast motion, backward motion, animation and superimposition.

'I am eye, I am a mechanical eye,' wrote Soviet film-maker Dziga Vertov, in his 'Kino Eye' manifesto. 'I, a machine, am showing you a world the likes of which only I can see ... Freed from the obligation of shooting 16 frames per second [standard silent film speed], freed from the frame of time and space, I co-ordinate any and all points of the universe, wherever I may plot them ... Thus I decipher in a new way the world unknown to you.'

The American avant-garde film-makers working after the Second World War also made slow motion part of their everyday vocabulary.

But it is probably only Andy Warhol and Ken Jacobs who have employed it in the same single-minded fashion that Gordon has in *24 Hour Psycho.*

In the late 1960s Ken Jacobs acquired an analytic projector that could show film at variable speeds from one to 24 frames per second. (During the 1970s, analytic projectors were used in university cinema-study courses where students were subjected to countless slow-motion screenings of the Odessa Steps sequence from *Battleship Potemkin* or, indeed, the shower sequence from *Psycho.*) Jacobs used the analytic projector to make the two-hour *Tom, Tom the Piper's Son* (1969), which he describes as a 'reverent re-examination' of a short 1905 film by Billy Bitzer. The original film was projected at different speeds and the projected images then filmed from different angles.

My camera closes in only to better ascertain the infinite richness ... searching out incongruities in the story-telling, delighting in the whole bizarre human phenomenon of story-telling itself, and this within the fantasy of reading any bygone time out of the visual crudities of film; dream within a dream!

The analytic projector became the mainstay of Jacobs's live 'Nervous System Film Performances', the first of which was *The Impossible: Southwark*

*Fair. The Impossible* begins with the opening image from *Tom, Tom, the Piper's Son*, a re-creation of Hogarth's painting of Southwark Fair, this being the place where the first film peep-shows were set up.

It was also Jacobs who, a decade earlier, had discovered Joseph Cornell's 1937 film *Rose Hobart*. Cornell had extracted from a print of the Hollywood B picture, *East of Borneo*, all the shots in which the notably androgynous actress, Rose Hobart, appears and had strung them together, thus applying the principles of his collage boxes to a time-based object. Jacobs and the film-maker/performer Jack Smith, both of whom had worked as studio assistants for Cornell, set up a private screening of *Rose Hobart*, fetishising this already amazingly fetishistic object by projecting it through a blue filter, slowed down to 16 frames per second and accompanied by a tacky 'Sounds of Spain' record.

*Rose Hobart* was undoubtedly amongst the avant-garde films Andy Warhol looked at while he was preparing to make his own. Almost everything Warhol would do in film is there in this Cornell throwaway: the paring down of a mass-culture object to its fantasy essence, the fetishising of the female star, the phantasmal effect achieved when film shot at sound speed

Rose Hobart in
*East of Borneo*,
Joseph Cornell
included her
image in his film
*Rose Hobart*.

is projected a third slower, at the speed of silent film.

The silent films that Warhol made during 1963 and 1964, notably *Kiss, Sleep, Haircut, Empire* and *Henry Geldzahler*, all use this slowed-down projection technique, which has the paradoxical effect of heightening the sensuous quality of the image while increasing our sense of distance from it. The film unwinds at a pace that is slightly out of sync with the rhythms of the viewer. This disjunction, between the body clock of the person *as image* and the body clock of the person watching, makes us aware of the image as 'other' and therefore unknowable. Hollywood codes of realism elide the gap between seeing and knowing; Warhol's films reinforce it.

Like Cornell (and like the Surrealists in general) Warhol was a fan of Hollywood films. For five years he moved effortlessly between painting and film-making, setting up a (per)version of the Hollywood studio system in his 'Factory', where he turned out hundreds of films for little more than the cost of stock and processing.

Conceptually *24 Hour Psycho* has something in common with Warhol's *Empire*, the Empire State Building filmed continuously from sunset to sunrise and then projected slowed down by a third; it is Hitchcock's *Psycho* projected not at 24 but at approximately 2 frames per second, so that it lasts for 24 hours. Both works are based on icons (one a building, the other a film) that everybody knows of, though not necessarily from first-hand experience. Both are of a length that exceeds the endurance of most viewers; they are not actually intended to be experienced from beginning to end.

But when one looks at *24 Hour Psycho* one notices immediately that the image does not conform to what we think of as slow motion. There is no ghostly glide as in a Warhol film; instead the movement, such as it is, seems jerky. By slowing the film to a 13th of its normal speed, Gordon shows us not a 'motion picture' but a succession of stills, each projected for about half a second. We become aware of the intermittency of the film image and the fragility of the illusion of real time in motion pictures.

Rather than isolating each image, however, the extreme slow motion heightens the tension between them. At the end of the driving scene, for example, Marion glimpses, through the pelting rain, the neon sign of the Bates motel and heads towards it like a moth to a flame. But is that attraction a property of the images

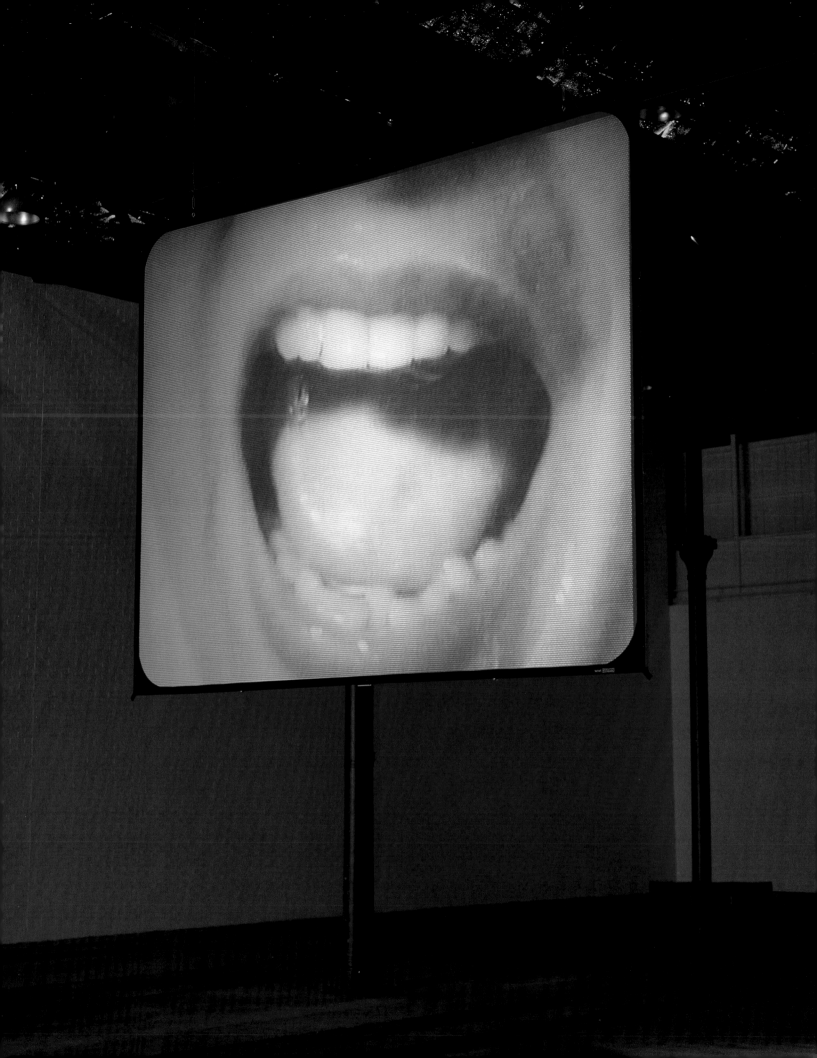

Andy Warhol's
*Empire* (1964).

Opposite:
installation shot
from *24 Hour
Psycho.*

themselves, or are we projecting our knowledge of the narrative into the gap between the images? One would think that slowing the film down would make the present more vivid. Instead it provides space for memory and anticipation to rush in. (I found myself running Bernard Herrmann's insistent score in my head, and of course out of sync, as I watched.)

To show the film (or more accurately a videotape copy of the film) Gordon employs an almost obsolete piece of video technology, an industrial Panasonic VHS desk with a jog mechanism that locks into a speed of more or less two frames a second. Because these machines are not entirely accurate, the piece might be more accurately titled *Roughly 24 Hour Psycho.*

Anyone with a top of the range VCR or laser-disc player could make a DIY version of *24 Hour Psycho.* Missing, however, would be the public dimension of the piece, for which a screen is crucial. Gordon hangs the screen on which *24 Hour Psycho* is projected high and slightly tilted towards the ground so that the image looms over the viewer. This echoes the spatial relationship in the film's most frightening images: the murderer's knife looming over

its victims, first Marion, then the detective Arbogast, frozen briefly before plunging downwards.

The placement of the screen also allows the viewer to walk behind it. From this vantage point one sees the image flipped left to right. The spatial confusion produced by this mirror image – the inversion of the memory one has of the film – suggests a metaphor for Norman's psychotic confusion of his sexuality and his inability to separate his own identity from that of his mother.

*Psycho* plays on unconscious and terrifying infantile sexual fantasies. If someone were to ask you who the murderer was in *Psycho,* you might picture not shy Norman but his 'mother', an uncommonly strong old woman with long grey hair twisted into a fetishistic knot at the nape of her neck and a very large knife poised about her head. It is this image of the castrating phallic mother that sticks in the memory and makes *Psycho* so disturbing.

Or rather, it is the image of the phallic mother combined with the viewer's guilt at being caught peeping. Like Warhol, Hitchcock implicates us in the perverse aspect of his own voyeurism. *Psycho* opens with a bird's-eye view that penetrates the window of a hotel room, where an unmarried couple is having a secret tryst. Hitchcock said he wanted *Psycho* to carry film into the 1960s and one of his strategies was to flout 1950s codes of censorship. Even today there is something illicit in the shot of Janet Leigh stretched out on the bed, quaintly garbed in a bra (unmistakably the focus of the shot) and a half-slip. Some 40 minutes later this shot is repeated, but this time we are put in the position of a psychotic serial killer spying on his victim as she undresses. This is the crucial shot that Gordon felt compelled to freeze-frame, as he watched within the safety of the family fold, in order to be sure exactly what it was or was not that he and Norman had glimpsed through the secret peep-hole.

*Psycho*'s iconic power extends beyond the psycho/sexual complications of its narrative, however. Like Robert Frank's photographs in *The Americans* (also 1959), *Psycho* depicts an aspect of American life disavowed by the shiny, saturated-colour images of a burgeoning suburbia that characterised the decade. It captures the sense of alienation and loss, of repression and claustrophobia that still pervades thousands of backwater towns where family life can be a horror story escapable only by death.

# Peter
# Greenaway

By Thomas
Elsaesser

The critic André Bazin once expressed a general dissatisfaction with films about artists and paintings in his essay, 'Painting and Cinema', but went on to claim that 'the cinema, far from compromising or destroying the true nature of another art, is, on the contrary, in the process of saving it'.[1] Nearly 50 years later, and a full century after the first presentation of the Lumière Cinématographe, a question arises that reverses Bazin's remark: is another art in the process of saving the cinema?

What prompts this question is the very success of cinema, an 'art' now so ubiquitous as to be all but invisible. Here I posit it as a possible way of looking at a series of strategic side-steps that Peter Greenaway has taken in recent years, by curating exhibitions and directing operas. As it happens, the steps fit into his project *The Stairs*.

In 1986 I wrote a ... film-script called *The Stairs* which ... hoped to discuss the provocations *ad nauseam* of the business of putting images with text, theatre with architecture, painting with music, selfishness with ambition. Stairs became the architectural motif and the general metaphor of the potential film (not ignoring the appropriate pun on a good hard look) ... it was to present a platform for display, like a theatre stage raked high for excellent visibility.[2]

The film was never made, but stairs have a symptomatic role in more than the Greenaway shows mounted in Geneva and Munich under that title. They point to what he has had in mind for some time, namely 'taking the cinema out of the cinema'.[3]

It transpires that the period of Greenaway's greatest triumphs as an established, indeed sustaining, pillar of the European art cinema, from *The Draughtsman's Contract* (1982) to *The Cook The Thief His Wife & Her Lover* (1991), coincided with his greatest dissatisfaction with the medium and its history: 'now that cinema celebrates its first centenary and is a medium ripe for the re-invention of itself, there is evidence to believe that all art moves towards the condition of film.'[4]

*On Leaving the Century of Cinema*
One exit at the top of Greenaway's stairs might be into a film museum like the National Film Theatre, in order to ponder once more Griffith or Gance, Paul Sharits or Jean-Luc Godard, an Antonioni film from the 1960s or a Hölderlin film by the Straubs. All other exits lead to the 'traditional' arts – opera, theatre, fine art – where, of course, much on view bears the unmistakable imprint of cinema. It is apposite, then, that a

A pillar of art:
*The Cook The Thief His Wife & Her Lover.*

*The Stairs*
projection
(1995), Munich.

painter turned film-maker should return from forays into television and dance, and present an installation reflecting on 'a century of propaganda for the cinematic experience'?

Each of Greenaway's feature films has an old-master style or single picture as its motif, self-consciously introduced and signposted.[5] But a wider view of his work suggests that Greenaway is actually travelling the other way, not towards examining what the cinema might have in common with the visual or performing arts, not even (like some recent French films dealing with the act of painting) making canvas and brush suitably ironic metaphors for the disappearance of celluloid and the camera-stylo from image-making. Rather, he is purging cinema, by confronting it both with itself and its 'others', recalling or insisting on a few conceptual features, in an attempt to rescue it from its self-oblivion by theatrically staging it across painting, sculpture, music, drama and architecture.

How does the Greenaway *oeuvre* look from these vantage points? Broadly speaking, two kinds of meta-commentary flank the five feature films that constitute his cultural capital. The early experimental work, culminating in the anti-films *A Walk Through H* (1978), *The Falls* (1980) and *Act of God* (1981), took cinema into the worlds of maps and archives, Borges and Calvino, missing persons and Babylonian libraries, stripping character and motive out of the narrative, and confronting film (through the voice of God broadcast by BBC announcers and the Central Office of Information) with its mythical documentary origins. The work for television (including *A TV Dante, M is for Mozart*) and *Prospero's Books* (1991) one could call post-films, in the sense that their concerns are neither narrative nor iconic-photographic. In keeping with the new technologies it deploys, the later work is graphic, concerned with trace and body, with surface, rather than space, and (absence of) body, as in the art films.

To these conceptual pillars can now be added an impressively proportioned project consisting of a series of installations/exhibitions, such as *The Physical Self* (Rotterdam, 1991), *Les bruits des nuages* (Paris, 1992) and *The Stairs* (Geneva 1994, Munich 1995), the latter keeping Greenaway at work, until the millennium, on public commissions for some of the world's major cities.

This focus on the city is significant because it announces an interesting and possibly crucial transfer. Much of Greenaway's work, I would argue, belongs to a British tradition of land(scape) art, an idiom not only intriguing for

its long history embracing an interest in shrines, gardens, vistas, secret paths and other invocations of the *genius loci*, but also offering a sophisticated conceptual vocabulary of trace, mark and index with which to explore perennially topical problems of aesthetics and semiotics. If Greenaway's art films, in their 'excessive Englishness'[6] pitch Britain as a set of codes and traditions into the Europe of the 1980s, so the city installations (so far planned and executed in such 'European' cities as Rotterdam, Vienna, Geneva, Munich and Barcelona) transfer a specifically 'English' language of landscape, site and history into urban environments.

*A Post-modernist turned Modernist?*
Is Greenaway keeping faith with modernism, or should he be regarded as one of the cinema's post-modernists? And if a modernist, does he belong to the American tradition of minimalism and conceptual art, or to the modernism that has, through poets and critics like T.S. Eliot or Ted Hughes, revived a 'metaphysical' or 'Jacobean' world of violence, masculinity and the extravagant conceit? Greenaway had already said of *The Draughtsman's Contract*: 'My film is about excess: excess in the language, excess in the landscape – which is much too green'.[7] The modernism/post-modernism divide may underestimate the force and diversity of the British/English concern with landscape, which has proved remarkably able to accommodate the most diverse strands of modernist thought.

A broader view of modernism allows one to draw a genealogy for Greenaway, and to situate him in the major post-war British tension between 'art school' modernism (David Hockney, Peter Blake, Richard Hamilton, R.B. Kitaj)[8] and 'art history' modernism (the Courtauld Institute, Anthony Blunt's *Poussin*, Niklaus Pevsner, Anthony Powell and William Golding) with its English gardens, the landscapes of neo-Romanticism, country houses set in ample grounds and stuffed with curio-cabinets and private collections. The tension also runs through the depiction of coastline and water (prominent in Greenaway) but difficult to place with any precision within British art and literature, for much – from Henry James and Virginia Woolf to Michael Powell and Derek Jarman – is haunted by the seascapes of Kent, Sussex or East Anglia, or obsessed with off-season resorts, 'learning from Blackpool'.

This British modernism, if it can count as such, of landscape and land art has arguably not proved the most fertile for cinema, or vice versa.

Re-presentation:
*The Draughtsman's Contract.*

Right:
*The Stairs* (1995),
Marstall
Installation,
Munich.

100 Objects to
Represent the
World (1992),
Vienna.

The modernism of art school 'pop' – its whimsy firmly plugged into the energy of commercial art, posters, fashion and design for the emergent mass-market – is probably the real partner in dialogue with cinema, if not its rival as the century's most prominent symbolic form. Pop and advertising certainly produced a generation of British film-makers whose international (read 'Hollywood') influence is undeniable. It brought the top end of British ad agency talent into direct contact with the Hollywood mainstream and contributed, importantly, to revitalising Hollywood itself in the 1980s.

By contrast Greenaway's work since *The Cook The Thief His Wife & Her Lover* presents a kind of meditation on the impossible dilemmas of a Thatcher-style Britain and on a British cinema caught between America and Europe. Even as he works with digital technology, Greenaway's mock-Victorianism sits uneasily with the pop-energies of a Hockney (also experimenting with electronic images and a digital paint box), just as his *A TV Dante* is in better company with land art such as Richard Long's or Hamish Fulton's visible and invisible walks[9] – where space, place and trace make a perfect geometry in four dimensions – than with Hockney's laser-printed portrait photographs.

*The cinema as kit: expanded or exploded view?* Morbid or cynical musings on the end of cinemas, or as Greenaway put it, on its 'sterility of concept, uniformity of execution,'[10] are not in short supply among either British or European film-makers. But when so much cinéaste ambition has had to write itself small and withdraw into the sulk corner of late-night television, Greenaway's successes have given him an opportunity to choose a larger canvas. He, too, starts with a sceptical assessment:

It is too late. Cinema is a one-way traffic: the best that can be hoped is to change the street furniture and the traffic-lights in readiness for the next attempt.[11]

A centenary is neither the worst occasion for an attempt to reinvent the cinema, nor is Greenaway a stranger to the magic of 100, the figure having served him well as the narrative architecture of *Drowning by Numbers*. Since then he has taken *100 Objects to Represent the World* to Vienna, *100 Stairs* to Geneva and, most recently, *100 Projections* to Munich. Even if at the Hayward Gallery the hundred is divided in two, a play of symmetry and seriality is nonetheless essential to the project.

And the idea of the 'folding' in half is

appropriate for a project that translates a temporal experience like the cinema into a spatial sequence. The order is reversible, the steps retraceable, the film can be rewound. What enfolds also unfolds. The labelled boxes, the white screens, the projections on to the buildings (Munich), the display tables and wall mounts (Rotterdam) the maps and instruments of vision and dissection (Geneva) that predominate in Greenaway's installations, all evoke a number of robust antinomies around removal and unpacking, storage and retrieval, inside and outside, before and after, evidence and argument, with both the cinema and the other arts alternately furnishing the *mise-en-abyme* into which each is Chinese-boxed (or Chinese-indexed).[12]

Another comparison also comes to mind. The Museum of the Moving Image – that modestly boastful monument to the movies' ubiquity, with its zoetropes and fantasmagorias, its agit prop train and blue-screens, its Western set and BBC newsroom – pays permanent homage to 'expanded cinema'. The Greenaway exhibit, so conveniently adjacent, might well be labelled 'exploded cinema'. A freeze-frame blast, or perhaps an explosion in the technical sense, as in an engineer's drawing, used for demonstrating the workings of a carburettor or a servo-system.

If we view Greenaway's installations as exploded cinemas in this sense, then our attention must be at once on the individual parts and on the fact that their arrangement is neither fixed nor arbitrary. Rather, they move along a number of determined axes, which represent their conceptual architecture. For his London kit, Greenaway proposes nine elements: 'artificial light, actors, props, text, illusion, audience, time, sound, changing imagery'. Some of these I would see as the 'working parts', laterally displaced, others as the imaginary axes, which allow the 'working parts' to transcend what we normally understand by the cinema machine. In this deconstructionist's shop the challenge is not to give away too soon which is which. Greenaway's props, in their profusion and surrealist incongruity, also seem to nod and wink at the spectator. But despite their comforting, archetypal associations, they are either gremlins bent on mischief or they are the defective parts of a plot, melancholic meta-mechanics of British cinema.[13]

A gallery space seems appropriate for such an exploded view of cinema because the installation is designed to give these elements a new materiality or to recall an original 'corporeality'

1. André Bazin, *What is Cinema?*, essays selected and translated by Hugh Gray, University of California Press, Berkeley, Los Angeles, 1967, p. 168. (Bazin's essay was written *c.* 1950.)

2. Peter Greenaway, *The Stairs*, Merrell Holberton, London, 1995, p. 11.

3. *Ibid.*, p. 9.

4. The passage continues: 'Painters, writers, playwrights, composers, choreographers – creators indeed who we could say should know better – have eager aspirations to make films, and if not to make them, then debate endlessly the possibilities of making them.' Quoted in Greenaway, *op. cit.*, p. 13.

5. A brief reminder: Vermeer (*Zed and Two Noughts*), Bruegel (*Drowning by Numbers*), Piero della Francesca (*Belly of an Architect*) and Frans Hals (*The Cook The Thief His Wife & Her Lover*).

6. See Peter Wollen, 'The Last New Wave' in Lester Friedman, ed., *Fires Were Started*, Minnesota University Press, Minneapolis, p. 46.

7. Quoted by Peter Wollen in Friedman, *op. cit.*, p. 45.

8. Wollen among others has argued that Greenaway fits this (1960s painter-poet-film-maker) avant-garde model perfectly: 'At heart, Greenaway, like Kitaj, is a collagist, juxtaposing images drawn from some fantastic archive, tracing erudite coincidental narratives within his material, bringing together Balthus and Borges.' Peter Wollen in Friedman, *op. cit.*, p. 44.

9. See, for instance, Stephen Bann's work on Richard Long.

10. Greenaway, *op. cit.*, p. 26.

11. Greenaway, *op. cit.*, p. 22.

12. Greenaway himself refers to Borges's famous Chinese encyclopedia quoted by Michel Foucault in *The Order of Things*, Greenaway, propectus for *In the Dark*.

divested by cinema. Temperature, texture or touch are aspects that do not seem to 'matter' to either cinematic projection or to the film itself, casting its spell of symbol and promise. Both live by the transparence of artificial light and both are parodied by a flashing electric torch that in a gallery – as Duchamp taught us – is at once a 'full' sign and an 'empty' object.

The second dimension, central to the cinema's repressed other, is also preserved or reinvented by the gallery space: that of a cinematic spectacle as live performance, yet fundamentally different from theatre, where body and voice can only be appreciated in the present tense. Greenaway 'explodes' this nexus, by having actors in showcase vitrines, but, as in cinema, separating body from voice and making sure that each day has a new programme. This recalls a crucial dimension of early cinema as itself a performance. At first, when films were bought and sold rather than exchanged or rented, the options were both 'materialist' and 'conceptual': either the same film to different audiences or different films to the same audience. Historically, the principle of 'different film/same audience' won the day, thus creating the unique commodity, the cinema, but Greenaway's installation recalls that this may not be inevitable, when all the other material parameters of cinema are being called into question.

*Dislodging the Frame*
Perhaps the most important reason for Greenaway passing (European) cinema through the art gallery in order that it should 'reinvent' itself is that constant irritant, the 'rigour of cinema's insistence on the rectangular frame, and ... that frame's fixed-aspect ratio.'[14] Something must surely give:

The ever decreasing choice imposed by commercial and industrial standards has tightened the frame-ratio to such a point that it must – in the same way as other tightening strictures have operated in other fields – explode. Painting, as always, has set the pace ... the last three decades have seen [the heavily framed painted image] largely evaporate.[15]

Interestingly, it was Bazin who proposed the classic distinction between the cinematic and the pictorial frame.[16] Bazin uses a rather traditional account of the picture frame to argue that the outer edges of the cinema screen are not strictly comparable to a frame at all, but function instead as a 'piece of masking that shows only a portion of reality ... part of something prolonged indefinitely into the universe'. He then goes on

to say that 'a frame is centripetal, a screen is centrifugal', thus bringing us back to the idea of Greenaway's 'exploded cinema' and leaving open the possibility that modern painting (having abandoned the 'centripetal' frame) can indeed redeem the cinema, if only to the extent of restoring to it the function Bazin claims for it: 'Thanks to the cinema and to the psychological properties of the screen, what is symbolic and abstract takes on the solid reality of a piece of ore.'[17] In so far as it is the cinema's ubiquity that makes it invisible, the question of the frame becomes central to its future, even though solutions for modern art's problems do not necessarily apply for cinema.[18]

Greenaway contests and tests the frame in a number of ways. One of his most interesting moves is the shift from 'wall-oriented, frontal-parallel-perpendicular' projection and display to a horizontal plane (the table tops as 'screens') and multi-dimensional screens 'behind' screens, showing not an image but the cone that cinematic lighting cuts into space. The installation at once suggests the complex geometry of the cinematic apparatus and acts as a projection-in-waiting, where the upright screen becomes a 'box' to be filled, rather than a surface to reflect an image and absorb a viewer. The glass vitrines, on the other hand, become cubic/cubist screens, on which the actor's roles – all the adulterers and kings they have played – unfold. A whole film is contained in a box, which is also a screen, without losing that ambiguity of objects/living things behind glass: 'don't touch, I'm valuable/dangerous'. Here we may have come full circle from when Orson Welles compared American film-making unfavourably to European cinema, saying that 'Hollywood treats the picture like a shop window behind glass, always stuffed to bursting'.[19]

*An Art of Projection: Scale and Ratio*
The question of dislodging the frame of the cinema screen seems urgent not so much because of Bazin's realist/illusionist problematics, or the preoccupations of the modernist avant-garde, but because it opens up that other dimension, perhaps the most crucial for Greenaway, of the audience. His worry about the frame as a function of the size and proportion of the screen, which sounds like the familiar grumble about cinema capitulating to television's aspect-ratio, may well touch the nub of his enterprise, because the frame implies scale and, through scale, the issue of cinema as public art.

Audiences have become noticeably important

13. 'Although a list of archetypes might be conceived in a larger number ... 100 of them have been chosen for consideration, to be recreated by actors ... with all their relevant attributes, props and gestures, in showcases, vitrines and small theatres ... The purpose is not only to celebrate the disciplined richness of this consensus collection, but to make connections and associations between the various ways the different media have established these 100 characters, and the limitations that might have ensued in the visual language necessary to identify and exploit them.' Greenaway, prospectus for *In the Dark*.
14. Greenaway, *The Stairs*, op. cit., p. 19.
15. *Ibid*.
16. 'Just as footlights and scenery in the theatre serve to mark the contrast between it and the real world so, by its surrounding frame, a painting is separated off not only from reality as such but, even more so, from the reality of what is represented in it ... This explains the baroque complexity of the traditional frame whose job it is to establish something that cannot be geometrically established – namely the discontinuity between the painting and the wall, that is to say between the painting and reality.' André Bazin, *What is Cinema?*, op. cit., p. 165.
17. *Ibid.*, p. 168.
18. The battle over verticality and horizontality of the picture plane in American modernism has recently been described by Rosalind Krauss in *The Optical Unconscious* (The MIT Press, Cambridge, Massachussetts, 1993). She argues that Andy Warhol mimetically moved Jackson Pollock's drip-paintings' picture plane (produced on the ground but crucially designed to be vertical, upright, eye-level) to the horizontal plane, putting canvases flat on the ground, to be stepped on, dripped on, pissed on ...
19. Quoted in James Naremore, *The Films of Vincente Minnelli*, Cambridge University Press, 1993.
20. Greenaway, *The Stairs*, op. cit., p. 32.

*Watching Water* (1993), Pallazzo Fortuny, Venice.

in Greenaway's *oeuvre*, to the point that they not only feature prominently in his most recent films, especially *Prospero's Books*, *A TV Dante*, *M is for Mozart* and *Darwin*, but have become their veritable subject. *The Baby of Macon*, for instance, is about what limits, if any, there are to an event, once one assumes that being observed by an audience makes something an event. Here the spectacularisation of contemporary social interaction is put to the test in order to see whether, indeed, 'events not witnessed by an audience are not only non-performances but non-events'. He sets out to prove that anything attended by an audience becomes a performance, and to question how this might alter our notion of the real, the possible and the tolerable (these 'limits of representation' are a major concern of modern cinema, from Pasolini to Fassbinder, and from Godard to Oshima).

Less traumatised, perhaps, by history and fascism, Greenaway, too, tests the limits of representation. Unlike earlier avant-gardes he goes into the gallery not for an intimate space but for the last of the big spaces. And he goes to spaces that are not just public but that are resonant of the power of the state – art and power. He wants to reach different kinds of audiences: shoppers, strollers, 'a man taking a dog for a walk, a dog biting a man, a man biting a dog'.[20]

Greenaway denounces the pseudo-community of today's cinema attendance, averring that even television scores higher as a form of sociability. He seems to have decided that there is no point in making European film unless one understands what creates audiences in our 'society of the spectacle'. Not until there is a new definition of the visual event will there be the material conditions for a new cinema. Are there spaces, he asks, between the museum and the '*grands travaux*', that are funded by the state for the general good, rather than relying on the market-place? In this sense *In the Dark and into the Light* might just be offering a vision of a new civic, potentially democratic, but as yet unrealised public function for the cinema. The contest for a new kind of presentational or representational space – 'art cinema', not for art's sake, but for politics' sake – has commenced.

# Damien
# Hirst

# By Gordon Burn

I never could stand the seriousness of life, but when the serious is tinted with humour it makes a nice colour.
Marcel Duchamp

Pity the poor baby-boomer, the inbetweenager. Too young to put down a marker in Swinging London the first time around, too old to be included in the 'Neo-Swinging' moment being enjoyed by the current crop of the lean and young and poptastically unencumbered.

The London art scene in the nineties has been pretty much a group one. And the group, by and large, has been the one that came out of Goldsmiths' College around 1988 or 1989 and showed at the two ground-breaking warehouse exhibitions that Damien Hirst curated: *Freeze* (1988) and *Modern Medicine* (1990).

There was an attempt to re-create the spirit of these shows in the winter of 1995 when the Walker Art Center in Minneapolis put on *Brilliant! New Art From London.* Nineteen of the artists included went over to America for the opening, and the party was still continuing several weeks later at various locations in London. One night, in the falling-down season just before Christmas, it surfaced in an industrial building close to Smithfield market, where it was the usual happy boil-up of heads, throats and

sweat-pasted hair. But with this crucial difference: the palpable sense, shared by everyone present, of living in an unrepeatable moment; of being there when.

'The kind of group synergy that can lead to great art – the synergy that once pulled first-rate pictures out of second-rate Abstract Expressionists – is nowhere in sight', Calvin Tomkins wrote in his review of *Brilliant!* in the *New Yorker.* But my intuition is that he is wrong.

This is a generation of artists who have internalised not only the history of modern art but also the history of popular culture. Angus Fairhurst (who plays 'Ian' in *Hanging Around*) has put together a 'band', which, in addition to himself, includes Mat Collishaw and Gary Hume, his contemporaries at Goldsmiths' College. Low Expectations' first public performance was the excuse for the party in the studio in Clerkenwell Road. And even those who had'nt been there before, had been there before. This was Warhol's *Exploding Plastic Inevitable* at the Electric Circus in 1966; it was Rauschenberg and Oldenburg and Rosenquist and Poons playing at Bob and Ethel Scull's party, described by Tom Wolfe in 'Bob and Spike', in the mid-1960s, around the time most of these people were being born.

The crummy building with the lurching lift,

Keith Allen and Damien Hirst on the set of *Hanging Around.*

10:03:12.20   02:11:27.04       002

Keith Allen as the disturbed and lethal Marcus in *Hanging Around.*

echoey stairs, sodden landings and poorhouse institutional walls ... The battered sofa, dumpster fridge and skittled bottles of Lowenbrau, Smirnoff and Jim Beam ... A great silver cycloptic Mitsubishi television, a drum-kit on a carpet and the tape of a gymnast looping over and over against a wall ... It was generic: 'excitement, parties, tragedies, masterpieces in lofts, etc.' - Allen Ginsberg to Lawrence Ferlinghetti, early 1950s. Artists in the band, artists out front (Sarah Lucas, Abigail Lane, Michael Landy, Tracey Emin, Angela Bulloch) supporting them.

It would be naïve to suppose that there weren't the usual undercurrents of competitiveness and petty jealousy and frustration circulating. But as a group, and for the time being, they present a conspicuous and almost unprecedentedly united front. They promote one another's work and help to hang one another's shows, and live and sleep and work together in shifting (and constantly intriguing) combinations. In Minneapolis, for example, Damien Hirst agreed not to show any of his dead animal pieces, and Jake and Dinos Chapman withheld their 'fuck-face' mannequins in the interest (it was said) of group solidarity: it was feared that the controversy they aroused would inevitably overshadow everything else in the show.

It is also possible that the reason Damien Hirst did not accompany the others to the opening of *Brilliant!* was because he felt that his appearance in Minneapolis would shift the balance of attention unfairly in his favour. Since his first short-listing for the Turner Prize in 1992 he has achieved the level of promiscuous Warholian celebrity that long ago transcended the coterie journals of the art press: he can turn up as a gossip column item, a game-show question or an op-ed cartoon. The first title for his contribution to *Spellbound* was 'Flying' ('Everybody in it was going to have their zips down'), a (possibly unconscious) reference to a career trajectory that has so far defied gravity. The film's central image is of a wartime Spitfire pilot flying mesmerically upwards into the blue beyond: 'You have no sense of time or distance or even gravity and there's a deadly silence. The engine cuts out and there is a sense of nothingness and then a sense of falling backwards ... back down to earth'. The Icarus plunge is the prevailing counter-image: a doctor is defenestrated; a butterfly burns its beautiful wings on an Insectocutor; in an early version of the script, a woman falls off a ladder and is impaled on a steel sculpture by Sol Le Witt.

Throughout the film there is constant heavy traffic in a skywards direction of the souls of the deceased – of everybody, in fact, unlucky enough to drift into the force-field of the dreamy, duffle-coated figure known as 'Marcus', a kind of unwitting, and then increasingly witting, terminator – a serial killer, or serial 'assister' in death. Way to go! His victims are turned into road rash, wrapped around lamp posts, pitched out of windows; they slit their wrists, stick their heads in the oven, go up in flames.

Any connection between 'Marcus Hellman' and Andy Warhol may be wholly accidental, but the visual referencing of Warhol images – a car crash, a mid-air suicide, other nods in the direction of Warhol's death-and-disaster series – is certainly not.

'Andy's Children: They Die Young' was the title of a magazine article, which appeared while Warhol was still alive. Since his death, a number of former Factory-hands have offered the view that Andy drew succour from watching what he regarded as the bits of human flotsam who hung around him go under. 'Andy loved to see other people dying', Emile de Antonio has said. 'This is what the Factory was about: Andy was the Angel of Death's Apprentice as these people went through their shabby lives with drugs and weird sex and group sex and mass sex'.

By this reckoning, Warhol (like Marcus Hellman) represents the obverse of the famous Schrödinger metaphor about the essence of life being the suction of negative entropy from the environment. 'I wonder if Edie will commit suicide?' it is claimed Warhol once asked of his former 'Superstar', Edie Sedgwick. 'I hope she lets me know so I can film it'. Warhol's film *Suicide*, his first experiment with colour, was based on a man who had tried to slash his wrists 23 times. (The person involved took out lawsuits and the film was never shown.)

Damien's preoccupation with death is now well established. But his involvement with film provides a new slant on the old relationship between death and photography (which Roland Barthes famously defined as the place where Death went when religion let it go). There is an obvious correlation between the rectangle of the film frame, which entombs the human image, and the clean geometry of the steel and glass vitrines, which 'frame' the artificially preserved carcasses of 'Damien Hirst' farmyard animals. The correlation lends a slightly sinister undertow to something Damien once said about his work: 'I like the idea of trying to understand the world by isolating something

Frankie Park in a Hirst spot dress in *Hanging Around*.

from it. You kill things to look at them'.

Marcel Duchamp had Rrose Selavy. Warhol had Ondine, Ultra Violet, Joe Dallesandro and his roster of spaced-out Superstars. During his first burst of fame he hired Alan Midgette, an actor, to impersonate him on a lecture tour, explaining that Midgette was 'more like what people expect me to be than I could ever be'. Damien's current alter-ego is his friend, the actor and Soho prankster, Keith Allen, who was in the Blur video Damien directed, plays Marcus in *Hanging Around*, and is involved in a projected feature film. Marcus represents the parallel existences, the sharer selves, that the film seems to be about. His is a fugitive identity: he has the name of one Damien Hirst friend, the physical form of another, and all his 'wives' are the same woman. 'I just wanted two identities, that's all', Duchamp said, explaining why he had his friend, Man Ray, photograph him as a woman. 'It was a sort of a readymadeish action'. (A Man Ray 'iron' sits on the desk in the psychiatrist's office in *Hanging Around*, alongside Meret Oppenheim's fur cup and saucer).

Duchamp did not allow his hand to interfere with his mind; an artist was 'just someone who signs things'. Many of the most well-known 'Andy Warhol' films were produced and directed by Paul Morrissey; probably half the paintings were created completely by assistants. It is an aesthetic Damien shares: 'Art without angst'.

As you would expect it to be, his approach to film-making is similarly unangsty. *Hanging Around* inevitably incorporates many of the motifs he has made familiar through his art – butterflies, ping-pong balls, dying cigarettes, dead meat, bug zappers – but it does not set out to be an art film. Unlike some of his contemporaries – who equate roughness of execution with rebelliousness and sometimes confuse the untrained look with sincerity, poverty, even seriousness of intention – Damien has always eschewed the gimcrack and the home-made. This was true even of the early shows he curated as a student, which were designed and catalogued to a professional standard. He has always gone in for technical perfection and 'finish', a kind of surface glamour. Even when working with the lowest form of material – dead matter, entrails, preserved flesh – he has always rated high production values over 'experimentalism'.

Just as his Blur video harked back unexpectedly to Benny Hill and Dick Emery and Saturday morning television, *Hanging Around* is a challenge in some ways to the usual notions and practices of the art film. There are no scratches or stains or multiple superimpositions. No arbitrary zooms, focuses, changes of angle, depth of field or light intensity. There is a narrative: actors and a story. It is realistic, naturalistic even. Reading it, you would expect the pivotal monologue of Philip, the old airman, to be delivered in a flat, uninflected, deadpan (art-house) manner. In fact, it is done in character, straight, with an accent, almost soap-operatically, like a scene from *Z Cars*.

In another scene in the film, a woman tells her husband: 'You have to come down. People are expecting you'. He replies, 'I'm not in a fit state Camilla ... Just go down and be a good hostess will you'. The man happens to be a junkie; the woman is wearing a Rifat Ozbek outfit based on a Damien Hirst spot painting. But it is an exchange that suggests *Emmerdale*, if not Terence Rattigan.

As David Thomson has pointed out, all but a few movie fanatics have seen more moving imagery on a television screen than 'at the movies'; television is on, 'like the light'. Like most of his generation, Damien is not a film buff but a channel-surfer. 'I'm more interested in Roald Dahl's *Tales of the Unexpected*, he says, 'than ... I don't know ... Richard Lester'. His film could be seen as belonging to the long tradition of 'found' objects, which achieve their power as works of art by being removed from their normal context and placed in a gallery setting. *Hanging Around* could be slotted into a normal evening's viewing without causing undue alarm.

The working title of the film, *Is Mr Death In*, is an anagram of 'Damien Hirst'. (Others, he points out, are 'A denim shirt', 'Near mid-shit' and 'Ten mad Irish'), so it is effectively 'Damien Hirst by Damien Hirst'. Lines of dialogue echo titles of pieces ('All day long telephone numbers come into my head and I get this strange urge to dial them'). The party in the film takes place in the Notting Hill house where he hosted a lavish party last year. An actress wears an outfit virtually identical to the one that Damien's girlfriend, Maia Norman, wore to the Turner Prize dinner in November. Marcus's son is Damien's son. Friends play the wives ... So how autobiographical is it? 'It's only autobiographical', he says, 'in the way that wiping your bottom is a self-portrait'.

The plot of *Hanging Around* is reminiscent of Cronenberg's *The Dead Zone*. Significantly, though, Damien says that the effect he was aiming for owes more to the closing sequence of John Huston's *The Dead*, with its ecstatic melancholy and ghostly light and the incantatory repetition of the single word: falling ... falling ... falling ...

Damien Hirst,
Keith Allen and
Eddie Izzard
(left to right)
on the set of
*Hanging Around*.

Following pages:
Shots from
*Hanging Around*:
Katrine Boorman
in the bath,
Eddie Izzard
falling from a
window.

10 :05 :09 .22     06 :27 :

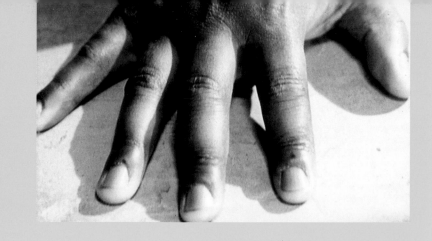

# Steve
# McQueen

By Martha Gever

I've been on the phone to Steve McQueen. Our conversation ranges widely, at times prompting references to various figures from our shared cultural lexicon, including such unlikely confederates as Jean Vigo, Andy Warhol and Sadie Benning. How these names entered our dialogue is impossible to reconstruct (although, it should be said, they were *not* uttered in reply to the standard artist-interview query 'Whose work has influenced you?'), but they may indicate the delightful feeling of intertextual promiscuity that McQueen's film-installation projects engender.

Take, for example, the overhead, high-contrast shot of five men and their shadow doubles performing the gyrations necessary to keep a hula hoop in motion in McQueen's *Five Easy Pieces* (can we imagine Jack Nicholson participating in such a childish sport?). It calls to mind the photographic experiments of Moholy-Nagy and other advocates of the use of the camera's mechanical 'eye', which established new forms of vision earlier in the century. But the analogy is called into question almost immediately, as soon as one of the men fumbles and disrupts the graceful rhythm of the shot. Another example: the camera offers a similarly startling view of an adult man slowly spinning a hula hoop, this time shot from below so that

his legs appear as two intersecting pillars, with the hoop circling around the centre of an undulating colossus – his crotch. Again, the odd camera angle echoes the stance taken in various photographs found in a Bauhaus textbook but recasts the Constructivist photographers' and film-makers' pristine fascination with optical innovation as an almost scandalous peep-show. And, as if that playful substitution were not irreverent enough, this image is replaced, by means of a simple edit, with a pair of legs and foreshortened torso occupying the same screen space but belonging to a man clad only in white underpants, who a little later in the film proceeds to pee on the camera, or so it appears. The moment the screen becomes flooded my cognitive faculties begin to go haywire: caught off guard, I am at once affronted by being visually deluged by what I know to be urine, captivated by the sensual imagery of the bubbling liquid and humoured by the outrageousness of this visual joke.

Having introduced this discussion of McQueen's film work with allusions to historical precedents and creative ingenuity that are staples of the art-critical enterprise, I cannot, however, continue in this vein, not because his work cannot sustain this sort of appraisal, but because

Hand of the Artist: Steve McQueen in *Stage*.

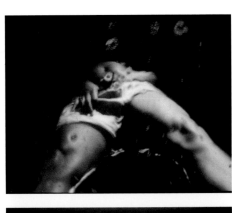

Dreams and Echoes: *Five Easy Pieces*.

my interest in it – and what I would contend is its strength – does not reside solely in its formal or technical virtuosity. Instead, I merely need to add that all of the performers in *Five Easy Pieces*, as well as the two men who feature in his film installation *Bear*, are black, and everything I have said about his work must be revised in the light of the racial politics operating in both art and cinema histories and institutional practices. If I then mention that McQueen himself is one of the protagonists in *Bear* as well as *Stage*, the fact that it is a black artist who conceived these compositions must also be taken into account.

But what does this mean? Does it mean that McQueen's imagery should be interpreted as commentary on black cultural identity or, conversely, as an attempt to redress the historical exclusion of black artists from the visual arts? Do the two male bodies on display in McQueen's *Bear*, for example, demand further reflection on problems related to demonic portrayals of black masculinity? Certainly, as numerous commentators have noted, representations of black men are perhaps the most dogmatic in Western culture. Not only do such portrayals make ascriptions of character traits based on racial criteria blatant, thereby underlining the power relations that produce

Face and Bodies: *Bear*.

Following pages: Margaret Kinnon and Steve McQueen in *Stage*.

and reproduce racial categories in Western societies, but they also infiltrate social relations by imposing on black men what Henry Louis Gates, Jr has expressed as 'the burden of being perceived through ... the already-read text of debasedness and animality.'[1] Thus, is it possible to view the aggressive physicality enacted in *Bear*, or the enigmatic encounter between the black man and the white woman configured in *Stage*, without becoming enmeshed in the kinds of fantasies concerning race, gender and sexuality that inform the insidious construct Gates describes?

Posing these questions in this manner suggests that politics rather than aesthetics provides the proper analytic framework for a discussion of McQueen's work. From this perspective, the two black men sizing each other up and wrestling in *Bear*, say, could be treated as a symbolic engagement with well-worn notions of the black male body as innately dangerous and violent. Since the naked men not only grimace but also smile and embrace tenderly as well as forcefully, the stereotype is invoked and undercut simultaneously. *Stage* ups the ante, as it were, by flirting with another anxiety ridden fantasy generated by racist social relations, this one with a cinematic pedigree dating back to *Birth of a Nation*: in a sequence of shots a white woman walks down a staircase, a black man awaits just out of her field of vision. With its nightmarish overtones of foreboding coupled with eroticism, this schematic rendering of a classic cinematic image from the file drawer marked 'film noir' could be interpreted as a canny pun that calls to mind the politically salient connotations of the word 'black'.

After producing these abbreviated observations to further an argument for a critique of racist stereotypes that could be extracted from McQueen's work, I am just as dissatisfied with the results as with my prior attempt to situate it in relation to Western art traditions. It is not that I think my comments are spurious, but somehow the analytic edifice they depend upon seems hopelessly inadequate here. And the problem is not mine alone; the impulse to consign recognisable representations of 'other' or 'deviant' perspectives to one or another brand of identity politics is all too common. Once such an operation has been performed, the cultural stratum, where debates over aesthetic strategies and forms of representation take place, can be split off and elevated above the messy world of struggles over resources and power. What intrigues me about McQueen's film installations, though, is that he manages to

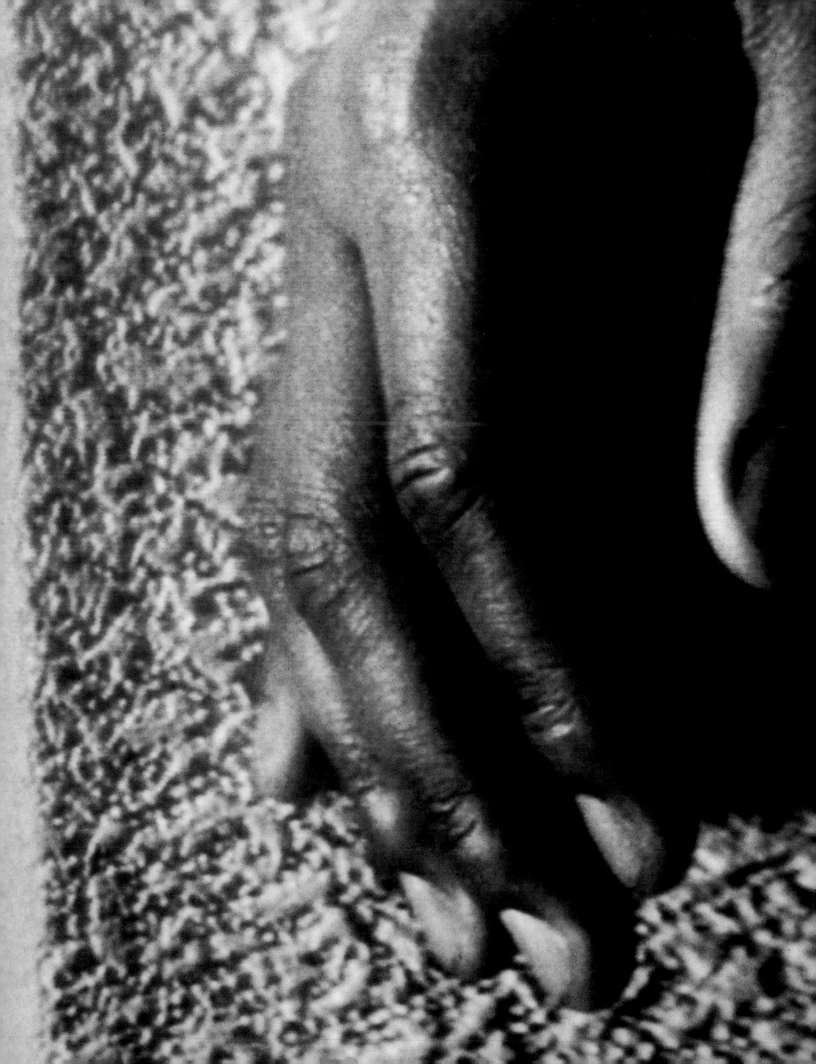

provoke a confrontation between these two supposedly incommensurable domains.

Consider the sequence from *Stage* mentioned earlier: the actors not only fail to fulfil their stereotypical roles, they are presented as equally complicit in a game of desire that is never resolved and where no actual meeting ever takes place. As the piece progresses, the culturally prescribed narrative of the endangered white woman, hinted at by the suspenseful *mise-en-scène*, dissolves in the face of her apparent autonomy, while the black man's body is subjected to a series of eccentric permutations, effected by a combination of remarkable camera manoeuvres and audacious montage that ultimately deflate any narrative expectations. This last observation might suggest that McQueen is frustrating spectatorial pleasure in order to expose the ideological operations of cinematic conventions (similar to radical avant-garde film-makers during the 1970s), but this would be misleading. Instead, his work fosters one of the mainstays of cinematic allure, voyeurism, by projecting immense, sensual, silent, black and white images of (for the most part) black bodies. And, by doing so, he opens up a space for reflections about whose fantasies, specifically, are allowed on the public stage

or in this case, the public screen.

Another way of approaching this is to ask what happens if we do not assume that artistic or cinematic discourses 'belong' to white men (although the privileged place white men have occupied in relation to these cultural territories should not be minimised). On this topic, Kobena Mercer's writings are most instructive, in particular his analysis of Robert Mapplethorpe's controversial homoerotic photographs of black men.[2] What Mercer challenges is not the interpretation of these photographs as fetishistic, aestheticised objects, but the notion that any pleasure a spectator might derive from these images automatically implicates him or her in an act of dehumanisation. The latter belief that the viewer is implicated in Mapplethorpe's photographs, Mercer points out, forecloses a host of considerations, including his own ambivalent responses and what he describes as a double identification – with both the black men transformed into objects of desire by Mapplethorpe's photographic artistry and with the desirous gaze of the viewer, whose identity is not predetermined (as it would be if these images were read as simple artefacts of racist social relations), and who may be, like Mercer, a gay black man.

Important ideas about the complicated interplay between sexuality and race in visual culture are generated by Mercer's eloquent analysis, but the exploration of these issues cannot stop with Mapplethorpe's images. Should that occur, white male subjectivity will retain its sovereignty, if not as the absolute dictator of meaning then at least as the standard against which all meanings are measured. Something more interesting starts to happen, though, when Mapplethorpe's now mythological images are employed as metaphor, as they are in Isaac Julien's film *Looking for Langston*. Projected on diaphanous panels of white fabric, stylised black male bodies (lifted from the pages of Mapplethorpe's *Black Book*) float like ethereal apparitions summoned from the gay spirit world by a psychic. Thus transplanted from the privacy of a book or an art gallery to a film concerned with power, voyeurism and sexual desire, these iconographic representations of 'the black male body' are incorporated into a more expansive context, where Julien confers on his characters the license to look and, therefore, the power to envision fantasies. In the process, he stakes the same claim for himself and, likewise, for the audiences for his film.

I have taken this detour via Mercer and Julien

High Anxiety:
*Stage.*

1. Henry Louis Gates, Jr, 'Preface' in Thelma Golden, ed., *Black Male: Representations of Masculinity in Contemporary American Art*, Whitney Museum of American Art, New York, 1994, p. 13.
2. Kobena Mercer, 'Reading Racial Fetishism: The Photographs of Robert Mapplethorpe' in *Welcome to the Jungle: New Positions in Black Cultural Studies*, Routledge, New York and London, 1994.

in order to make a case for McQueen's film installations as a further elaboration of the vexed issue of voyeurism. Put like that, this undoubtedly overworked word seems deserving of its dictionary definition as a sexual perversion, a guilty gratification of a troubled psyche. But it is just as reasonable to understand voyeurism as an everyday activity that anyone who watches a movie or peruses a gossip column indulges in; if that means that all of us who do such things are sexual perverts, so be it, although it does not follow that all voyeuristic conceits are identical. However, McQueen's art is not concerned so much with the quotidian dimensions of the desire to *look* and, in looking, possess the unattainable object of fascination, as it is with the desire to *see* – see what two men with their arms tightly clasped around each other's heads look like when the camera is pointed upward from between their legs; see how the sole of a white athletic shoe, carefully making its way along a cable that bisects a black frame horizontally, appears when rotated 90 degrees and projected as a gargantuan image that spans an entire wall; in other words, see what happens when a few actors performing simple actions are filmed in indeterminate locations using all kinds of improbable angles, unorthodox framing, an

unruly editing style and lots of close-ups; and see what happens when these fragmentary gestures are assembled to produce what I can best describe as illusionist spectacles that are both intimate and larger than life.

I am also tempted to call them oversized mini-dramas, but that implies that there are plots or at least characters in McQueen's film installations, neither of which is accurate, but there *are* moving pictures, which is, after all, where cinema began. In a sense McQueen recapitulates the restless investigation of visual phenomena and the fascination with projected images of movement that preoccupied the earliest years of film production and exhibition, and which has resurfaced sporadically whenever a new kind of vision, differing from those offered by entertainment brokers, has been called for. For McQueen this means speculating about what it takes to defy the pull of gravity, especially the centripetal force of history, without denying its power. As his work demonstrates, setting aside the historical equation of vision with unambiguous knowledge can be a risky undertaking, but what makes the chance worth taking is the sensation of navigating a visual field oriented to a new compass that points in more than one direction at a time.

Robert Mapplethorpe. *Ken Moody* (1983), © The Estate of Robert Mapplethorpe.

Isaac Julien's *Looking for Langston* (1989).

# Eduardo
# Paolozzi

# By Martin Kemp

The ancient 'Art of Memory' exploited our propensity to recall one thing by association with another. Astonishing feats of recollection were achieved by locating items to be remembered in specific places, in real or imaginary settings. Frances Yates's classic book, *The Art of Memory*, showed how the associative architecture of the mnemonic art reached its peak of philosophical elaboration in the extraordinary 'Theatre of Memory' constructed in wood by Giulio Camillo and described in his *L'Idea del Teatro* of 1550. Conceived as a semicircular theatre in the ancient manner, it served as a storehouse for a vast, classified and compartmentalised collection of cosmological wisdom, preserved as images, variously located in the seven tiers of its structure. As a contemporary reported:

He pretends that all things that the human mind can conceive and which we cannot see with the corporeal eye, after being collected together by diligent meditation, may be expressed by certain corporeal signs in such a way that the beholder may at once perceive with his eyes everything that is otherwise hidden in the depths of the human mind. And it is because of this corporeal looking, that he calls it a theatre.

The cinema serves as a kind of twentieth-century memory theatre for Eduardo Paolozzi, not of the static kind created by Camillo but of ceaselessly mobile images, plastic and vivid, unstable yet insistent, residing in collapsed time and dislocated locations. It is a locus in which he voraciously devours, dismembers and reassembles the images that are to be recalled by his inner eye. His own collections and assemblages in turn act as sites for the exercise of associative memory, which we are invited to share.

I remember as a boy entering those excitingly exotic cinema halls – bustling through the gilded foyer, floating up the brassy stairs, hung with signed photographs of soft-focus stars, into an upper saloon of great plaster columns, pale-cream sphinxes, unidentifiable reliefs of semi-clothed gods and muses, grimacing masks, ziggurat friezes, marbled panels and plush russet carpets humming with odours of sweet buns and stewed tea. And on, through the swinging doors into the breathy darkness, stale with dribbled ice cream and dusty farts – waiting for the rucked curtain to raise its rich satin skirts; for that transportation beyond the world of late afternoon drizzle; for those journeys to lands of huge distances, livid colour and livid action, unimagined configurations of nature and artifice, in which a huge American car was both as real

*Bunuel Head (1996).*

The movie-prop store, The Trading Post, in Southall, London.

and as incredible as a space ship, a quick-draw cowboy as intimate and as alien as a lumbering Egyptian mummy come to exact its revenge.

The cinema opened doors into a parallel universe. Yet for all the illusion of reality, for all that we brought to this restless world of zooming perspectives and sinister corners, for all our willingness to collude with the deception, the screen world somehow remained irredeemably removed from tangible experience – a world in which blood was bloody but not blood, in which six-shooters shot without pause for reloading, and in which great classical temples collapsed and bounced without stony crunch. Sensory logic was seduced, leaving us dizzy as we stumbled on to the moist pavements that led prosaically to home and school.

The stores of film studios are littered with the debris of defunct illusions, hollow columns whose gravity is only illusory, the 'empty horses' that provided the title of David Niven's autobiography, cannonballs devoid of destructive potential, and the plastic barbed-wire that Paolozzi recalls from his visit to the Trading Post, a warehouse of movie props for hire. The surfaces of sham stone revealed their ironic insubstantiality to his enquiring knuckles. Mingled with the detritus of such artful confections are the humble 'real' objects: discarded ropes, paint-splattered ladders, torn corners of gaudy cloth, once proud conspirators in the transformation of dross into visual magic. As an artist who is self-professedly in the business of 'the metamorphosis of rubbish', Paolozzi continuously alerts us to the eloquent pathos of the discarded object, which, now being devoid of function, presents a less prescriptive field for associative memory. This pathos, which emerges both from the individual item and even more intricately from its association with other fragments from obsolete visual inventories, he characterises as the 'psychopathology of the everyday object' – a lateral transfer from Freud's 1901 essay on 'The Psychopathology of Everyday Life', which analyses what are now known as 'Freudian slips', such as the misnaming of a familiar object on the basis of deep, often symbolic, associations. The ordinary is somehow made so unreal by lateral slippage of its name or function, or by a subtle realignment of viewpoint, that it becomes paradoxically super-real, or even sur-real, as in Buñuel and Fellini.

Throughout his career Paolozzi has intuitively sought to exploit the resonant and unexpected associations that dislocated objects may acquire. They can be seen, through his eyes, to be in the

Painting curiosities: *Scarabattolo* (*trompe l'oeil*), attributed to Domenico Remps.

Boris Karloff in Karl Freund's *The Mummy* (1932), a key film for Eduardo Paolozzi.

Right: *'Reefer Madness'* (1996).

process of 'becoming art', and 'becoming poetry', above all in the strange aggregations of incongruous entities, which, like the greatest still lifes, become lyric poems to the ambiguity of objects. It is this sense of resonance by collective displacement that lies behind his fascination with museums, with the way that collections act as arenas for visual recollection. Faced with the constricting disciplinary apartheid of the modern museum system, he looks particularly to those collections in which our taxonomies of knowledge are subverted. The early history of collections – the study of the *Wunderkammer* or cabinet of curiosities – provides an insight into a world of visual conjunctions where the artifice of nature and human creativity stand side by side to reveal a cosmos of things united by philosophical insight rather than functional necessity. His use of racks – of the kind of storage racks used by film studios and in the reserve collections of museums – provides a paradoxical image of order within which perceptual disorder reigns, an alternative taxonomy, perhaps unsystematic to our eyes. The objects in his racks become reflections of dismembered histories, biographies and autobiographies, as if seen in a shattered mirror. They become relics pillaged from undocumented reliquaries, like the shelved

*Props for a Blue Movie* (1996), part of Paolozzi's exhibit in *Spellbound.*

collections of funerary artefacts robbed from unidentified Egyptian tombs and now treasured in Western museums. The loss of the defined eloquence of original context is replaced by other kinds of visual voice. His own seminal piece of exhibition-making, his *Lost Magic Kingdoms* at the Museum of Mankind in 1985, pointed to the lyric transformation of everyday consumer objects by 'primitive art' into images of wonder. The act of displacement, say, of removing a light bulb from its light-giving function, subverts naming and classification in a way that relies upon the special characteristics of the visual rather than the verbal. That is why the use of the word 'metaphor' to define the mechanism for such visual transfers of form and content does not, in the final analysis, work.

The freeing of meaning through displacement inevitably carries resonances of temporal transformation. Film is a time-based medium. A classic definition was given in Bazin's 1945 essay on 'The Ontology of the Photographic Image'. Bazin argued that, whereas photography 'embalms time',

the film is no longer content to preserve the object, enshrouded as it were in an instant, as the bodies of insects are preserved intact, out of the distant past, in amber. The film delivers baroque art from its convulsive catalepsy. Now, for the first time, the image of things is likewise the image of their duration, change mummified as it were.

The time of film, as it acts on the memory, is not real time. It is collapsed time, intense images of dynamic continuities segmented into discontinuous sequences, sometimes terminated, and sometimes suspended, as in the great serials that once played such a role in popular cinema. It is one of the paradoxes of the moving image that our memory still relies on 'pictures' – we did, after all, talk of 'going to the pictures'. The pictures that burn most deeply in our minds are often concerned with trauma: the wrapped mummy shambling inexorably towards its tormentor, judderingly resistant to the bullets that cause erupting pustules in its layered bandages; the 'black spot' of Long John Silver in *Treasure Island*, transformed from the unwanted blot on my homework into a black nothingness of burgeoning anxiety. Both images I remember with frissons of fear. They are shared with Paolozzi, and with how many others?

Paolozzi's images often involve classic archetypes. They are often paired: Adam and Eve, iconically stiff; the top-hatted man beating the 'little woman' and the corseted dominatrix beating the submissive male (suggested by *American Gigolo*, with echoes of Pasolini?); the animals of the Ark, passing by two by two. Sometimes they are multiples, asserting their power through repetition, as in the teeming legions of rats, black- and red-eyed, resonant with memories of *Nosferatu* (and of the *Pied Piper*, of the breaking point of Winston Smith in Orwell's *1984*, of Freud's 'Rat Man', of the sewers in *The Phantom of the Opera*). Exotic images play a conspicuous role in his memory: the Manchurian Warrior, orientally grotesque; the Shanghai Express; and the Thief of Baghdad. Bodies are schematised, with physiognomic masks, boxily inflated chests, segmented abdomens, the caricatured limbs of the comic-book muscle-man, all redolent of the gigantism of late Roman art and Chinese festival figures. The enigmatic sphinx becomes the screen on to which photographic images are projected, its undulating plaster surface becoming a site for illusion, which perpetrates a double unreality. Robotic manikins, marionettes and dolls are placed in implicit dialogue with 'real' people, at once stiffly inanimate by comparison and yet – as in Heinrich von Kleist's 1810 essay 'On the Marionette Theatre' – capable of logarithmic geometries of perfect motion beyond the human range. Travel, and the very machinery of travel in time and space, is ever present by implication or illustration: the trains of Hitchcock, and most particularly of Sternberg's *Shanghai Express*; the great liners within which microcosmic societies perpetrate love and murder; the wonderful hybrid of the flying boat (echoes of Howard Hughes's *The Spruce Goose*?); and images of wheels, cogs and cams as the icons of mechanical motion. The rackety reels and clicking shutters of the projectors, the mechanised flicker of early moving images, the jerky gesticulations of the human puppets of the silent movies, are all suggested.

Are they merely suggested as figments in the mind of the viewer, or are they part of Paolozzi's intention? I think 'intention' is the wrong word in this context. Unlike Marcel Broodthaers's *Musée de l'Art Moderne*, with its alternative taxonomies and bureaucracies, Paolozzi's recollections do not posit a new order, not even a subversive one. When Broodthaers established his 'Département des Aigles', in which all kinds of 'high' and 'low' portrayals of eagles were housed together, he orbited the visual conjunctions around an idea. Paolozzi orbits ideas around the visual suggestiveness of the

object. In the final analysis, Paolozzi's visual aggregations are not museum-like, since the contents of his collections are determined by expressive association rather than by any of the predetermined categories necessary for systematic activities of collection and display. In his parallel universe of the visual, he conducts multiple dialogues of a subversive nature – between high and low culture, exclusively expensive and cheaply available, sophisticated and primitive, Western and non-Western, European and American, private and public, original and reproduction, art and technology, humans and machines, the fine and the vulgar. Across all his extraordinarily diverse fields of activity – as a sculptor in many media, a maker of prints, exhibitions, films and books, as a designer of murals, mosaics, stage sets, furniture, ceramics and tapestries, and as an author – he has been creating fields for interpretation in which the fluid eloquence of objects is liberated rather than constrained.

His fragmentary script or scripts for the imaginary movie and its assemblages of props – some on the move, some stored in opportunistic disorder, some gathered together in enigmatic tableaux – apparently provide the archaeological evidence for a great cinematographic event. But the event is not identifiable as having occurred in the past, nor happening in the present, nor coming in the future. Like his *Props for a Musical about the 'Life & Death of Hieronymus Bosch'*, exhibited in Munich in 1990, the evocative material signs belie the existence of the elusive movie. His ambiguous theatre of movie memories provides a stage for our combinatory and associative imaginations in which the linear realities of time and place – the taxonomic measures provided by the clock and the map – are suspended in favour of allegories that are endlessly open.

*Props for a Musical About the 'Life & Death of Hieronymus Bosch'*, part of the 1990 *Arche Noah* exhibition, Munich.

# PauLa
# Rego

**By Marcia Pointon**

A visit to the cinema was the standard treat for children growing up in western Europe immediately before or after the Second World War. The moving image had not yet been familiarised by television and video, and the matinée showing of a Disney film was eagerly anticipated: a pleasure tinged with anxiety. The terror of the forest fire that threatens to engulf Bambi, and the horrifying swamp, in which the fleeing Snow White encounters logs that transform into the ravenous mouths of great beasts, are unforgettable. The occasion of cinema, the unrepeatable (in that era) nature of the experience, and the characteristic Disney synthesis of conventionalised social banality and elemental psychic disturbance ensures that Disney is, for adults of this generation, a source not only of pleasure but also of powerful associations with parental authority. The scene of the Disney-animated film evokes, moreover, through nostalgia, a fascination with the unfathomable relationship of the 'then' and the 'now', of memory and the passage of time, marking the physiological body with its changes and transformations. Disney, in short, invokes infantile terror and fantasy in a world that is both familiar and horrifying.

Rego propels her audiences into that world precipitately, unapologetically and without ceremony. Magnificently exploiting the capacity of the static image for heraldic clarity of statement, ignoring cartoon-type pictorial progression in favour of iconic sequences – in which gaps and hiatuses, repeated motifs and sharp surprises grip the viewer – Rego generously pays homage while powerfully subverting the much-loved entertainer of children across the world. Suddenly, and without prelude or overture, the black-clad ballet-dancing ostriches from *Fantasia* surround us: their ungainly bodies are compressed into relentless square spaces, thrust against the picture plane, while the immediacy of the pastel medium conveys an urgency of execution (the dynamic of the dance and the intensity of Rego's engagement with it). In *Fantasia* Disney created a wild parody of classical ballet, performed by hippos, alligators and ostriches. Ballet displays as natural what is most artificial: the dancing bear is therefore seen nowadays as a travesty in a world where performance is the prerogative of humans, and animals are relegated to 'other', against which culture is measured, to be lauded or condemned. In Disney's *Fantasia* the highly conventionalised choreography devised for the human body is transmogrified into the

Working drawing for *Snow White*.

Paula Rego working in her studio on one of the 'Ostrich women' works.

grotesque, if hilarious, cavorting of birds in ballet shoes and hippos in tutus.

Rego reclaims Disney's cast for a tragic, and unspoken, drama. Fracturing the team discipline of *Fantasia*, while retaining its orgiastic mood, Rego gives us melancholy dancers trying, hopelessly, to fly, arms outstretched like harpies, a silent and ageing chorus whose bright new satin shoes fail to mask the sadness of life. Like a sympathetic Circe she transforms Disney's animals (with their human attributes) into humans who retain their animality. In so doing she offers an implicit commentary upon dance as a human (and particularly as a female) discipline and also upon Western audiences' fascination with the romance of ballet imagery. Deftly and brilliantly drawing in the medium Degas himself so often used for ballet subjects, Rego's *Fantasia* shatters the chocolate-box fantasy of a popular pictorial tradition. Degas' dancers are trained professionals in motion: their faces are occluded, their torsos a mere approximation, their legs and arms are the focus of attention. Rego by contrast endows her ostrich dancers with facial expressions, physical imperfections, corporeal mass and, above all, sexuality. With obdurate expressions, with stubby fingers clenched and rounded bellies, they inhabit a space in which

they cannot stand full-height, and from which they gaze out searchingly to the absent audience.

Dance is often formalised and ritualised courtship; traditionally it 'signifies matrimony'. But in Rego's ostrich world, dance is performed in the absence of male partners; Rego dismantles the Disney façade with its parade of identical appearances to reveal the schoolgirl in her bow who will never grow up, the flirtatious older woman and the young girl hoping for adventure. Here the discipline of dance is half-learned and ill-rehearsed; the body's craving for love and affection takes precedence over the acquisition of dance steps. Magical pink ballet shoes, tutus and *pas de deux* – key elements in many a little girl's imaginative life – structure the adult's desires and her struggle to survive. Nowhere is this more apparent in Rego's extraordinary images than in the depiction of a single figure with feet so wounded that she has discarded her ballet shoes (like some suffering female Philoctetes, outcast and in pain), and in the lewd open-mouthed hippo in bra and dirty ballet shoes who sprawls in her chair waiting for her prey.

The similarities between animal and human bodies that are a feature of all the great narratives of creation are a source not only of humour and delight but also of anxiety and fear. When Goya

Edgar Degas,
*Female Dancer
Viewed From
Behind.*

Artist's drawing
for *Fantasia*.
© Disney

*Dancing Ostriches from Walt Disney's Fantasia* (1995), pastel on paper mounted on aluminium, 59 × 59 ins.

paints a plucked turkey, its legs rigidly stretched out above its head, we are reminded of a human body. The wings become arms and the crossed feet possess a certain elegance. For centuries such slippages have been the stock-in-trade of cartoonists. Moreover the fabulous traditions of animal narratives by authors such as Aesop, La Fontaine, Beatrix Potter and, most famously Disney, with mythic characters like Rupert Bear, Sam Pig, Mickey Mouse and Donald Duck, are inextricably tied to forms of moral didacticism. The declaration with which Ovid's *Metamorphoses* opens, 'My purpose is to tell of bodies which have been transformed into shapes of a different kind', might almost be a manifesto for Disney's inventive career. But in Ovid, to be transformed into an animal is a punishment or, at the very least, a misfortune. Those transformed by gods into trees or animals weep in anguish and struggle to regain their human shape and voices. Their transformation is witnessed by fellow humans who lament their loss. In the Aesop tradition, on the other hand, animals are wily strategists or gullible simpletons, actors in dramas where innocence invariably triumphs over guile.

It is significant that in the case of *Snow White and the Seven Dwarfs* Rego has ignored Disney's seething (and deeply sentimental) animal kingdom to focus on the battle between Snow White and her stepmother. Disney's saccharine anthropomorphism is filtered out through Rego's bold confrontation with the main theme: jealousy. In Disney's operetta Snow White asks: 'What do you do when things go wrong?' The question is disingenuous, serving to soften a series of appalling events, including the heroine's loss of home, her threatened murder and the effects of wicked spells. The reassuringly friendly dwarfs, bunnies and birdies, and the pantomime 'royal' costumes with their Bavarian bodices and white blouses, are similarly thoroughly *heimlich* or homely. As Freud pointed out in his essay on the uncanny (the un*heimlich*), fairy tales are associated with instantaneous wish fulfilment. He thought, however, that stories like *Snow White* were not character-istically uncanny. Had he lived to see Disney – and certainly had he survived to see Rego – he might have revised his view. For underpinning the tale of the beautiful and innocent girl, so cruelly treated by her father's second wife and eventually rescued by her Prince Charming, is a family drama of extreme violence.

Without the dwarfs and the animals Rego re-stages the Snow White story in a series of

*Dancing Ostriches from Walt Disney's* Fantasia (1995), pastel on paper mounted on aluminium, 63 × 47 ½ ins.

images in which the uncanny – that something which ought to have remained hidden but has come to light – is painfully present. If men are absent from Rego's *Fantasia* images (except for the elegant and sinister alligator that dances with the nubile hippo), in her four *Snow White* scenes their presence is felt acutely but symbolically. Snow White's filmic father is, to all intents and purposes, Disney himself. He 'replaces' her lost father and ensures that Snow White is rescued by the good animals and birds and befriended by the dwarfs. Rego's Snow White, however, remains deeply attached to her parent. Rego's 're-writing' produces a prehistory to the Snow White story in which the heroine, still at this time a princess (in a white flowered silk dress), plays with her father's hunting trophy, which she holds in her lap. This memorable image interpolates the absent father as a presence between Snow White and her stepmother. The trophy, which (in the best Disney tradition) might well have been borrowed from the *treppenhaus* of some Hohenzollern Castle, reminds us not only of the deer killed in the forest by the huntsman and of the cuckold's horns but also, by extension, of the Ovidian metamorphosis in which the powerful God Jupiter turns himself into a bull in order

El Greco, *Resurrection of Christ* (1596).

*Dancing Ostriches from Walt Disney's* Fantasia (1995), pastel on board mounted on aluminium, 59 × 59 ins.

*Snow White and
her Stepmother*
(1995), pastel on
paper mounted
on aluminium,
70 × 59 ins.

Goya, *Still Life.*
*A Plucked Turkey*,
(1810/1823).

*Swallows the*
*Poisoned Apple*
(1995), pastel on
paper mounted
on board,
70 × 59 ins.

Working drawing
for *Snow White*.

to make love to the human Europa. Snow White's Prince Charming can never hope to compete with this. Snow White's preoccupation with her father, which Rego forcefully brings out, helps to explain the impossibility of adequately representing the Prince (regarded as a failure or loss of nerve even in Disney's version) or his horse. Snow White, in Rego's dénouement, finds autoerotic satisfaction in the space of fantasy left vacant by the loss of her father. Meanwhile the presence of the ultimate father, Jove or God, a figure of absolute authority, casts a shadow over the whole series. Thus the poisoned Snow White falls, like a fallen angel in a biblical scene or like Eve with the apple this time stuck in her throat, while clutching her skirt around her buttocks in a gesture of modesty. The homely (*heimlich*) parts of the body are distinctly uncanny (un*heimlich*) when unlawfully revealed.

What, then, are the social laws governing the body and its boundaries and how do they work to construct us as subjects? Rego substitutes a girl suffering the pangs of puberty for Disney's eternally infantile Snow White: deep is the humiliation to which her grey-faced stepmother subjects Snow White when she inspects at arm's length the girl's white cotton knickers. Hanging in the background is Snow White's crimson

party dress and in her hair (Olympia-like) is a crimson ribbon. In its associations with all those other stained cloths – Christ's loin-cloth, Veronica's handkerchief, the holy shroud – the stepmother's inspection is like some fetishistic act in a religious drama. The whiteness of Snow White's stand-up 'Tudor' collar in the film is translated into the whiteness of the girl's knickers, and innocence is overtaken by knowledge. Disney intends, it seems, to offer us a secular alternative to the Fall, a prelapsarian paradise where jolly asexual dwarfs work and Snow White cooks and sews, and where, despite the deathly blow dealt by the Satanic witch in her jealous rage, regeneration is delivered by an androgynous Prince. But Rego's world is distinctly post-lapsarian. Knowledge is sexual, and jealousy, we may deduce, drives Snow White as well as her stepmother. In the struggle between them jealousy is explicitly sexual; they compete for the perfection of physical appearance that will win them the attention of men: of fathers and lovers. This is a deeply self-referential drama. The mirror on the wall eventually tells the stepmother that she must cede to the younger woman. To be no longer 'fairest of them all' is a problem of self-identity. The solution is murder.

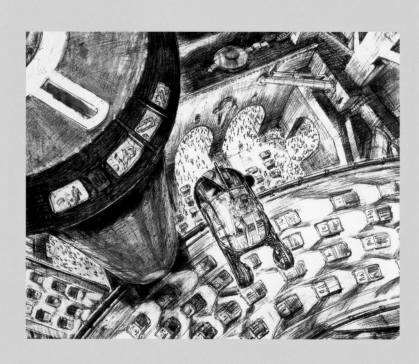

# Ridley
# Scott

By Christopher Frayling

Fritz Lang, it has been said, had a painter's eye and an architect's pen: the one aspect of his *Metropolis* (1926) that still lives is its design; the closing words of the fade out, about the unity of head, heart and hand, now seem both pernicious and sentimental. Vincent Korda also had a painter's eye and the technical skill of an interior architect, plus a social network that included several avant-garde European designers. Korda provided 'the settings' for *Things to Come* (1936), and the design, once again, is the only aspect of the film that lives on; the underlying message – that advanced technology will sort out our lives, especially when it 'tears out the wealth of this planet and exploits its giant possibilities' – now seems crassly naïve. Ridley Scott was educated as a fine artist and then as a graphic designer during the explosion of 'Pop' in British art. His films *Alien* (1979) and *Blade Runner* (1982) have been described as key examples of 'the designer as author' and as having the same relation to post-modernism as *Things to Come* and *Metropolis* had to Modernism. Their design will doubtless last, whatever the fate of their scripts.

Science-fiction author Robert Silverberg has described the cityscape of Los Angeles in the year 2019, as revealed – through the chiaroscuro of artificial light on acid rain – in *Blade Runner*:

'It is not', wrote Silverberg, 'the familiar city of palm trees and perpetual bright sunshine. Above us loom colossal, sloping, high-rise buildings of intricate and alien designs, patterned, perhaps, after Aztec temples or Babylonian ziggurats, that turn the narrow, congested streets into claustrophobic canyons and hide the dark, pollution-foul sky. Down here on surface level we move warily through a densely packed district, largely Oriental in population and in architecture, a crazy, hyped-up version of Hong Kong or Tokyo, where a dizzying multitude of flashing electronic signs seeks insistently to draw our attention to games parlours, massage houses, noodle counters, drug-vending shops, and a thousand other commercial establishments.'[1]

Hampton Fancher wrote the first screenplay for *Blade Runner*, but left during preproduction (having rewritten the script over and over he eventually 'just disengaged from the project'). His initial drafts were written when the film was known, variously, as *The Android* and *Dangerous Days*. The title *Blade Runner* came, according to the credits, from William Burroughs (as did the well-known phrase or saying 'Heavy Metal'). These initial drafts had treated the story as 'a thing set in rooms, a dramatic piece; but

Opposite:
Artwork for
*Blade Runner* by
Sherman Labby.

Fritz Lang's
*Metropolis*
(1926).

Ridley said "what's going on *outside* the windows?"... and we developed things from there'.[2]

Actually, Ridley Scott probably *drew* this message rather than communicating it in words; all the main contributors to the look of the film *Blade Runner* have recalled how Scott's ability to make fast and focused pen drawings (known among the staff as 'Ridleygrams') saved a lot of time and misunderstanding during pre-production. 'A picture really *is* worth a thousand words', he once said to me, 'and I did after all spend a long time in art school'. But the drawings were intended purely as tools rather than as ends in themselves. Some of them have been published in *Blade Runner Sketchbook* and look like office memoranda in sketch form; all have been superseded by what ended up on the screen. As Picasso said of *Les Demoiselles d'Avignon* (1906-7), when asked whether he thought of his painting as a form of visual research, 'the point is to show what I have found, not what I am looking for'. The same goes for films.

In Philip K. Dick's novel there were surprisingly few visual clues as to what the city of San Francisco would look like after 'World War Terminus': some scattered references to the grey and sun-clouding dust of the nuclear winter; to streets clogged with 'kipple' or useless junk; to empty apartment blocks in the suburbs where a half-occupied building 'rated high in the scheme of population density'; to vidphones, hovercars landing on roofs, people wearing 'the huge new sun-filtering glasses', artificial animals and above all the terrifying 'silence of the world'.

To help transform these scattered references into the actual – and completely literal – world, which big-budget cinema demands, Ridley Scott and his team had two classic films to use as reference points. First, Fritz Lang's *Metropolis*, where the director's training as both a painter and an architect had enabled him to mobilise his Berlin designers to create a sectored and stratified city consisting of workers' dwellings and catacombs (down below), consumer base and flyovers (street level) and the bosses' quarters and pleasure gardens (up above). The view from the skyscraping pyramid-like Tyrell Corporation in *Blade Runner* owes a great deal to the view from the 'New Tower of Babel', where the Master surveys his *Metropolis*. And second, William Cameron Menzies' *Things to Come*, where the director was really an *art* director, and where 'designer of settings' Vincent Korda (a graduate of Budapest's College of Industrial Art and

Into the abyss: Fritz Lang's *Metropolis* (1926).

Academy of Art before he practised as a painter in France) made full use of Le Corbusier's *Vers une Architecture* (1927) and Norman Bel Geddes's *Horizons* (1932) when visualising the classless gleaming-white underground piazza of 'Everytown' in the year 2036: a grandiose fusion of Le Corbusier and American streamlining, of European and American Modernism.

Both *Metropolis* and *Things to Come* had envisioned the city as somewhere *new*, somewhere that had managed to start from scratch in the foreseeable future – a fallacy, which Scott has referred to as 'the diagonal zipper and silver hair syndrome': 'I think the mistake a lot of futuristic films make when they attempt short leaps forward in time is that they devastate whole cities and erect hokey-looking utopias'.[3]

Instead, he reacted *against* the bleak, pristine, austere look of previous cinematic versions, to create a more credible city of 40 years hence, which has what he calls 'a reality of its own', a city full of afterthoughts:

Think of Chicago or New York City right now, the over-saturation, how impossible it is to maintain some of these buildings. Think how expensive it is going to be to take down the Empire State Building. It will cost as much as building it. Eventually, you'll just have to 'retro-fit' things on the face of the building rather than having to pull half the side off, re-house the air conditioning or re-wire it. The cost will get so high it is going to be simpler just to smack things on the outside. So maybe the buildings will start to be designed from the inside out. You wear your guts on the outside. That gives us a picture of a textured city.

So to help visualise what may be going on 'outside the windows', Scott turned to industrial designer and product planner Syd Mead,[4] who had specialised in convincing his clients (such as U.S. Steel, Chrysler, Volvo and the Loewy office) that his air-brushed illustrations of the future were acceptable and marketable, and to production designer Lawrence G. Paull and art director David Snyder. It was important that Los Angeles 2019 seemed *possible* and *tangible*, and a designer working in industry was a useful place to start. In communicating with this team, Scott used as reference materials 'Hogarth drawings, 1930s photographs and the contemporary comic strip work of Jean Giraud (better known as Moebius) [from the magazine *Heavy Metal*]'.[5] He also referred to the 'Viewing Theatre' sequence from Orson Welles's *Citizen Kane* (1941), in which the reporters' cigarette smoke is cross-lit by shafts of light from the projection booth. He wanted, he

Artwork for
*Blade Runner* by
Sherman Labby.

He wanted, he said, 'a Philip Marlowe/Sam Spade environment ... a film set 40 years hence, made in the style of 40 years ago'. An environment where, as Raymond Chandler put it in 1950, 'the streets were dark with something more than night'. Instead of Philip K. Dick's deserted streets, he wanted street life. Instead of 'the silence of the world', a lot of noise. Instead of TV ads, a huge video wall promoting Coca-Cola and a blimp, with flashing lights, that exhorted people to emigrate off-world. It was Ridley Scott's background as an artist and designer that helped him realise his visualisations.

Ridley Scott did his foundation year and fine-art course at West Hartlepool College of Art in the mid-1950s, then studied at the Royal College of Art in South Kensington from 1958 to 1961.[6]

I was a painter and then a designer in art school, which totalled a period of seven years' training ... [Then] I was a set designer for a number of years, so whatever film I do, I always have great input into the decision on how the sets and the atmosphere will be ... I consider myself a good designer, therefore I require an *extremely* good designer.

One of his tutors at West Hartlepool, Stephen Crowther, has recalled that Scott's work was 'like the best American illustrators; in fact some of the staff thought his work was a bit on the slick side, not really suitable for painting'. He refers to the subsequent films as the work of 'a narrative artist who uses a camera instead of a brush'. Scott went on to the RCA's postgraduate School of Graphic Design at a key moment in its development: a course devoted to 'Television and Film Design' (taught by George Haslam) was introduced in October 1958 just as Scott was beginning; the role of 'photography as a design medium' was billed in the prospectus as a 'recent addition' (and, it could have added, a controversial one, since it was almost a moral precept in the School that everything had to be done by hand); and the College's student magazine *Ark* was quite literally in the throes of discovering America. Looking back, in 1963, Mark Boxer (by then Editor of the *Sunday Times* Colour Section) contrasted the pallid early days of *Ark,* when 'page after page was devoted to wet English romanticism, pretty yacht designs and Betjemanesque collections of old trains', with the late 1950s *Arks* when 'the concern has been for images and patterns of life today': photographic covers featuring Brigitte Bardot, celebrations of the iconography of New York, a link-up with the concerns of the Independent Group at the Institute of Contemporary Art, and an end to 'latter-day Victorianism'.

Mark Boxer attributed this turning point to the influence of Fine Art within the College:

The reason for all this must surely be not unconnected with the Painting School. The Pop Art movement certainly owes a great deal to graphics. But in its turn it has enriched graphics and *Ark* in particular... The Pop-graphic movement may be instant nostalgia, but this is the very guts of visual magazines.

For it was in October 1959 that Ridley Scott's fellow students David Hockney, Peter Phillips, Allen Jones, Derek Boshier and Patrick Caulfield all arrived in the Painting School at Exhibition Road and the Principal, Robin Darwin, wrote of a 'two-way traffic' between the fine and the applied arts.

Scott has recalled of his time at the College:

I went there as a Graphic Design student, but what interested me most of all was the opportunity to develop into something I hadn't really touched on before – which was photography. I had already started to get fairly pre-set that I wanted to do film ...

When the 'Television and Film Design' course started, students had to imagine the camera's range of vision by miming with four wooden mock-ups on broomstick tripods. Three graphic designers, four painters and one interior designer enrolled on the first one-year programme. The facilities were not that great. By 1961, the year Scott graduated, the Film course was (in his words) still 'a cupboard with a Bolex camera in it'; but it had at least matured into a department in its own right, based in the Queensgate common room recently vacated by Ceramics students. And the atmosphere helped Scott 'draw out things I hadn't really thought about before'. It was a period in the College's history that has recently been called 'the development of a post-modern sensibility'. Pop Art/Pop graphics. Uptown Pop/Downtown Pop. Grainy blow-ups/the origins of the colour supplement. One of the first screenings of *The Wild One* in Britain, at the student film society. Photographic *Ark* covers featuring Bardot, a motorcyclist tearing through a forest and a Coca-Cola advertisement; another cover featuring a line drawing of Tony Hancock. A poster project entitled *Design in Britain* (with swinging variations on the Union Jack, the Mini Cooper and the Jaguar appearing everywhere). Visits by recent ex-students who had moved on to television or film design: Clifford Hatts, the head of design at the BBC (and an ex-tutor); Peter Newington, producer of the first *Monitors* in 1958 (who took over the 'Television and Film Design' course four years later, on George Haslam's death); Richard Macdonald, who was in the process of designing the sets for Joseph Losey's

The Criminal (1960); and Bernard Lodge, title designer for *Dr Who* and *Z Cars*.

The course had been started because 'so many College students were entering the industry [mainly television] without any previous training'; so there were close relationships between the College and BBC Design, as well as ABC Television (which donated an annual scholarship). In a catalogue entitled *Graphics RCA: fifteen years' work at the School of Graphic Design, Royal College of Art*, published in 1963, a still from Ridley Scott's film *Boy on a Bicycle* ('made as part of the Diploma Examination' and showing a young boy trudging across a muddy estuary, with belching factory chimneys set against a grey sky) appeared with Edward Day's poster for *The Quare Fellow* (1960), the photographic cover of Len Deighton's *The Ipcress File* (Deighton had been a student at the College in the mid-1950s), a still from television's *Quatermass and the Pit* (which Hatts had designed), the titles of *Z Cars* and a package design for *Square Deal Surf More Shining Whiteness*.

The course enabled Scott to experiment with photography – producing, among other things, a 1961 poster for SKj, made up of a row of shining silver balls on a white background with red lettering. He was also able to write, direct and photograph the 16mm *Boy on a Bicycle* (for £250) about a boy, played by his younger brother Tony, who takes the day off school and cycles around a town in the north-east of England to the strains of the theme tune to *Housewives' Choice*: during the day he visits a fairground, sits on a jetty and smokes a cigarette, imagines he is 'the only kid not in school in the land' and meets Ridley Scott's dad. Above all, the course encouraged Scott to study design *in an art environment* (Darwin's 'two-way traffic'), introduced him to post-modern culture in a greenhouse atmosphere, and helped focus his ambitions on film. Not unexpectedly he joined the BBC Design Department (1961-5) after graduating. There, as a training exercise, he directed a potted half-hour version of Kubrick's *Paths of Glory*. This was followed by 12 years of directing television commercials – including the famous Hovis ad of 1974, featuring another boy with a bicycle, a hill in Shaftesbury, Dorset (standing in for Yorkshire) and Dvorak's *New World Symphony* played by a brass band – before he made his first feature film *The Duellists* (1977).

'My training in commercials', he has said, 'was *really* my film school. It helped build my awareness of how to present and – "manipulate"

Opposite:
The spinner in
*Blade Runner*.

CUT/ ROY LANDS JUST BEYOND D.

CUT/ ROY WALKS TO EDGE - LOOKS DOWN AT D.

CUT/ C.U. OF D. LOOKING DESPERATE

CUT/ D. POV OF ROY SMILING DOWN

*Blade Runner*
drawings.

is a bad word – *fascinate* the audience and hold it in a kind of dramatic suspension. I learned how to communicate immediately, to use every conceivable visual and aural device to work on the scenes and grab the audience's attention'.

The combination of Scott's background as a postgraduate student at that particular time, his apprenticeship as a BBC set designer and his 'film school' training in commercials – sometimes several a week ('I still think of ads as little films') – certainly helps explain his unusually *visual* approach to big-budget movie making. A clichéd criticism of his work is that design comes first, with words a poor second, to which Scott has replied that film is, after all, supposed to be a visual medium. He is confident working with artists such as the Swiss Surrealist Hans Rudi Giger, who produced the bio-mechanical *Alien* concept in 1978 out of bones, Styrofoam, Plasticine, fibreglass and coiled wire, creating the atmosphere of Fuseli's *Nightmare* with special effects.[7] Or with illustrators such as Jean 'Moebius' Giraud, who designed some of the costumes for *Alien*, or industrial designers such as Syd Mead on *Blade Runner*. This can be a combustible combination, comparable to working in a Renaissance *bottega*.

Alan Raymond, who documented the making of *Blade Runner* for ABC News, has referred to Scott as 'basically an obsessional director'. Lawrence Paull, the production designer, has recalled that 'Ridley brought out the best in everybody, but he was difficult. I'd say 40 per cent of those in relationships who worked on *Blade Runner* got separated or divorced during the production. The pressure was incredible'. It took two storyboard artists, a production designer, an art director and an industrial designer to get near his vision of what went on outside the window in the year 2019.[8] But, in retrospect, nearly all the participants reckon the results were well worth the effort. The sketches and Ridleygrams had turned into art. As art sometimes does, *Blade Runner*, for better or worse, had provided a new way of seeing.

A bar based on the film opened in Tokyo, a city that had itself been a source of inspiration for the film. And ten years after the filming Ridley Scott visited the Bradbury Building (where part of the ending had been shot):

When we shot in front of the Bradbury Building in downtown L.A., we dressed the street by trashing it. Recently, I went down there again, and the real street looks as I wanted it to look for the film in 1982. Nature imitating art?

The end of the line: the replicant snake dancer in *Blade Runner*.

Opposite: Harrison Ford as Deckard in *Blade Runner*.

1. Robert Silverberg, 'The Way the Future Looks' in *Screen Flights/Screen Fantasies*, New York, 1984, pp. 187–92.
2. Interview with Hampton Fancher for Christopher Frayling's BBC Radio Four programme *Print the Legend*, November 1995.
3. Ridley Scott's comments are from 'Blade Runner – design and photography' in *American Cinematographer*, July 1982, pp. 684–93, 715–32, and 'Directing *Alien* and *Blade Runner*', in *Screen Flights/Screen Fantasies, op. cit.*, pp. 293–302.

4. On Syd Mead's contribution, see 'Designing the Future' in *Screen Flights, op. cit.*, pp. 199–213, and *American Cinematographer, op. cit.*
5. *Blade Runner Sketchbook*, San Diego, 1982, pp. 61–4.
6. This account of Ridley Scott's time at the Royal College of Art has made use of Christopher Frayling, *The Royal College of Art, one hundred and fifty years of art and design*, Barrie and Jenkins, London, pp. 156–60, 166–71, 188–9; Alex Seago, *Burning the Box of Beautiful Things*, Oxford University

Press, 1995 (especially pp. 77–174 on *Ark* in this period); Richard Guyatt, ed., *Graphics RCA*, Royal College of Art, 1963; and *College Annual Reports*, 1958–61.
7. On *Alien*, see Paul Scanlon and Michael Gross, *The Book of* Alien, Heavy Metal Communications, New York, 1979, and Hans Rudi Giger, *Giger's* Alien *film design*, Titan Books, 1979.
8. Quotes by Alan Raymond, Lawrence Paull and Ridley Scott (on the Bradbury Building) are from 'Blade Runner - ten years on' (in *Details* magazine, *op. cit.*, pp. 110–15, 177).

# Boyd Webb

By Michael O'Pray

In Boyd Webb's film *Love Story*, a piece of popcorn comes to life and attempts to breed. There on the tacky carpeted floor, beneath the rows of seats, constantly in danger of being crushed by waves of moving feet, this bit of nature struggles for existence in the most artificial of worlds: the cinema. Surrounded by the sounds and flickering shadows of the great themes and emotions of mankind being played out on the screen – love and death, joy and despair – and by the fetid atmosphere of the theatre itself, nature finds the conditions for its survival, at least in Webb's version of the world. The film's theme takes us back to Webb's *Herbert Groves* (1973), a diptych comprising two colour photographs (reproduced in black and white below), one of a betting shop exterior and the other of a man's mouth being prised open, by what looks like a medical instrument, to reveal it filled with lichen. In Webb's words, 'the nutrients essential for this lichen's survival are filtered from the humid fug of despair, jubilation and nervous human effluvium peculiar to betting shops'. It is in the similarly fetid and hyper-emotional atmosphere of the cinema that he has set his new film.[1]

Over the years Webb's work has moved from photographs with a disturbing element added by the artist (*Eels,* 1971) through photographs and text (*Herbert Groves*) to cibachrome fabrications, and finally the more anthropomorphic, animation-like work of recent years. If *Love Story* is a continuation of his longstanding exploration of the vicissitudes of nature, it also embodies the paradoxical qualities common to much of his photographically based work. For instance, in *Love Story* the 'natural' popcorn is an animated element, whereas the threatening feet are live action. While the human emotions played out on screen unravel in accordance with the laws of narrative – tying up all the loose ends of imaginary lives – it is the story of the popcorn, at the mercy of the accidental (a wayward shift of a foot might squash it), that is more like life itself. In this scenario the cinema audience plays the role of gods to the unfortunate popcorn and it lives its life before us.

As the critic Greg Hilty has remarked, Webb has created 'a poetic experimental universe ... governed, like our own world, by conditions which are at once self-perpetuating: stasis and migration, growth and decay, life and death'. At the heart of this is what Hilty describes as Webb's desire to conjure up 'a world where the everyday is rendered marvellous'.[2] It therefore seems almost predictable that he should turn to

Herbert Groves, an amateur lichenologist, has successfully developed and introduced a lichen (*Sponsio Grovesiaceae*) to the moist lining of his throat in order to become eligible for disability compensation.
A keen punter, he now studies form in earnest, investing sometimes to advantage, sometimes not.

Through skilful husbandry the lichen *Sponsio Grovesiaceae* has adapted successfully to the inclement environment of the human throat.
Nutrients essential for this lichen's survival are filtered from the humid fug of despair, jubilation and nervous human effluvium peculiar to betting shops.

Left and following pages: Early working manipulations: popcorn.

Opposite:
*Mother* (1992).

animation, through which he can not only conjure up the marvellous but also explore two of his ongoing concerns: the animating of the inanimate and the omnipotence of the creator. In his book *Totem and Taboo*, Freud suggests that the projection of human properties on to animals and objects is key to art as a human activity, and that our need for art and magic is rooted in an infantile mechanism. Like children, we believe that our frustrated desires have been fulfilled, however impossible or untrue that might be: the omnipotence of thought. Webb's work projects a sense of the 'impossible', presented as solace for disappointment with the world as it is. So often in his photographic work we glimpse other worlds that lurk beneath the surface or just around the corner, as with the objects that peep out from behind ambiguous constructions and 'landscapes'. In film, animation is the most effective way of creating such 'impossible' worlds and the act of animation itself is one of omnipotence, in that the control of the animator is total: unlike live action, anything is possible – gravity and the laws of nature can be jubilantly defied.

In an essay on cinematic décor the Surrealist writer Louis Aragon described the way the use of objects, sets and other actors in the films of

Charlie Chaplin creates a 'vision of the world, which, together with the discovery of the mechanical and its laws, haunts the hero to such an extent that by an inversion of values each inanimate object becomes a living thing for him, each human person a dummy whose starting-handle must be found'.[3] Like Chaplin, Webb not only animates the inanimate but also 'de-animates' the animate, at times treating figures, animals and plants in the same way as the objects they engage with. His figures' frozen gestures, actions or poses often suggest not so much the captured moment of a narrative as the existence of another world in which their status is unclear, as in *Trophy* (1985), where the god-like man floating in the universe hurls a model of the world at the world itself. But the clearest precedents for Webb's work are to be found in Surrealist photography: Bellmer's brutalised dolls and Man Ray's love-making mannequins (*Untitled, c.* 1936), enigmatic landscape (*Waste Land/Terrain vague*, 1929) or wrapped and bound objects (*The Enigma of Isador Ducasse,* 1920). His acknowledgement of the influence of Victorian genre painting and mail-order catalogue photography aligns him with a further Surrealist trait exemplified by the collages of Max Ernst (*A Week of Happiness,*

Fleshy Moments:
Man Ray,
*Untitled* (1936).

Unnerving
Victoriana:
Max Ernst,
a collage from
*A Week of
Happiness*
(1934).

1. This paragraph owes much to a conversation with the artist on 25 January 1996 and the essay as a whole to the critical suggestions of Sarah Hill, Philip Dodd and Ian Christie. I have also referred to Stuart Morgan's excellent essay 'Global Strategy' in *Boyd Webb*, Whitechapel Art Gallery, London, 1987.

2. Greg Hilty, 'A Degree of Unease: The Work of Boyd Webb' in *Boyd Webb*, VII Indian Triennale catalogue, British Council, 1994.

3. Louis Aragon, 'On Décor', first published in 1918 and reprinted in Paul Hammond, ed., *The Shadow and Its Shadow*, Polygon, Edinburgh, 1991, pp. 55–9.

4. Hilty, *op cit*.

*Tutelar*
(1993).

1934), who created a macabre, erotic and bizarre world by subversively integrating his own 'perversions' into standard Victorian images. Webb's heady mix of people (or fragments of them), household objects, *mise-en-scène* and odd camera angles similarly disturbs, elates and lends fresh insight.

In the past few years, when objects rather than people have taken a central place in Webb's art, the notion of 'substituting something for the subject'[4] has become pivotal. But despite the animation and anthropomorphism employed to this end, Webb's objects never lose their integrity as objects. They are not cancelled out by their 'role' but rather it is their very mundanity and idiosyncracy that provide much of the humour. The carrots of *Entrechat* (1992) are just that – carrots – but sticking out from beneath a skirt they are suspended between their 'objectness' and their transformation into a pair of legs. It is their vulnerability, their comicalness as vegetables as well as their physical similarity to legs that makes them such a witty choice. (Interestingly, the sixteenth-century painter Arcimboldi, a precursor of the Surrealists, also constructed portraits composed of vegetables and flowers that drained the human subject of life while at the same time animating the objects employed through their location in a new context.)

Another distinctive characteristic of Webb's photographs is his use of scale, the way his mock-sublime figures or objects are set against fragments of larger, not quite decipherable surfaces, as in *Salvage* (1984), *Nourish* (1984) or *Shell Shock* (1983). This is a further way that he constructs another possible universe: his images contain enough information for us to gauge its scale, dominant materials, perimeters and perhaps even its physical laws. His use of space is at times reminiscent of Giorgio de Chirico, Salvador Dalí, Dorothea Tanning (*Eine kleine Nacht Musik*, 1944) or the more abstract but spatially invigorating work of Joan Miró.

It should come as no surprise that Webb is fascinated by film and has returned, after his first film made with Philip Haas in 1984 (*Scenes and Songs from Boyd Webb*), this time to animation. Two traditions of animation come to mind when looking at photographs such as *Ebb* (1993), *Salvo* (1993) or *Smother* (1992): first, early cartoons such as Emile Cohl's *Fantasmagoria* (1908) or the anarchic and inventive films of early Disney, so admired by Eisenstein, and second the East European Surrealist-influenced school of the Czech Jan Švankmajer (*The Flat*, 1968) and Polish

film-maker Walerian Borowczyk (*Renaissance*, 1963), who anthropomorphise real objects (chairs, nails, potatoes, stones, doors and so forth) using stop-frame methods. Webb's deflated balloons/ contraceptives (*Miasma and Ampoule*, 1993) and Plasticene germs and sperm (*Tutelar*, 1993) look ready to wriggle into life, to gallivant around the frame performing impossible feats for our entertainment. They are reminiscent of the lines that take a cinematic walk in Disney's *Silly Symphony* series of the late 1920s and early 1930s, animated to a point of chaos and anarchy, or of Švankmajer's nails, socks, screws and bits of raw meat that malevolently invade our complacent world of Newtonian gravity, Darwinian selection and traditional morality. In other words, they are not simply performing impossible tricks but are disturbing occupants of our world whose ways defy our expectations. They fill us with unease.

It is perhaps the pre-eminent sign of Webb's modernity that he has transplanted the grand concerns of art into mundane objects such as deflated balloons or popcorn without forfeiting the capacity to create universes filled with magical possibilities. As he has said of his own work, 'nothing is as it seems'.

Walt Disney, 'Skeleton Dance', one of the *Silly Symphony* series.

**Fiona Banner** was born in 1966 in Merseyside. She studied at Kingston Polytechnic from 1986–89 and at Goldsmiths' College of Art, London, from 1991–93, and now lives in London. Banner's first solo exhibition was at City Racing, London, in 1994 and she has participated in group exhibitions including *BT New Contemporaries 1994*, *4 Projects* at Frith Street Gallery, London, *Viewing Room* with Christopher Wool at Luhring Augustine, New York, and *General Release*, an exhibition of young British artists at the Scuola di San Pasquale, Venice, in 1995.

**Terry Gilliam** was born in Minneapolis, Minnesota, USA, in 1940. From 1958–62 he majored in Political Science in Los Angeles, and moved to New York. After travels and work as a freelance illustrator, he moved in 1967 to London, where he now lives. Work as a cartoonist and animator for television led to his involvement in *Monty Python's Flying Circus*, beginning in 1969. The first Monty Python film, *And Now for Something Completely Different*, was made in 1971 followed three years later by *Monty Python and the Holy Grail*, which Gilliam co-directed, and in 1978 by *Life of Brian*, which he designed. In 1976 he directed *Jabberwocky*, and his subsequent films have included *Time Bandits* (1981), *Brazil* (1985 – the film received two Oscar nominations), *The Adventures of Baron Munchausen* (1989 – winner of BAFTA awards for Production Design, Costume Design, and Make-up, Oscar Nominations for these categories and for Special Effects), and *The Fisher King* (winner, Oscar for Best Supporting Actress). In 1995 Gilliam directed *12 Monkeys*.

**Douglas Gordon** was born in 1966 in Glasgow where he still lives, having studied at Glasgow School of Art from 1984–88 and The Slade School of Art, London, from 1988–90. His first solo show was *24 Hour Psycho* at Tramway in Glasgow in 1993, subsequently shown in Berlin, Leipzig, Vienna, and now London. He has had further solo shows at ARC in Paris in 1993; at Lisson Gallery, London, and the Kunstlerhaus, Stuttgart, in 1994; in New York, at the Van Abbemuseum, Eindhoven, and the Centre Georges Pompidou in Paris, in 1995. Gordon has taken part in group exhibitions throughout Europe and in Japan, including *Self-Conscious State*, Glasgow, 1990; *Guilt by Association* , Dublin, 1992; *Prospekt 93*, in Frankfurt, and *Watt* in Rotterdam in 1993; *General Release* in Venice, *Wild Walls* in Amsterdam, and the *Biennale de Lyon*, all in 1995, and *The British Art Show 4*, a National Touring Exhibition from the Hayward Gallery which opened in Manchester in 1995 and travelled to Edinburgh and Cardiff in 1996.

**Peter Greenaway** was born in Wales in 1942. He trained as a painter, and began working as a film editor in 1965, spending 11 years cutting films for the Central Office of Information. In 1966 he started making his own films, and since then has continued to produce paintings, novels and illustrated books. Along with numerous short films and innovative productions for television, he has directed the following feature films: *The Draughtsman's Contract* (1982), *A Zed and Two Noughts* (1986), *The Belly of an Architect* (1987), *Drowning by Numbers* (1988), *The Cook The Thief His Wife & Her Lover* (1989), *Prospero's Books* (1989*), The Baby of Mâcon* (1993), and *The Pillow Book* in 1995. In 1994, in Amsterdam, Greenaway directed *Rosa, A Horse Drama*, an opera in 12 scenes. Over the past five years he has curated exhibitions including *The Physical Self* in Rotterdam (1991), *100 Objects to Represent the World*, Vienna and *Le Bruit des Nuages* at the Louvre, Paris (both 1992), *Watching Water* in Venice, *Some Organising Principles* in Swansea, and *The Audience of Mâcon*, in Cardiff (all 1993), and *The Stairs, Geneva, the Location* in Geneva in 1994, and *The Stairs, Munich, Projection* in 1995. He has exhibited his own work in galleries from Toyko to Tempe, Arizona.

**Damien Hirst** was born in Bristol in 1965. He studied at Goldsmiths' College of Art, London, from 1985–89, and now lives in London and Devon. Solo exhibitions include *In & Out of Love* in Woodstock Street, London, in 1991, and *Internal Affairs* at the ICA, London, the same year; he has also had solo exhibitions in Paris, New York, Cologne, Los Angeles, Milwaukee, at the Mattress Factory in Pittsburgh, the DAAD Gallery in Berlin, and White Cube/Jay Jopling, London. Hirst has curated and participated in a number of exhibitions in London, including *Freeze* in 1988, *Modern Medicine* in 1990, and *Some Went Mad, Some Ran Away* at the Serpentine Gallery in 1994. He has taken part in other group shows around the world including in 1992 *Young British Artists* at the Saatchi Gallery, London, and the Turkish Biennial in Istanbul; the Aperto section of the Venice Biennale in 1993; *From Beyond the Pale* at the Irish Museum of Modern Art in Dublin in 1994; and *Brilliant! Art from London* at the Walker Art Center in Minneapolis in 1995. In 1992 Hirst was a nominee for the Turner Prize, which he won in 1995.

**Steve McQueen** was born in 1969 in London where he currently lives, having studied at Chelsea School of Art from 1989–90, Goldsmiths' College of Art from 1990–93, and Tisch School of the Arts, New York University, New York, from 1993–94. McQueen has exhibited his film works in the exhibitions *Acting Out: the Body in Video, Then and Now* at the Royal College of Art, London , in 1994; *Mirage: Enigmas of Race, Difference and Desire*, ICA, London, *The British Art Show 4*, a National Touring Exhibition travelling to Manchester, Edinburgh, and Cardiff, and *X/Y* at the Centre Georges Pompidou, Paris, all in 1995.

**Eduardo Paolozzi** was born in Leith, Scotland, in 1924. He studied at Edinburgh College of Art in 1943, and at Slade School of Art from 1944–47. From 1947 until 1950 he worked in Paris. Paolozzi has had a distinguished teaching career, and is currently visiting Professor at the Royal College of Art in London. His first one-person exhibition was at the Mayor Gallery in London in 1947 and his many other solo shows have included a retrospective in the British Pavilion at the 30th Venice Biennale in 1960 and exhibitions at the Museum of Modern Art, New York (1964), the Tate Gallery, London (1971), and the Städtische Galerie im Lehnbachhaus, Munich (1984). Paolozzi created the exhibition *Lost Magic Kingdoms and Six Paper Moons* at the Museum of Mankind, London, in 1985 and touring through Britain in 1988–89. Most notable among his many commissioned works are the glass mosaics for Tottenham Court Road underground station, London, made between 1980 and '86. Paolozzi has made four films*: The History of Nothing* (1960–62), *Kakafon Kakkon* (1965), *Mr. Machine* (1971), and *1984 – Music for Modern Americans* (1983), and has himself appeared in two films.

**Paula Rego** was born in 1935 in Lisbon, in Portugal, and came to London to study at the Slade School of Art in London from 1952–56. Rego has exhibited regularly in Lisbon and Oporto since the mid 1960s. Her first solo show in Britain was at the AIR Gallery, London, in 1981, followed by yearly exhibitions at Edward Totah Gallery, London. Rego's 1988 retrospective exhibition at the Fundacao Calouste Gulbenkian in Lisbon travelled to the Serpentine Gallery in London. *Nursery Rhymes*, an exhibition of graphic work, opened at Marlborough Graphics in 1989 and has toured extensively through the British Council in Europe, as a South Bank Centre Touring Exhibition in Britain, and in Australia and the United States. Rego was Associate Artist at London's National Gallery from 1990–91, and her exhibition *Tales from the National Gallery* also toured widely. She exhibited *Peter Pan and Other Stories* in 1993, and her *Dog Woman* series in 1994, both at Marlborough Fine Art, London. Rego's work has been included in many thematic and survey shows throughout the world, including most recently *Unbound: Possibilities in Painting* at the Hayward Gallery and *John Murphy, Avis Newman, Paula Rego* at The Saatchi Gallery, both in 1994.

**Ridley Scott** was born in South Shields, Northumberland, in 1937. He studied graphic design at the West Hartlepool College of Art in 1956 and the Royal College of Art, London, from 1958–61, where he made his first film, *Boy on a Bicycle*. Graduating with honours, Scott travelled through the United States for a year, working with documentary film-makers Richard Leacock and D.A. Pennebaker. Returning to Britain, he joined the BBC first as a production designer and then on the directing team. Scott left the BBC to form his own company. He has directed over 2,000 commercials, many of them award winners at the Venice and Cannes Film Festivals, and

remains managing director of RSA. Scott's first feature film was *The Duellists* made in 1978, and winner of the Jury Pize at Cannes. His second film, *Alien*, in 1979, won an Academy Award for its special effects, and was followed by *Bladerunner* in 1981. Subsequent features have included *Legend, Someone to Watch Over Me, Black Rain, Thelma and Louise, 1492: Conquest of Paradise*, and *White Squall*, for release in Britain in May 1996.

**Boyd Webb** was born in Christchurch, New Zealand, in 1947, and lives in Brighton. He attended Ilam School of Art from 1968–71 and the Royal College of Art, London, from 1972–75. He has exhibited extensively throughout the world since the late 1970s. Notable solo exhibitions include those at the Anthony d'Offay Gallery, London, since 1981; the Centre Georges Pompidou, Paris, and the Stedelijk van Abbemuseum, Eindhoven, both in 1983; the Whitechapel Art Gallery, London, 1987 and travelling throughout 1988; F.R.A.C. du Limousin, France, and the Hirshhorn Museum and Sculpture Garden, Washington, D.C., in 1990; Harris Museum and Art Gallery, Preston, 1994, travelling in Britain and India under the auspices of the British Council. Among the many group exhibitions in which Webb has participated are the Sydney Biennales of 1982 and 1990; Documenta 7, Kassel, 1982; the Aperto Section of the Venice Biennale in 1985; and *British Art Now*, a British Council exhibition travelling through Japan in 1990. In 1984 Webb made a film, *Scenes and Songs from Boyd Webb*, with director Philip Haas.

**Fiona Banner**
Hadrian Pigott
Schiela Lawson
Emily Perkins
Venessa Holtham
Frith Street Gallery

**Terry Gilliam**
*The Road to Monkey Heaven is*
*a: Paved*
*b: Littered*
*c. Barricaded*
*with Good Intentions!*
J. Glyn Williams
Charles Roven
Ian Robinson and
Peter Maccrimmon at
Ranks Laboratories
James Saunders at Grand Central
Imogen Pollard
NATS Post-production
Nick Williams at Animated Extras
Gilbert James of The Peerless
Camera Company
Maggie Gilliam
Darren Willis at Video
Imaging Supplies
Sally Shelton at Don Whitley
Scientific
Slingsby
Lucy Darwin

**Douglas Gordon**
Sharon Essor
Nicola White
Charles Essche at Tramway
Christine van Assche
Alfred Hitchcock
Lisson Gallery, London

**Peter Greenaway**
*In the Dark*
Cast:
The actors
Production:
Lighting Designer: Reinier van
Brummelen
Assistant: Eliza Poklewski Koziell
Anton R.D. Fielmich Jr.
Props: Constance de Vos, Rupert
Jones and Ashley McCormick
Casting: Kate Rudman
Casting Assistant: Oliver Porter
Composer: Patrick Mimran
Sound: Nigel Heath
Haydn Bendall
Ian Sylvester
Paul Hicks
Abbey Road Studios

**Damien Hirst**
*Hanging Around*
Written and directed by
Damien Hirst
Produced by Nira Park
Director of Photography:
John Metcalfe
Production Designer: Kit Line
Production Manager/2nd Unit
Director: Stephen Malit
Editor: John Mayes
Cast (in order of appearance):
Marcus: Keith Allen
Wife 1: Finola Geraghty
Anna: Katrine Boorman
Wife 2: Julia Royse
Baby: Connor Hirst
Philip: Trevor Peacock
Firemen: John Thomson,
Anthony Genn
Girl on ladder: Alice Smith
Boy: Alfie Owen-Allen
Camilla: Frankie Park
Ian: Angus Fairhurst
Wife 3: Amanda Symonds
Children: Finn, Oriel and
Ivo Carew
Consultant: Eddie Izzard
Consultant's wife: Theresa Hickey
Stunts: Rod Woodruff, Bill Davey
Production:
First Assistant Director:
Ben Hughes
Second Assistant Director:
Andrea Brown
Third Assistant Director:
Phil Booth
Production Assistant: Nora Meyer
Sound Recordist: Howie Nicol
Boom Operator: Malcolm Rose

Dubbing Mixer: Billy Mahony
Sound Design: Stephen Griffiths,
Kevin Brazier
Focus Puller: Jasper Fforde
Clapper Loader: Sam Browne
Arial Cameraman: Simon Werry
Arial Co-ordinator: Mark Hanna,
The Flying Machine Company
Camera Grip: Andy Edridge
Gaffer: Terry Edland
Best Boy: Ashley Palin
Telecine Grader: Tareq Kubaisi
Animation: Angus Fairhurst
Titles: Jonathan Barnbrook
Production Buyer: Anna Kasabova
Standby Props: Clive Pegg
Costume Designer: Rebecca Hale
Make-up and hair: Karen Hyams
Wardrobe Assistant:
Mark Bouman
Location Manager: Adam Black
Continuity: Annie South
Stills Photographer: John Jefford
Costumes supplied by: Patrick
Cox, Flyte Ostelle, Dispensary,
Katherine Hamnett, Browns,
Zoe Moore, Rifat Ozbek, Paul
Smith, John Richmond, Ghost
Make-up supplied by:
MAC Cosmetics
Skin care products supplied by:
Clarins
Hair products supplied by:
Paul Mitchell
Camera equipment: Cine Europe
Lighting equipment:
AFM Lighting
Film stock: Kodak
Laboratory: Metrocolor
(London) Ltd

Music:
*Hanging Around*:
Words and music by Alex James,
Charlie Bloor, Stephen Duffy,
Justin Welch
Published by MCA Music,
Copyright Control, Sony Music,
EMI Music Publishing
*Summer in Siam*:
Performed by The Pogues
Published by Perfect Songs Ltd
Courtesy of Warner Music UK Ltd
*A Fine Piece of Madeira*:
Performed by Radar
Additional music composed by
Guy Pratt and Azna, courtesy of
Island Music

Special thanks to:
Richard and Judith Greer,
Daniel Moynihan, Neal Brown,
Jay Jopling, 192 Restaurant,
The Ivy Restaurant,
The London Butterfly House

**Steve McQueen**
*Stage*
Directed by Steve McQueen
Produced by Polly Nash
Cast:
Margaret Kinnon
Steve McQueen
Production:
Production Co-ordinator:
Joanna Macklin
Photographer: Noski Deville
Focus Puller: Steve Smith
Loader: Peter Bathurst
Camera Assistant: Naylor El-Solh
Gaffer: Nick Green
Grip: Judith Stanley Smith
Production Designer:
Astrid Sieben
Art Director: Dina Goldman
Additional Art Department help
from: Clifford Bingham,
Mark Cairns, Cath Wadling,
Dot Young and Susie
Editor: Jaime Estrada-Torres
Avid Operator: Angie Shortt

Special thanks to:
Nick Green Lighting
Grip House

The Production Design Company
Greenwich Council
Panavision
Head First Facilities
Film and Television Department,
Royal College of Art
Mary McQueen
Anthony Reynolds Gallery

**Eduardo Paolozzi**
*The Jesus Works and Store:
an attempt to describe an
indescribable film*
Ray Watson
Nick Gorse

Special thanks to:
Frank Thurston
Sabina Grinling
Marynka
Clinton Eichelberger
Martin Moore
Stuart Moore
The Trading Post, Southall,
London
The Museum of the Moving Image

**Paula Rego**
John Erle-Drax of Marlborough
Fine Art (London) Ltd.
Ron Mueck

**Ridley Scott**
Julie Payne
Sherman Labby
Henry Chancellor
Tim Miller, Film and Television
Department, Royal College of Art
Ken Morse
Mark Shillum
P3 Post: Avid Offline and
Online Facility (11 Kingly Street,
London W1)

**Boyd Webb**
*Love Story*
Directed by Boyd Webb
Produced by Pamela Asbury
Production:
Production Manager: Lucy Glyn
Production Designer: Anne Tilby
Editor: Peter Beston
Assistant Editor: Bill Smedley
Model Maker: Scott Brooker
Lighting Cameramen: Clive
Norman and Graham Pettit
Animators: Derek Mogford and
Daryl Marsh
Camera Assistants: Stephen Sadler
and Harpie
Lighting Assistant: Phil Griffith
Construction Manager:
Nick Bloom
Costume: Suzi Pride
Props: Andrew Green
Runners: Dan Davies and
Matt Buck
Artistes: Jay Simon and
Mira
Music by De Wolfe Music

Special thanks to:
Jayne Pilling, Director of the
British Animation Awards
Roger Law of Spitting Image
Susan Moore, Elaine and Anne
Cartwright from the Spitting
Image workshop
Charles Rubenstein & Vadid at
the Rio Cinema, Dalston
Framestore
Panavision
Samuelsons
Film Stock Centre Blanx
Metrocolor Ltd.
AFM Lighting
TG Snacks
Red or Dead
Dr Martens
The Tape Gallery
Colour Processing Laboratories
Anthony d'Offay Gallery

**Gordon Burn's** first novel, *Alma Cogan*, won a Whitbread Award. His second *fullalove*, made the final twelve for the 1995 Booker Prize. He is the author of *Somebody's Husband, Somebody's Son*, a study of Peter Sutcliffe. His current projects include a book about the West murders in Gloucester, and a novel whose title, *A Celebration At Least*, is taken from a work by Damien Hirst. He lives in London and writes infrequently on art.

**Thomas Elsaesser** is Professor at the University of Amsterdam and Chair of the Department of Film and T.V. studies. From 1972–1991 he taught English, Film and Comparative Literature at the University of East Anglia. Recent books as author and editor include *New German Cinema: A History* (1989), *Early Cinema: Space Frame Narrative* (1990), *Writing for the Medium: Television in Transition* (1994), and *Double Trouble* (1994). He has recently completed editing a volume on *German Cinema: The First Two Decades.*

**Christopher Frayling** is Professor of Cultural History and Pro-Rector at the Royal College of Art in London. He has worked in television and radio, making the two historical series *The Face of Tutankhamun* and *Strange Landscape – the Illumination of the Middle Ages* for BBC2. His published works have included *The Vampyre* (1976), *Spaghetti Westerns* (1980), *The Royal College of Art: 150 years of art and design* (1987), *The Art Pack* (1992) and *Things to Come* (in the *Film Classics* series for the British Film Institute, 1995).

**Martha Gever** is an art and media critic whose writing has been published in *Afterimage, October, Screen* and *Art in America,* as well as a number of anthologies. She co-edited *Queer Looks: Perspectives on Lesbian and Gay Film and Video* (with John Greyson and Pratibha Parmar), *How Do I Look? Queer Film and Video* (with the Bad Object Choices collective), and *Out There: Marginalisation and Contemporary Cultures* (with Russell Ferguson, Trinh T. Minh-ha and Cornel West). She is currently working on a study of lesbian celebrities in the context of contemporary U.S. culture and politics.

**Martin Kemp** is British Academy Wolfson Research Professor and since October 1995 has been Professor of the History of Art at the University of Oxford. He studied Natural Sciences and Art History at Cambridge and at the Courtauld Institute of Art, London. He is the author of *Leonardo da Vinci. The Marvellous Works of Nature and Man* (1981), *The Science of Art. Optical Themes in Western Art from Brunelleschi to Seurat* (1990), and numerous studies of the relationships between representation in art and science.

**Michael O'Pray** has published widely on avant-garde film, video, animation and film theory, and has edited *Andy Warhol: Film Factory* (1989) and *Inside the Pleasure Dome The Films of Kenneth Anger* (1990). In 1981 he joined the editorial collective on *Undercut* and in 1983 he formed the Film and Video Umbrella. From 1992 to 1995 he was Chair of the Arts Council's Artists' Film and Video Committee. His book *Derek Jarman: Dreams of England* is to be published in 1996 and he has recently edited *The British Avant-Garde Film 1926–1990.*

**Marcia Pointon** is Pilkington Professor of History of Art at the University of Manchester. Her recent published works include *Naked Authority: the Body in Western Painting 1830–1908* (1990), *The Body Imaged: the Human Form and Visual Culture since the Renaissance* (1993, edited with Kathleen Adler) and *Hanging the Head: Portraiture and Social Formation in Eighteenth Century England* (1993). Her forthcoming book, *Strategies for Showing: Women, Possession and Representation in English Visual Culture 1650–1800* will be published in 1997.

**Amy Taubin** writes film criticism for the *Village Voice* and is a contributing editor for *Sight and Sound.* Her writings have been published in the anthologies *Women and Film* (edited by Pam Cook and Philip Dodd) and *Debating Sexual Correctness* (edited by Adele M. Stan). In the sixties she appeared in avant-garde films by Andy Warhol, Jona Mekas and Michael Snow, and in 1981 she made the short film *In the Bag* (in MOMA's collection). From 1983 to 1987, she was the film and video curator of the New York art centre, The Kitchen. She is currently finishing a monograph about Martin Scorsese's *Taxi Driver* and a book on American Independent Film.

**Linda Ruth Williams** is lecturer in film at Southampton University. She is author of *Sex in the Head: Visions of Femininity and Film in D.H. Lawrence* (1993), *Critical Desire: Psychoanalysis and the Literary Subject* (1995), and has written many articles on cinema, feminism and modern fiction. She is now writing a book on erotic thrillers.

**Peter Wollen** has written on and worked in a wide range of cinema. His published works include *Signs and Meaning in the Cinema, Raiding the Icebox,* and *Singin' in the Rain.* He co-directed a series of films with Laura Mulvey, including *Penthesilea,* and *Riddles of the Sphinx* and co-wrote (with Mark Peploe) the script for Michelangelo Antonioni's film *The Passenger.* He has curated a number of exhibitions including *Frida Kahlo and Tina Modotti* and *The Situationist International.*

Compiled by
Vicky Allan

Since the earliest days of cinema
in Britain, there has been an
intimate relationship between art
and film. This chronology intends
not to set out a single, seamless
narrative of that relationship,
but to provide the materials out
of which a number of diverse
narratives might be made.
The selection of material
has generally tried to register
the range of factors that
have shaped art and film's
relationship, including:

the early importance of European
Modernism and avant-garde film-
makers; Neo-Romanticism; the
response to American culture
(both 'high' and popular); the
awareness that an extraordinary
variety of cultures, not only
American and European,
have produced art and films.

Where non-British films are
mentioned, a two-letter code for
the country of origin is given
(e.g. It = Italy).

# Chronology

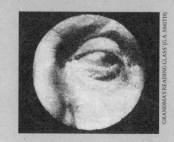
GRANDMA'S READING GLASS (G.A. SMITH)

## 1896

● January
Birt Acres (who had collaborated with Robert William Paul in the development of the Kinetoscope) holds the first public screening of moving pictures in Britain for the Lyonsdown Photographic Club. This is soon followed by a screening at the Royal Photographic Society (14 January). The programme consists of films made by Acres, among them *The Derby* and *The Opening of the Kiel Canal.*

● March
R.W. Paul (scientific instrument maker who was the first in Britain to manufacture an Edison Kinetoscope) and Birt Acres attempt to establish the first public cinema at the corner of Piccadilly Circus and Shaftesbury Avenue.

● Birt Acres spends the rest of the year touring the country, lecturing and giving moving picture performances.

● Birt Acres produces a series of films that feature the popular magazine and stage cartoonist, Tom Merry, performing his 'lightning cartoons', including *Tom Merry, Lightning Cartoonist: Lord Salisbury.*

● R.W. Paul uses a hand-colouring process to tint film portraits of the Royal Family.

● The National Portrait Gallery building in St. Martin's Place opens, housing its collection which was founded in 1856.

● The narrative painter Hubert von Herkomer uses photographs as the basis for his portrait of Herbert Spencer.

● The Central School of Arts and Crafts (London) opens under W.R. Lethaby and George Frampton.

### Births
Michael Balcon
William Cameron Menzies

### Deaths
John Everett Millais

## 1897

● Walter Sickert resigns from the New English Art Club (founded in 1886 in opposition to the Royal Academy), which is becoming increasingly conservative.

● In New York J. Stuart Blackton establishes the Vitograph company with Albert E. Smith and William T. Rock. Their first film is *Burglar on the Roof.* J. Stuart Blackton, who was born in Sheffield, emigrated to the United States in 1885 to become an illustrator in New York.

● The Tate Gallery opens as the National Gallery of British Art. Built on the site of the demolished Millbank Prison, it is designed to hold the collection of nineteenth-century painting and sculpture, given to the nation by Sir Henry Tate, and some paintings transferred from the National Gallery.

● *Comic Faces* (G.A. Smith) A film of Vaudeville turns.

### Publications
Cecil Hepworth (pioneer film maker) publishes *The ABC of the Cinematograph*, the first British book to be published on moving pictures.

### Births
Alberto Cavalcanti (Brazil)
Hein Heckroth (Germany)

## 1898

● The British branch of Gaumont Company is set up by A.G. Broomhead and T.A. Welsh.

● Many early moving pictures feature the theme of art or the figure of the artist. Those made in 1898 include *The Artist and the Flower Girl* (R.W. Paul) and *Come Along Do!* (R.W. Paul), a comedy in which a couple from the country visit an art gallery.

A STRIP FROM R.W. PAUL'S ANIMATED FILM, THE KITCHEN

● *Animated Portrait – Miss Marie Lloyd* (Warwick Trading Co.) Filmed at the Alhambra Theatre of Varieties, Brighton.

● Wyndham Lewis studies at the Slade School of Art (1898–1901).

● Camberwell School of Arts and Crafts is founded.

### Births
John Grierson
Henry Moore

### Deaths
Aubrey Beardsley
Edward Burne-Jones

## 1899

● The first animated film is an advertisement, created by Arthur Melbourne Cooper. In *Matches: An Appeal* a box of Bryant and May's matches opens and the matches chalk up this appeal: 'For one guinea Bryant and May will forward a case containing sufficient to supply a box of matches to each man in a batallion, with the name of the sender inside.'

● Walter Sickert lives in Dieppe, France (1899–1905).

### Births
Noël Coward
Alfred Hitchcock

## 1900

● *Grandma's Reading Glass* (George Albert Smith) An eccentric 'trick' film, with extreme close-ups as seen through a magnifying lens.

● *Miss Ellen Terry at Home* (Warwick Trading Co.) This film of the actress at home was one of many on the theatre (or music hall) and its stars.

● *The Last Days of Pompeii* (R.W. Paul). Adaptation of Lord Lytton's novel.

### Births
Lazare Meerson (Poland)
Roland Penrose

### Deaths
John Ruskin

PHOTO-SERIES FROM EADWEARD MUYBRIDGE'S 'THE HUMAN FIGURE IN MOTION'

# 1901

# 1902

# 1903

# 1904

# 1905

● *The Human Figure in Motion*, a collection of Eadweard Muybridge photographs, is published in London. It contains facsimile signatures of subscribers to Muybridge's earlier *Animal Locomotion, an electro-photographic investigation of consecutive phases of animal movement* (a collection of serial instantaneous photographs published in 1887).
Among these are Hubert von Herkomer, James Abbott McNeill Whistler, John Ruskin and Lawrence Alma-Tadema.
● *The Devil in the Studio* (W.R. Booth). An artist in his studio squeezes a tube of vermilion paint, from which Mephisto emerges in smoke and flames. A large portrait of the artist appears on the canvas; seconds later the devil makes it vanish. Further tricks follow: the artist's model fades from her platform and becomes visible on the canvas like a slowly developing photograph.
● *The Famous Illusion of De Kolta* (W.R. Booth). Trick film in which Pierrot starts to sketch upon a board. A drawing of an old drunkard appears with marvellous rapidity. The drawing comes to life, and the drunk lifts a bottle of whisky to his mouth. A short comic sketch follows.
● *Fire!* (James Williamson) Story of a house on fire, with sequences tinted red.

**Births**
Len Lye (New Zealand)
Christopher Wood

● Duncan Grant studies at the Westminster School of Art.
● William George Barker buys two large houses on Ealing Green in West London and starts making films in the gardens.

**Births**
Anthony Asquith
Emeric Pressburger (Hungary)

● *Alice in Wonderland* (Cecil Hepworth, Percy Stow) One of the longest films of the period, it has 16 scenes and is based on the drawings by Sir John Tenniel. 'Every situation was dealt with with all the accuracy at our command and with reverent fidelity, so far as we could manage it, to Tenniel's famous drawings'. (Cecil Hepworth in *Came The Dawn*).

**Births**
Kenneth Clark
Thorold Dickinson
Roger Furse
Barbara Hepworth
John Piper
Ceri Richards
Graham Sutherland

**Deaths**
James Abbott McNeill Whistler

● First issue of the *Optical Lantern and Cinematograph Journal*.
● Colonel Broomhead's theatre is built in Bishopsgate as a special theatre for films.
● The art school set up at Bushey by the painter Hubert von Herkomer closes.
● *The Sculptor's Jealous Model* (R.W. Paul). A love-crazed model smashes a statue, stabs the sculptor and then kills herself.

**Publications**
*Impressionist Painting* by Wynford Dewhurst.

**Births**
Cecil Beaton
Terence Fisher

● An exhibition of 305 Impressionist paintings, including works by Monet, Degas and Renoir is organised by Durand Ruel and held at the Grafton Galleries.
● Vanessa Stephen (later Bell) organises the Friday Club.

**Births**
Edward Burra
Anthony Gross
Tristram Hillier
Michael Powell

## 1906

● *The Hand of the Artist* (W.R. Booth). Animated cartoon based on 'Lightning Sketches'. The hand of an artist produces portrait sketches that come to life. The hand then crumples up the paper and throws it away as confetti.
● The Fitzroy Street Group, an informal association, with members including the Rothensteins, Walter Russell, Spencer Gore and Walter Sickert, is formed.
● G.A. Smith and Charles Urban patent their colour process, Kinemacolor
● Duncan Grant and Matthew Smith attend the Slade School of Art.

**Births**
Carol Reed

## 1907

● Augustus John sees *Les Demoiselles d'Avignon* at Picasso's studio in Paris.
● *Comedy Cartoons* (W. R. Booth). A sequel to *The Hand of the Artist*
● *The Sorcerer's Scissors* (Walter R. Booth). A pair of scissors appears in front of the title and cuts out a woman's form. This comes to life and is then altered by an intervening paintbrush.

**Births**
Humphrey Jennings
Laurence Olivier
Claude Rogers
Paul Rotha
Basil Wright

## 1908

● Foundation of the Allied Artist's Association, a non-jury exhibiting body (an alternative to the New English Art Club). Formed by Frank Rutter and supported by Walter Sickert, Spencer Gore, Lucien Pissarro, Walter Bayes and others, its first annual exhibition is held at the Royal Albert Hall.
● Malcolm Arbuthnot arouses controversy with a large group of semi-abstracted photographs at the London Photographic Salon.
● Walter Sickert teaches at the Westminster School of Art (1908–12 and 1915–18). David Bomberg attends his evening classes.
● C.R.W. Nevinson and Stanley Spencer study at the Slade School of Art (1908–12).
● Arthur Cooper makes the animated film *Dreams of Toyland*.

**Births**
William Coldstream
David Lean
George Pal (Hungary)
Victor Pasmore
Carel Weight

## 1909

● Malcolm Arbuthnot holds his first one-man show of photographs.
● Wassily Kandinsky exhibits annually at the Salon from 1909 until 1911.
● *The Sporting Mice* (Charles Armstrong) A silhouette film featuring performing mice. 'Professor' Armstrong was the first animator to work in cut-out silhouettes, also producing the silhouette work *Votes for Women: A Caricature* in the same year. He made many short films, including advertisements, at his studio, the Cumberland Works, in Kew.

**Births**
Francis Bacon

**Deaths**
William Powell Frith

## 1910

● November
Roger Fry's *Manet and the Post-Impressionists* exhibition opens at the Grafton Galleries. Manet's work is already known and respected, but works by Cézanne, Van Gogh, Gauguin, Picasso and the Fauves Matisse, Vlaminck and Derain are also included. The exhibition causes outrage among the British art world and public.
● Walter Sickert paints his *Camden Town Murder* series, which provokes widespread disapproval.
● *Birth of a Flower* (Kineto Company, director Percy Smith) The growth of a flower is filmed using time-lapse photography.
● Paul Nash and Ben Nicholson study at the Slade School of Art.

## 1911

● May
Formation of the Camden Town Group, including Wyndham Lewis, Duncan Grant, Spencer Gore and other English Post-Impressionists. Its first exhibition is held in the Carfax Galleries in London.
● *Animated Putty* (W. R. Booth). A lump of putty shapes itself into an eagle's head, a bunch of roses, a windmill, a girl in a hat, a devil and a boy.
● Wyndham-Lewis paints his *Smiling Woman Ascending a Stair*, which is Cubist/Futurist in style.
● Ezra Pound, T.E. Hulme, F.S. Flint and Richard Aldington launch Imagism.

**Births**
Val Guest
Mervyn Peake
Vincent Price

**Deaths**
Henry Wallis

## 1912

● October
The *Second Post-Impressionist Exhibition of English, French and Russian Artists* opens at the Grafton Galleries. The French artists are selected by Roger Fry, the English by Clive Bell, and the Russian by Boris von Anrep. Central to the exhibition are 19 paintings by Matisse, including *Le Luxe* and *La Danse*. 13 Picasso paintings are displayed, including the Cubist *Tête d'Homme*. Bell's selection of English art includes works by Eric Gill, Spencer Gore and Wyndham Lewis.
● The artist Hubert von Herkomer sets up studios at Bushey and begins making films.
● Duncan Grant exhibits a series of paintings in London under the title *Compositions in Colour-Music and studies in line and shape*.
● Ezra Pound coins the term Vorticism.
● Members of the Camden Town Group including Spencer Gore, Wyndham Lewis and Jacob Epstein decorate Madame Strindberg's Soho theatre club, The Cave of the Golden Calf, in a fauvist style.

**Births**
John Halas
Keith Vaughan

**Deaths**
Lawrence Alma-Tadema

## 1913

● January
The British Board of Film Censors (B.B.F.C.) begins operating with Joseph Brooke Wilkinson as its Secretary.
● October
*The Post-Impressionist and Futurist Exhibition* is organised by Frank Rutter at the Dore galleries. Works by Jacob Epstein (*Marble Doves*), Wyndham Lewis, Edward Wadsworth and C.R.W. Nevinson are included.
● November
Filippo Marinetti visits London at Nevinson's request.
● Formation of the London Group (a fusion of the Camden Town Group and smaller artists' groups).
● The Camden Town Group organise the *English Post-Impressionists, Cubists and Others* exhibition in Brighton.
● Foundation of the London Film Company by Dr R.T. Jupp.
● Gino Severini (Italian Futurist) exhibits at the Marlborough Gallery.
● Roger Fry founds the Omega Workshops.
● Marinetti writes a manifesto on 'The Variety Theatre', describing how the music hall can exploit all modern machinery, including cinematography. The manifesto is published in the *Daily Mail*.
● Vanessa Bell, Roger Fry and Duncan Grant establish the Grafton Group, a splinter society from The Friday Club.
● Charles Chaplin leaves Britain for the United States.
● Jacob Epstein makes the sculpture *The Rock Drill*, incorporating an insect-like robot creature.
● *The Old Wood Carver* (Hubert von Herkomer) The film (now lost) is supplemented by a book, *The Old Woodcarver*, by J. Saxon Mills.

**Other films**
*Quo Vadis?* (Enrico Guazzoni, It)

**Births**
John and Roy Boulting

## 1914

● March
Foundation of the Rebel Art Centre for Futurist British artists is headed by Wyndham Lewis.
● July
First copies of the Vorticist magazine *Blast* ('Review of the Great English Vortex') appear in London.
● *Peace and War Pencillings by Harry Furniss* (Harry Furniss) Film of the popular cartoonist drawing topical sketches at accelerated speed.
● Duncan Grant makes his *Abstract Kinetic Collage Painting with Sound*, an abstract scroll painting that Grant describes as suggesting that 'movement played a great part in establishing the relationship of pictorial forms'.
● Official War Artists' Commission is established by C.F.G. Masterman, Director of Propaganda.
● Paul Nash joins the Artists' Rifles and David Bomberg serves with the Royal Engineers.

**Other films**
*The German Spy Peril* (Will Barker)
*A Little Lady Cartoonist* (Walter R. Booth)

**Publications**
● *Vital English Art*, a Futurist manifesto written by C.R.W. Nevinson and Filippo Marinetti, is published in the *Observer*.
● *Art* by Clive Bell.
● *Des Imagistes*, first anthology of Imagist poetry, edited by Ezra Pound.

**Births**
Joy Batchelor
Robert Colquhoun
Norman McLaren

**Deaths**
Spencer Gore
Hubert von Herkomer

## 1915

● March
Exhibition of Vorticist paintings at the London Group, including works by Edward Wadsworth, C.R.W. Nevinson and Henri Gaudier-Brzeska.
● First production by Ernest Anson Dyer of *Dicky Dee's Cartoons No. 1*. Anson Dyer previously worked as a stained-glass artist and was to become the leading animator in British cartoons before the Second World War.
● *John Bull's Animated Sketchbook No 1* (Dudley Buxton) Animated cartoon and the first production by the Cartoon Film Company (the first British company devoted purely to animated films). Six of the series were produced in 1915. Anson Dyer worked in collaboration with Buxton.
● *His Winning Ways* (George E. Studdy) Lightning cartoon included in Gaumont's film newsreels.
● John Grierson attends Glasgow University.

**Publications**
*Blast 2* is published as a War issue and includes Lewis's 'War Notes' and his essay 'Artists and War'.

**Births**
Terry Frost

**Deaths**
Henri Gaudier-Brzeska
Arthur Hughes

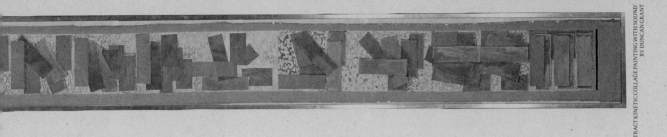

# 1916

● July
*Charlie, the Perfect Lady*
(Charles Chaplin, US) is released
after having been rejected by the
B.B.F.C. in 1915.
● Exhibition of C.R.W.
Nevinson's paintings of military
subjects is held at the Leicester
Galleries.
● *The Real Thing at Last*
(J.M. Barrie) is made in Bushey
studios. A parody of Shakespeare
written by Barrie, it is premièred
as a charity show for British
troops. The film shows how
*Macbeth* might be filmed in both
Britain and Hollywood; the latter
includes dancing girls and an
appearance by 'Charlie Chaplin'.

## Other films
*The Battle of the Somme*
(Geoffrey Malins, J.B. McDowell)

# 1917

● David Bomberg is transferred
to a Canadian regiment as a
war artist.
● Edward Wadsworth works on
schemes for dazzle camouflage
for ships.
● Exhibition of Alvin Langdon
Coburn's Vorticist photographs
and paintings, is held at the
Camera Club, London. The
'Vortographs' are photographs
taken using a prismatic
construction of mirrors.
● Paul Nash is appointed an
official war artist.

## Births
Leonora Carrington
John Francis Minton

# 1918

● A Henri Gaudier-Brzeska
memorial exhibition is held at
the Leicester Galleries.
● *Hearts of the World*
(D.W. Griffith).
American end of the War film,
made with co-operation from the
British Government.
● Henry Tonks (originally a
surgeon) becomes Professor at
the Slade School of Art.

## Births
Peter Lanyon

## Deaths
Birt Acres

# 1919

*Romeo and Juliet* (Anson Dyer,
produced by Cecil Hepworth)
Animated film of the Shakespeare
play in which the figures of
Charlie Chaplin and Mary
Pickford are used as Romeo and
Juliet.
● Wyndham Lewis has his first
one-man show at the Goupil
Gallery, London.
● Foundation of the Seven & Five
Society (which contains seven
painters and five sculptors,
including Ivon Hitchens).
● Closure of the Omega
Workshops.

## Publications
*The Caliph's Design* by
Wyndham Lewis

## Deaths
Harold Gilman

# 1920

March
● The Vorticists attempt to
reform as the X Group, exhibiting
at Heal's Gallery. This, their only
exhibition, features works by
Wyndham Lewis, William
Roberts, Edward Wadsworth
and others.
● Alfred Hitchcock's first job in
the film industry is as title
illustrator for Lasky's Famous
Players, a branch of the American
company Paramount, which
has set up in Islington.
● Roger Furse (theatre and film
designer) studies at the Slade
School of Art under Henry Tonks.

## Publications
*Vision and Design*, a collection of
25 essays by Roger Fry.

## Births
Dirk Bogarde
Alan Davie
Lewis Gilbert
Patrick Heron
Gerald Thomas

## 1921

● Charles Chaplin makes a triumphant return visit to Europe, visiting London.
● Frank Dobson's first one-man sculpture show is held at the Leicester Galleries.
● Graham Sutherland studies graphic art at Goldsmith,s college (1921–6).
● Ben Nicholson visits Paris, where he sees a 1915 Picasso that has 'a great impact on him.
● William Rothenstein becomes Principal of the Royal College of Art.

**Births**
Ken Adam (Germany)
Peter de Francia
John Latham

## 1922

● 24 January
The ballet *Façade, an entertainment* is first performed at the Sitwells' house, 2 Carlyle Square, London. It is choreographed by Ashton, to music by William Walton (who will later compose for the cinema) and based on the poem by Edith Sitwell.

**Publications**
*Since Cézanne* by Clive Bell

**Births**
Lucian Freud
Richard Hamilton
Christopher Lee
William Turnbull

## 1923

● With the help of Dudley Murphy (who directed Fernand Léger's *Le Ballet Mecanique*), Ezra Pound attaches a Vortoscope (prismatic lens used by Vorticist Alvin Langdon Coburn) to a movie camera with the intention of making an abstract film. The idea is abandoned.
● Michael Balcon produces his first film, *Woman to Woman*, hiring Alfred Hitchcock as writer, art director and assistant director.
● David Bomberg leaves Britain for Palestine, as unofficial artist for the Zionist Organisation.

**Other films**
*Comin' Thro' the Rye* (Cecil Hepworth)
*La Roue* (Abel Gance, Fr)

**Births**
Lindsay Anderson
Richard Attenborough
Jeff Keen

**Deaths**
Sarah Bernhardt

## 1924

● Henry Moore takes up a part-time post as instructor at the Royal College of Art.
● John Grierson moves to the United States to take up a position as a Rockefeller Research Fellow in social science.
● The anti-soviet film *Red Russia* is rejected by the B.B.F.C. because it has already led to Communist disturbances in Amsterdam and Bordeaux.

**Births**
Anthony Caro
Eduardo Paolozzi

## 1925

● The Film Society is founded to screen works that are not otherwise viewable (generally because of censorship), including many European avant-garde films. The initial executive council is made up of Iris Barry (who was to become the first director of the film department at M.O.M.A., New York), Sidney L. Bernstein (later director of Granada Television), Adrian Brunel, Frank Dobson (sculptor), Hugh Miller, Ivor Montagu and W.C. Mycroft. Founder members include Augustus John, E. McKnight Kauffer, Roger Fry, J. Isaacs, Dame Ellen Terry and H.G. Wells.
● The first screenings of the Film Society take place on 25 October. For the remainder of the year they show a selection of films including British work (for example *Typical Budget* by Adrian Brunel), French avant-garde films (for example *A Quoi rêvent les Jeunes Films* directed by Henri Chomette and featuring cine-portraits by Man Ray), 'bionomic' films (of nature and microscopic life) and American Comedy (Chaplin and Mack Sennett).
● The start of Film Society screenings marks the appearance in Britain of European and Russian avant-garde films.
● Michael Powell is introduced to Harry Lachman, an American painter and member of Rex Ingram's film unit (Ingram would later take up sculpture).
● Leonard and Dorothy Elmhirst buy Dartington Hall and set up an alternative art school.

**Other films**
*The Pleasure Garden* (Alfred Hitchcock)
*The Rat* (Graham Cutts)

**Births**
Richard Burton
Peter Sellers

## 1926

● February
Paul Leni exhibition of designs for film sets is held at the Mayor Gallery, London.
● October-December
*Drawings, Etchings & Woodcuts by Samuel Palmer and Other Disciples of William Blake* is held at the Victoria & Albert Museum.
● The Film Society continues its policy of showing a wide range of films, including *Entr'acte* (directed by René Clair, for the French modernist ballet *Relâche*), scientific films, *Le Ballet Mécanique* (Fernand Léger and D. Murphy), *The Cabinet of Dr Caligari* (Robert Wiene), *Dr Mabuse, the Gambler* (Fritz Lang), and *Greed* (Erich von Stroheim). *Le Ballet Mécanique*, *Entr'acte* and *The Cabinet of Dr Caligari* are extremely influential on young artists.
● Oliver Messel (film and stage designer) designs masks and décor for Cochran's Revue. Messel is also painting portraits at this time. (He will paint portraits of many film stars, including Vivien Leigh and Merle Oberon.)
● John Grierson first uses the term 'documentary' in a review for the *New York Sun*.
● William Coldstream studies at the Slade School of Art.

### Other films
*Metropolis* (Fritz Lang, Ge)
*The Lodger* (Alfred Hitchcock)

### Publications
● *Let's Go to the Pictures* by Iris Barry.
● 'The Cinema' by Virginia Woolf is published in *Nation and Athenaeum*, 3 July.

### Births
Bryan Forbes
Leon Kossoff
Karel Reisz (Czechoslovakia)
John Schlesinger

## 1927

● July
First issue of the film review *Close Up* is edited by Kenneth Macpherson and Winifred Bryher and published in Switzerland.
● Screenings at The Film Society include *Emak Bakia* (Man Ray), *Crossing the Great Sagrada* (Adrian Brunel) *Symphonie Diagonale* (an 'Absolute Film' by Viking Eggling), *Rhythmus* (Hans Richter), *Nana* (Jean Renoir), *Cinderella* (a silhouette film by Lotte Reiniger) and *L'Inhumaine* (Marcel L'Herbier).
● The Film Artist's Guild is founded.
● 'Pool' films sponsors the imagist poet H.D.(Hilda Doolittle) to make the first free-verse film-poem, entitled *Wing Beat*.

### Other films
● *I Do Like to Be Beside the Seaside* (Oswell Blakeston) Film made with the poet H.D.

### Publications
*Towards A New Architecture*, translation of the French text by Le Corbusier.

### Births
Bruce Lacey
Ken Russell

## 1928

● 1 January
The Cinematograph Films' Act comes into operation and imposes a quota on the number of foreign films shown.
● August
Christopher Wood and Ben Nicholson meet Alfred Wallis, the fisherman painter – on a trip to St Ives.
● 27 September
*The Jazz Singer*, the first all-synchronised film, introducing dialogue, has its British première at the Piccadilly Theatre, London.
● Screenings at The Film Society include *Filmstudie* (Hans Richter), *Nosferatu* (Murnau), *La Petite Lili* (Alberto Cavalcanti) and *Mother* (Vsevlod Pudovkin).
● After its Film Society screening (21 October), the B.B.F.C. rejects Pudovkin's *Mother*.
● First one-man show of John Armstrong paintings (Armstrong designed eight films for Alexander Korda).
● First one-man exhibition of Henry Moore at the Warren Gallery.
● John Grierson is appointed head of the Empire Marketing Board Film Unit.
● *Moulin Rouge* (E.A. Dupont) A British International Production, filmed using a European crew, to create a 'Continental' look. Alfred Junge, the former theatre designer and artist from Germany, is art director.

### Publications
*Through a Yellow Glass* by Oswell Blakeston, critic and associate editor of *Close Up*.

### Births
Michael Andrews
John Berger
John Bratby
James Ivory
Stanley Kubrick
Tony Richardson
Nicolas Roeg
Joe Tilson

### Deaths
Charles Rennie Mackintosh

## 1929

● April
*Close Up* features an article by Robert Herring on 'A New Cinema, Magic and the Avant-Garde' and photographs by Francis Bruguière, director of *The Way*.
● August
Dora Carrington makes the short film *Dr Turner's Mental Home*.
● John Grierson makes his first film, *Drifters*, a documentary about the Scottish herring fisheries. The sculptor John Skeaping works as art director on the film.
● Len Lye makes his first film *Tusalava*, financed by The Film Society.
● The Film Society screenings include *Battleship Potemkin* (Sergei Eisenstein), *Bed and Sofa* (censored film by Room), and *Tusalava* (Len Lye). *Battleship Potemkin* is screened with *Drifters* (John Grierson) and a Disney film (*Barn Dance*). Eisenstein is present at the screening.
● The Cinematograph Films' Act establishes a minimum quota for the distribution and screening of British-made films.
● At the Château of La Sarraz, near Lausanne in Switzerland, a meeting of independent/avant-garde film-makers (at which Ivor Montagu and Jack Isaacs of the Film Society represent Britain) forms the International League of Independent Cinema.
● *Blackmail* (Alfred Hitchcock) Hitchcock's (and Britain's) first sound film features a murder scene in an artist's studio.

### Other films
*Piccadilly* (E.A. Dupont)

### Publications
*Film Problems of Soviet Russia* by Winifred Bryher (published by Pool) registers the impact of Soviet montage cinema on artists and intellectuals throughout the world.

### Births
John Osborne

## 1930

● 1 April
B.B.C. makes first official dual-wave Baird television broadcast.
● 4 August
First Odeon Cinema opens at Perry Barr. Oscar Deutsch is the founder of what will become the Odeon circuit.
● The Film Society screenings include *The General Line* (Sergei Eisenstein), *The Passion of Joan of Arc* (Carl Dreyer), *The Mechanism of the Brain* (Vsevolod Pudovkin), *Conquest* (Basil Wright and John Grierson) and *Fashions for Women* (Dorothy Arzner).
● Edward Carrick works as a painter and commercial artist.
● The Second International Congress of Independent Cinema takes place in Brussels. Oswell Blakeston is one of the British representatives. Kenneth Macpherson's *Borderline* and Francis Bruguière and Oswell Blakeston's *Light Rhythms* are screened.
● Formation of the Society of Industrial Artists (Nash becomes President in 1932).

### Publications
*The Film Till Now* by Paul Rotha.

### Births
Robyn Denny
Elizabeth Frink
Peter Hall
Harold Pinter

### Deaths
Christopher Wood

FROM THE ANIMATION 'LA JOIE DE VIVRE' (ANTHONY GROSS)

# 1931

- April
Henry Moore has a one-man show at the Leicester Galleries.
- The Film Society screenings include *Man With a Movie Camera* (Dziga Vertov), *Enthusiasm* (Dziga Vertov) and *Little Red Riding Hood* (Alberto Cavalcanti).
- *Recent Developments in British Painting* is held at Tooths Gallery; it includes works by Paul Nash, Edward Burra, J.W. Power, Edward Wadsworth, Ben Nicholson and others.
- The Granada cinema in Tooting, London, opens. It is a 'super-cinema' in Venetian-Gothic style, designed by the Russian director-designer Theodor Komisarjevsky.
- Alexander Korda joins Paramount British studio and settles in Britain.
- British sound newsreel *British Paramount News* begins regular release.
- *Modern Pictorial Advertising by Shell* is held at the New Burlington Galleries.
- Herbert Read becomes Professor of Fine Art at Edinburgh University.

**Other films**
*The Skin Game* (Alfred Hitchcock)
*Tell England* (Anthony Asquith, Geoffrey Barkas)

**Publications**
*The Meaning of Art* by Herbert Read

**Births**
Frank Auerbach (Germany)
Malcolm Morley
Bridget Riley
Richard Smith

**Deaths**
William Orpen

# 1932

- 14 February
Alexander Korda establishes the company London Films.
- February
*Seven & Five* exhibition is held at the Leicester Galleries (including works by David Jones, Ivon Hitchens and Ben Nicholson).
- May
Opening of Shepperton studios.
- 16 September
English actress Peg Entwhistle commits suicide by jumping from the H of the Hollywood sign.
- The periodical quarterlies *Sight and Sound* (Great Britain) and *Film Quarterly* (United States) are first published.
- Film Society screenings include *Bluebottles* (Ivor Montagu) and *Lichtspiel Schwartz-Weiss-Grau* (László Moholy-Nagy).
- Paul Nash writes articles on 'Advertising and Contemporary Art', 'Art and Photography' and 'The Artist and Industry' (in the *Weekend Review*).
- Henry Moore accepts invitation to set up a new department of sculpture at Chelsea School of Art.
- The artist Anthony Gross, in partnership with the American film-maker Hector Hoppin, begins making cartoon films in France. He makes the cartoon *La Joie de Vivre*, between 1932 and 1934.
- Henri Fluchère writes an article in the third issue of *Scrutiny*, attempting to explain Surrealism to the British Public.

**Births**
Peter Blake
Howard Hodgkin
Richard Lester

**Deaths**
Dora Carrington

# 1933

- September
The British Film Institute (B.F.I.) is launched.
- Foundation of the art group *Unit One* with Herbert Read as spokesman. Members include Henry Moore, Ben Nicholson, Barbara Hepworth and Paul Nash.

KINETIC FEATURE (PAUL NASH), SHOWN AT MAYOR GALLERY

- 'Super de-luxe' movie theatres proliferate in Britain and U.S., incorporating café restaurants and Wurlitzer electric organs.
- While at Glasgow School of Art Norman McLaren makes an untitled film, a hand-painted abstraction made with colour dye.
- The Artists International Association (A.I.A.) is formed with about 20 left-wing artists and writers, including Clifford Rowe (illustrator and founder), Ronald and Percy Horton, Peggy Argus, James Boswell (illustrator), James Fitton and Mischa Black (industrial designer).
- The Central School of Art, where James Fitton teaches, becomes the recruiting ground for the A.I.A.
- László Moholy-Nagy makes his first visit to London at the invitation of Herbert Read.
- The Mayor Gallery reopens with a Surrealist exhibition in which British Surrealists (eg. Paul Nash, Henry Moore) exhibit with Dalí, Ernst and others.

**Publications**
*Art Now* by Herbert Read

**Births**
John Boorman
Stuart Brisley

# 1934

- November
Formation of the Workers' Film and Photo League.
- William Coldstream stops painting and begins work for the General Post Office (G.P.O.) Film Unit. The unit, which has the function of producing information films for the Post Office, is headed by John Grierson. Len Lye also joins the unit.
- Humphrey Jennings paints scenery for Alberto Cavalcanti's *Pett and Pott*. Jennings also directs *Locomotives* and plays a heroic telegraph boy in Cavalcanti's *The Glorious Sixth of June*.
- *Unit One* exhibition at the Mayor Gallery. Artists included are Henry Moore, John Armstrong (film-set designer), Edward Burra (who would later do paintings of cinematic subjects in America), Paul Nash, Ben Nicholson and Wells Coates.
- At London's Zwemmer Gallery, an exhibition entitled *Objective Abstractions* includes the works of William Coldstream, Victor Pasmore, Ivon Hitchens and others.
- The British Council is founded.
- The Film Society screenings include *October* (Sergei Eisenstein) and *Das Testament von Dr Mabuse* (Fritz Lang).
- Walter Gropius, founder of the Bauhaus, moves to London.

**Other films**
*The Man Who Knew Too Much* (Alfred Hitchcock)
*Evergreen* (Victor Saville)

**Publications**
*Art and Industry* by Herbert Read

**Births**
Mark Boyle
Bob Law

**Deaths**
Roger Fry

# 1935

- Myfanwy Evans produces the first issue of *Axis*, with the assistance of John Piper.
- Bill Brandt's Surrealist photographs are first published in *The News Chronicle*.
- Norman McLaren makes *Camera Makes Whoopee* and *Colour Cocktail*. He shows them at the Scottish Amateur Film Festival, judged by John Grierson. *Colour Cocktail* wins a prize.
- Len Lye makes *Colour Box* without a camera (painting directly on to film), which wins a special prize at the Brussels International Film Festival.
- The artist and designer Hein Heckroth is invited to London to design the Kurt Weill opera, *A Kingdom*.
- László Moholy-Nagy makes the documentary film *Life of the Lobster*.
- The A.I.A. hold the exhibition *Artists Against Fascism and War*, including work by Paul Nash and Henry Moore.
- *Coal Face* (Alberto Cavalcanti) A collaboration with the painter William Coldstream (as editor). Verse by W.H. Auden, music by Benjamin Britten.

'COAL FACE' (ALBERTO CAVALCANTI)

**Other films**
*Shipyard* (Paul Rotha)

**Publications**
- *A Short Survey of Surrealism* by David Gascoyne

**Births**
Paula Rego
Peter Watkins

# 1936

- June
London's first *International Surrealist Exhibition*. On the organising committee are Herbert Read, Hugh Sykes Davies, David Gascoyne, Humphrey Jennings, Henry Moore and Paul Nash.
- Shell commissions artists to design pastoral posters.
- James Boswell (founder member of A.I.A.) becomes Art Director for Shell.
- Norman McLaren, Ivor Montagu and others go to Spain where they film the Spanish Civil War.
- Naum Gabo moves to England where he exhibits in *Abstract and Concrete* at the Lefèvre Gallery.
- *The Birth of a Robot* (Len Lye). Humphrey Jennings works in collaboration with Lye on this film for Shell.
- *Rembrandt* (Alexander Korda) starring Charles Laughton Vincent Korda, himself a painter, designs the sets.
- *Things To Come* (William Cameron Menzies, produced by Alexander Korda) Britain's first big science-fiction film. Vincent Korda is chiefly responsible for the set design, but other design talents including John Bryan, Frederick Pusey and Menzies himself, work on the film. The Bauhaus artist László Moholy-Nagy works as visual consultant on the Work Sequence.
- Norman McLaren makes the anti-war film *Hell Unltd.* with Helen Biggar.

**Other films**
*The Secret Agent* (Alfred Hitchcock)
*Night Mail* (Harry Watt, Basil Wright)

**Publications**
- 'England's Climate', John Piper and Geoffrey Grigson's critique of modernism, is published in *Axis*.
- *The English at Home*, a book of photographs by Bill Brandt, is published by Brian Batsford.

**Births**
Patrick Caulfield

# 1937

- First issue of *Circle*, an 'International Survey of Constructive art' is edited by Ben Nicholson and Naum Gabo.
- The Euston Road School is founded. It is orientated towards 'realist' painting. Claude Rogers, Victor Pasmore and William Coldstream set up an independent 'School of Painting and Drawing'.
- Anthony Gross returns to Paris and begins work on the cartoon adaptation of *Round the World in 80 Days*. It is abandoned in 1939.
- The Odeon Leicester Square opens on the site of the old Alhambra music hall (torn down in 1936). Designed by Harry Weedon and Andrew Mather, it differs from the rest of the Odeon chain.
- Walter Sickert paints *Jack and Jill* (Edward G. Robinson and Joan Blondell), probably based on a publicity still for the New York mobster movie *Bullets or Ballots*

**Other films**
*Edge of the World* (Michael Powell)
*Young and Innocent* (Alfred Hitchcock)

**Publications**
- A study of Samuel Palmer by Geoffrey Grigson is published in *Signature*.

**Births**
Derek Boshier
David Hall
David Hockney
Allen Jones

**Deaths**
Henry Tonks

# 1938

- 16 March
A.I.A. holds a discussion between the Surrealists (Herbert Read, Roland Penrose, Humphrey Jennings and Julian Trevelyan) and the 'Realists' (Anthony Blunt, William Coldstream, Graham Bell and Alick West).
- 30 March
Cinematograph Films' Act 1938 sets new lower quota regulations for British cinemas.
- 4–29 October
Exhibition of Picasso's *Guernica*, with preparatory paintings and sketches, is held at the New Burlington Galleries 'to raise support for the fight against Fascism'. About 3,000 people visit.
- December
Picasso's *Guernica* moves to the Whitechapel Art Gallery. There are 12,000 visitors in a fortnight.
- Michael Balcon succeeds Basil Dean as the head of Ealing Studios.
- Walter Sickert paints his *High Steppers* from a still from *A Little Bit of Fluff* (1927), starring Syd Chaplin and Betty Balfour.
- John Grierson invites Norman McLaren to join the G.P.O. film unit. The first film he makes is *Book Bargain* about the manufacture and printing of the London telephone directory.
- The Euston Road School sets up its teaching 'school', where artists including Victor Pasmore and William Coldstream work alongside their students.
- Ben Nicholson designs *These Men Use Shell*, an advertising poster for Shell.
- Oskar Kokoschka (b. Austria) moves to England.

**Births**
Oliver Reed

**Deaths**
Lazare Meerson

# 1939

- February–March
The A.I.A. organises a travelling exhibition of Surrealist and other works, which tours 12 towns including Bradford, Southport, York, Newcastle and Carlisle.
- November
The War Artists' Advisory Committee (W.A.A.C.) is established under the chairmanship of Sir Kenneth Clark.
- 3 September
All British cinemas close at the outbreak of the Second World War; cinemas outside urban districts reopen on 11 September.
- With the outbreak of the war, the Tate Gallery and National Gallery close, and their contents are moved to places of safety.
- Edward Carrick begins to work as Art Director in charge of the Crown Film Unit and Army Film Unit Art Departments.
- Norman McLaren moves to New York.
- Ben Nicholson and Barbara Hepworth move to Cornwall.
- *Spare Time* (Humphrey Jennings, produced by Alberto Cavalcanti). A Mass Observation film about how the British use their spare time.

**Other films**
*The First Days* (Humphrey Jennings, Harry Watt, Pat Jackson)
*Jamaica Inn* (Alfred Hitchcock)

**Births**
Terry Atkinson
Germaine Greer

**Deaths**
Mark Gertler
Gwen John

# 1940

- January
The magazine *Horizon*, which will serve as a platform for Neo-Romanticism, is published under the editorship of Cyril Connolly.
- 27 February
First British propaganda film for mainstream cinema opens in Britain.
- The Ministry of Information's Film Division plans a programme of 'film propaganda', incorporating documentaries, newsreels and feature films.
- 23 April
The last screening of films by the Film Society features Eisenstein's *Alexander Nevsky*.
- August
Britain's G.P.O. Film Unit becomes the Crown Film Unit.
- August
Paul Nash photographs the wreckage of Nazi aeroplanes, which he will later use for his painting *Totes Meer*.
- The National Gallery opens its first War Artists' Advisory Committee room exhibiting paintings by Paul Nash and Graham Sutherland.
- The Film Section of the Ministry of Information, initially under the direction of Kenneth Clark, decides to sponsor feature films as propaganda. Powell and Pressburger are the first and only beneficiaries of this plan.

**Other films**
*Welfare of the Workers* (Humphrey Jennings)
*London Can Take It!* (Humphrey Jennings)
*Rebecca* (Alfred Hitchcock, US)

**Births**
Terry Gilliam
Malcolm Le Grice
John Lennon

**Deaths**
Eric Gill

## 1941

● *Words for Battle* (Humphrey Jennings). The film is set to a series of British poems and includes shots from a war artist's exhibition.
● April/May
Heaviest German bombings of London, more than 1,000 die in each raid. Henry Moore works on his shelter drawings through the year.
● August
The Royal Air Force Film Production Unit is formed.
● October
Exhibition of works by Henry Moore, John Piper and Graham Sutherland at Temple Newsam, Leeds.
● December
The British Army Film and Photographic Unit is formed, later taking on Roy Boulting.
● John Minton collaborates with Michael Ayrton on designs for John Gielgud's *Macbeth*.
● Works by Ben Nicholson and Barbara Hepworth are photographed using a Rolliflex.

**Other films**
*The Heart of Britain* (Humphrey Jennings)
*Newspaper Train* (Len Lye)

**Births**
Barry Flanagan
Stephen Frears
Mary Kelly
James Scott

**Deaths**
J. Stuart Blackton
Virginia Woolf

## 1942

● A Surrealist exhibition organised by Toni del Renzio is held at the International Art Centre.
● Michael Powell and Emeric Pressburger set up their own production company, The Archers.
● J.M. Keynes becomes chairman of the Committe for the Encouragement of Music and the Arts (which later becomes the Arts Council).

**Films**
*Went the Day Well?* (Alberto Cavalcanti)
*One of Our Aircraft is Missing* (Michael Powell and Emeric Pressburger)
*Work Party* (Len Lye)
*Kill or be Killed* (Len Lye)

**Publications**
● *Life of William Blake* by Alexander Gilchrist (new edition of an earlier publication)
● *British Romantic Artists* by John Piper

**Births**
John Bellany
Peter Greenaway
Derek Jarman
Terry Jones
David Larcher
George Passmore
(of Gilbert & George)

**Deaths**
Walter Richard Sickert
Alfred Wallis

## 1943

● The set designer Hein Heckroth exhibits Surrealist paintings at the Modern Art Gallery, Charles Street, London.
● Artists International Association exhibition *For Liberty* is sponsored by the *News Chronicle* and announces 'a new integration of art and life'.
● Eduardo Paolozzi studies at the Slade School of Art.
● Franciszka and Stefan Themerson make the experimental film *Calling Mr. Smith*. A 'tragic film-dream' set to music by Bach, Szyanowski and a distorted Horst Wessel Lied, in which war-time texts are integrated with documentary fragments, pictures and static objects.

**Other films**
*Fires Were Started* (Humphrey Jennings)
*The Life and Death of Colonel Blimp* (Michael Powell and Emeric Pressburger)

**Publications**
● *William Blake/A Man Without a Mask* by Jacob Bronowski.
● *Horizon* magazine publishes an article by Ben Nicholson on Alfred Wallis.

**Births**
Ian Breakwell
Gilbert Broesch
(of Gilbert & George)
Mike Leigh
Michael Palin

**Deaths**
R.W. Paul
Beatrix Potter

## 1944

● February
Arthur Rank founds the company Eagle-Lion for international distribution of British films.
● April
Toni del Renzio's Surrealist manifesto 'Incendiary Innocence' is published.
● Mervyn Peake designs poster for the Ealing studio film *Black Magic*.
● *A Canterbury Tale* (Michael Powell, Emeric Pressburger). Set in the British countryside with references to the heritage of English literature.

**Publications**
Henry Moore's *Shelter Notebook* is published.

**Other films**
*The Way Ahead* (Carol Reed)

**Births**
Alan Parker
Michael Nyman
Tony Scott
Bruce McLean

**Deaths**
Lucien Pissarro
William Heath Robinson

## 1945

● April
Francis Bacon exhibits *Three Studies for Figures at the Base of a Crucifixion* at the Lefèvre Gallery.
● British Federation of Film Societies formed, with 46 member organisations.
● John Piper designs Ealing studio film posters, *Pink String and Sealing Wax* and *Painted Boats*.
● *Henry V* (Laurence Olivier) The film has a musical score by William Walton and art direction by Roger Furse.
● John Bryan acted as art director on this film, using Oliver Messel's designs. Hein Heckroth acted as costume consultant.
● The Arts Council of Great Britain is incorporated under Royal Charter 'to develop a greater knowledge, understanding and practice of the fine arts exclusively, and in particular to increase the accessibility of the fine arts to the public.' It becomes the central grant-making organisation for the arts.
● *Spellbound* (Alfred Hitchcock, US) includes dream sequences designed by Salvador Dalí.

**Other films**
*Dead of Night* (Alberto Cavalcanti, Charles Crichton, Robert Hamer, Basil Dearden)
*Brief Encounter* (David Lean)

**Births**
Terence Davies
Mike Leggett
Richard Long

POSTER FOR KIND HEARTS AND CORONETS BY JAMES FITTON

# 1946

● 30 January
First meeting of the Museum of Modern Art Organising Committee (which would form the Institute of Contemporary Arts). Present are Roland Penrose, Herbert Read, E.L.T. Mesens (the Surrealist), Peter Watson (founder of *Horizon* magazine), E.C. Gregory, the experimental film-maker Jacques Brunius and G.M. Hoellering who ran the Academy Cinema in Oxford Street.
● March
Laurence Olivier's *Henry V* receives a special Academy Award (as only US films were then competing).
● 7 June
B.B.C. resumes television broadcasts with transmission of Victory parade.
● August
The first Edinburgh Festival is held.
● Large exhibition of Picasso and Matisse paintings is held at the Victoria and Albert Museum.
● Establishment of Bath Academy of Art, Corsham Court, Wiltshire, by Lord Methuen. Film, music and drama are taught alongside fine art.
● William Turnbull studies at the Slade School of Art.
● David Bomberg begins teaching at the Borough Polytechnic.
● *A Matter of Life and Death* (Michael Powell and Emeric Pressburger)
Alfred Junge is production designer and Arthur Lawson art director .

**Publications**
*Penguin Film News* is first published, edited by Roger Manvell.

**Births**
Bill Forsyth
Annabel Nicolson

**Deaths**
John Maynard Keynes
Paul Nash

# 1947

● John Piper designs sets and costumes for Benjamin Britten's opera *Albert Herring*.
● The Institute of Contemporary Arts (I.C.A.) is founded in a small office in Charlotte Street.

**Films**
*Black Narcissus* (Michael Powell, Emeric Pressburger)

**Publications**
● *Sequence*, a film journal edited by Lindsay Anderson and Gavin Lambert, is published at Oxford University. Penelope Houston and Karel Reisz will later join them.
● László Moholy-Nagy's *Vision in Motion* is published.

**Births**
David Bowie

# 1948

● 9 February
*Forty Years of Modern Art: 1907–1947. A Selection from British Collections*. I.C.A. exhibition of European avant-garde art and Surrealism held in George Hoellering's Academy Hall in Oxford Street, London.
● 21 December
*40,000 Years of Modern Art*
I.C.A. exhibition demonstrating the links between modern art and 'primitive' non-Western art from earlier periods, featuring Picasso's *Les Demoiselles d'Avignon*. Conceived by Herbert Read, this was held in the Academy Cinema basement.
● Francis Bacon begins his 'Heads' series. The open-mouthed scream of the figures is partly inspired by the screaming nurse in Sergei Eisenstein's *Battleship Potemkin*.
● Hammer Films is formed as a production arm for Exclusive Films (distribution company set up in 1935).
● Frank Auerbach persuades Leon Kossoff to attend classes at the Borough Polytechnic.
● Henry Moore wins the International Sculpture Prize at the Venice Biennale.
● *The Red Shoes* (Michael Powell, Emeric Pressburger)
Hein Heckroth, who had previously designed for ballet, works as art director on the film. He wins an Oscar for Colour Art Direction.

**Births**
Mike Figgis
William Raban
Chris Welsby
Bill Woodrow

# 1949

● *Passport to Pimlico*, first of what became known as the Ealing comedies, is released.
● British stage musical, *Maytime in Mayfair* showcases top fashion designers, including Norman Hartnell.
● William Coldstream begins Professorship at the Slade School of Art.
● Bridget Riley studies at the Royal College of Art.

**Other films**
*The Third Man* (Carol Reed)
*Kind Hearts and Coronets* (Robert Hamer)

**Births**
John du Cane
Tony Cragg
Sally Potter

**Deaths**
Edward Wadsworth

# 1950

● May
The I.C.A. acquires 17 Dover Street, Piccadilly. Its first exhibition is *James Joyce: His Life and Work* and the building is refurbished by architect Jane Drew, artist Neil Morris and Eduardo Paolozzi.
● December
*1950: Aspects of British Art*
The official opening exhibition of the I.C.A. at Dover street includes works by three members of the future Independent Group: Eduardo Paolozzi, William Turnbull and Richard Hamilton.

**Films**
*Sunset Boulevard* (Billy Wilder, US)

**Births**
Neil Jordan

**Deaths**
Humphrey Jennings

# 1951

- The Festival of Britain opens, with the aim of telling 'one continuous, interwoven story ... of British contributions to world civilisation in the arts of the people'. The organising committee includes Hugh Casson (Director of Architecture), Huw Wheldon (Arts), Cecil Cooke (Exhibitions) and others.
- Neo-Romanticism is the most widely represented style in the Arts Council's *60 for 51* exhibition at the Festival of Britain.
- The Telecinema, designed by Wells Coates, shows documentary films made that year. The programme includes *A Solid Explanation* (Peter Bradford), *Royal River* (Brian Smith), *The Black Swan* (Leonard Reeve) and the Norman McLaren films *Around is Around* and *Now is the Time*.
- *Ten Decades of British Taste* is held at the I.C.A. and includes British paintings from 1851–1951.
- The I.C.A. maintains an international and Surrealist orientation, exhibiting the works of Roberto Matta and Picasso, and screening French Surrealist films.
- Dorothy Morland is appointed Director of the I.C.A.
- *Painter & Poet* (John Halas, Joan Maude, Michael Warre) Four films using artists' images set to poems. They include images by Michael Rothenstein, Mervyn Peake, Henry Moore, Michael Ayrton, Ronald Searle and others.
- The Scottish experimental film-maker Margaret Tait makes the film *One is One*.

## Other films
*The Man in the White Suit* (Alexander Mackendrick)
*The Tales of Hoffmann* (Michael Powell and Emeric Pressburger)

## Deaths
Ivor Novello

# 1952

- 23 September
Charles Chaplin arrives in London, his re-entry permit to the United States having been rescinded.
- 10 December
Max Ernst exhibition at the I.C.A.
- 16 December
Lecture by David Sylvester on Francis Bacon at the I.C.A.
- Peter de Francia is appointed head of Fine Arts programming at B.B.C. television.
- Formation of the 'Young Group', later known as the Independent Group, with Reyner Banham as its Secretary. At its first meeting Eduardo Paolozzi feeds a series of coloured images taken from American magazine advertising through an epidiascope.
- Michael Powell plans to combine the talents of Dylan Thomas, Graham Sutherland and Stravinsky for a film set in the South of France. This project is never realised.
- The Telecinema (from The Festival of Britain) becomes the National Film Theatre.
- John Berger organises the first of his exhibitions entitled *Looking Forward* at the Whitechapel Art Gallery, which will include 'realist' works by John Bratby, Peter de Francia, Josef Herman and others.

## Films
*Singin' in the Rain* (Stanley Donen, Gene Kelly US)

## Deaths
Charles Ginner

# 1953

- September
*Encounter* magazine is launched. It is edited by Stephen Spender and Irving Kristol.
- B.B.C. Radio presents *The Goon Show*.
- Victor Musgrave opens the future Gallery One in Covent Garden. His first show features works by John Christoforou, Peter Danziger and Sam Kaver, and indicates the gallery's orientation towards unknown international artists.
- Anthony Caro begins to teach sculpture part-time at St. Martin's School of Art.
- William Turnbull makes the film *Tired = 83B with A.*
- *O Dreamland* (Lindsay Anderson). Documentary giving a personal view of a crowd at a funfair.
- *The Drawings of Leonardo da Vinci* (Adrian de Potier) Produced by Basil Wright, this is the first of a series of collaborations between Wright and Michael Ayrton. The artist wrote the script, which weaves an essay on Leonardo around selected images, and stems from Ayrton's already developed interest in animation film-making. It is funded by the B.F.I.
- Peter Blake studies at the Royal College of Art.

## Other films
*Wakefield Express* (Lindsay Anderson)
*It Came from Outer Space* (Jack Arnold, US)
*Gentlemen Prefer Blondes* (Howard Hawks, US)

## Births
Russell Mulcahy (b. Melbourne, Australia)
Julien Temple

## Deaths
Cecil Hepworth

# 1954

- Events and meetings related to American cinema and popular culture take place at the I.C.A. throughout the year, including a lecture on science fiction by Lawrence Alloway (19 January), *Ambush at the Frontier* and a dialogue on the Western film by Toni del Renzio and Lawrence Alloway (1 July).
- *Man versus Machine* exhibition is held at the Building Centre, London.
- Victor Pasmore becomes Master of Painting at the Department of Fine Art, Durham University, and sets up the abstract foundation course 'The Developing Process'.
- *Figures in a Landscape* (Dudley Shaw Ashton) Examples of Barbara Hepworth's sculpture are seen against the settings that inspired them. Barbara Hepworth herself is seen at work in her garden, and the commentary is spoken by Cecil Day Lewis
- *The Wild One* is rejected by the B.B.F.C. on the basis of possible incitement of juvenile crime. It is not given a certificate until 1967, though numerous screenings occur despite its censorship.

## Other films
*Thursday's Children* (Lindsay Anderson, Guy Brenton)
*On the Waterfront* (Elia Kazan)
*Rear Window* (Alfred Hitchcock)

## Births
Alex Cox
Ian Davies
Anish Kapoor

## Deaths
Edward McKnight Kauffer

# 1955

- Events at the I.C.A. include a film seminar on *Postwar American Movies* chaired by Lawrence Alloway (24 February), a seminar on *Recent American Movies* (10 March), a symposium on movie heroines (24 March) and a lecture by Lawrence Alloway on *The Movies as Mass Medium* (7 April).
- January
Britain's first feature-length cartoon, *Animal Farm*, made by John Halas and Joy Batchelor, is screened.

- 22 March
*A Communications Primer*, a film by Charles Eames, is screened at the I.C.A.
- *E. McKnight Kauffer* exhibition at the Victoria and Albert Museum includes posters for Shell and B.P.
- Richard Hamilton works for Sidney Bernstein as consultant designer for Granada Television before the company begins transmissions.
- Lawrence Alloway becomes Assistant Director of I.C.A.
- *The Quatermass Experiment* (Val Guest). It is the first major success for Hammer Films and is adapted from the television series written by Nigel Kneale.

## Other films
*Rebel Without a Cause* (Nicholas Ray, US)
*The Seven Year Itch* (Billy Wilder, US)

## Births
Rowan Atkinson

## Deaths
James Dean (US)

NUMBER 23 BY JACKSON POLLOCK

# 1956

● January
*Modern Art in the United States* opens at the Tate Gallery. The final room of the exhibition, devoted to Abstract Expressionism makes a powerful impact on British artists and the public.
● February
The first 'Free cinema' programme is screened at the National Film Theatre. It includes Lorenza Mazzetti's *Together* (featuring Eduardo Paolozzi and Michael Andrews), *O Dreamland* (Lindsay Anderson) and *Momma Don't Allow* (Karel Reisz and Tony Richardson).
● 9 August
*This is Tomorrow* exhibition opens at the Whitechapel Art Gallery. Based on the idea of collaboration between 'one architect, one sculptor and one painter' it involves 36 participating artists. Richard Hamilton, John Voeckler and John McHale's contribution is a combination of popular imagery (Marilyn Monroe and Robbie the Robot cut-out) and Op art (soft floors and fluorescent paint). *This is Tomorrow* reflects the widespread interest in American popular culture, which is evident in both art and film throughout the 1950s.
● Stuart Brisley (film and performance artist) attends the R.C.A.
● Bruce Lacey stops painting and begins making short films and performing a comic cabaret act in London night clubs.

**Other films**
*Invasion of the Body Snatchers* (Don Siegel, US)
*Et Dieu ... créa la femme* (Roger Vadim, Fr)

**Births**
Danny Boyle

**Deaths**
Alexander Korda

# 1957

● March
Roger Coleman becomes editor of *Ark*. Issue no. 19 concentrates on Hollywood culture and pop.

FRONT COVER OF ISSUE 19

● 21 May
Paris Situationists come to the I.C.A. for a screening of Guy Debord's film *Hurlements en faveur de Sade*.
● 27 July
Ralph Rumney becomes the only British founding member of the Situationist International.
● September
Roger Coleman becomes assistant editor of *Design* magazine.
● October
*Reveille* magazine publishes a life-size pin-up of Brigitte Bardot.
● December
*Dimensions* exhibition is held at the O'Hana Gallery. Lawrence Alloway curates the show, which includes Richard Smith, William Green and Eduardo Paolozzi.
● Basil Wright asks Michael Ayrton to come to Greece and assist on a film he is making called *The Immortal Land*.
● *The Curse of Frankenstein* (Terence Fisher) is the first Hammer production in the genre of Gothic horror.

**Other films**
*Every Day Except Christmas* (Lindsay Anderson)

**Deaths**
David Bomberg
William Cameron Menzies
John Minton
Percy Wyndham Lewis

# 1958

● January
*Five Young Painters* exhibition at the I.C.A. includes works by Richard Smith, William Green and Peter Blake.
● 30 July
William Green appears on the *Tonight* programme in Ken Russell's film *Painting an Action Painting*.
● July
A programme of films by Charles and Ray Eames is screened at the I.C.A.
● Francis Bacon paints his *Study for the Nurse in the film Battleship Potemkin*.
● First of the *Carry On* series *Carry On Sergeant* (Gerald Thomas).
● John Bratby makes paintings for the film *The Horse's Mouth*, directed by Ronald Neame, in which Alec Guinness plays a hard-up painter. Screenplay by Joyce Cary.
● *Coventry Cathedral* (Dudley Shaw Ashton) Film following the development of the plans for Coventry Cathedral. It features Graham Sutherland and his designs for the altarpiece.
● Richard Williams completes the animated film *The Little Island*, declared as revolutionary for its use of allegory.

**Other films**
*Amelia and the Angel* (Ken Russell)
*Dracula* (Terence Fisher)
*Tom Thumb* (George Pal)
*Vertigo* (Alfred Hitchcock, US)

**Publications**
*Art and Illusion* by Ernst Gombrich.

**Births**
John Maybury
Nick Park
Cerith Wyn Evans

# 1959

● January
*Room at the Top* (Jack Clayton), from the novel by John Braine, is released and is one of the first examples of 'northern realism' in films.
● 4 February
*The New American Painting* opens at the Tate Gallery. A M.O.M.A. touring exhibition, put together by Porter A. McCray, it includes works by Jackson Pollock, Mark Rothko and Willem de Kooning.
● April
*The Developing Process*, an exhibition at the I.C.A., includes work by Victor Pasmore, Richard Hamilton, Thubron and Tom Hudson.
● May–June
Duncan Grant retrospective is held at the Tate Gallery.
● December
William Green's *The Errol Flynn Show* is held at the New Vision Centre Gallery.
● B.B.C. runs the series *Art-Anti-Art*, including a programme on the links between Futurism and the Independent Group by Reyner Banham.
● John Piper designs costumes for Benjamin Britten's opera *Turn of the Screw*, filmed by Peter Morley for television.
● David Hockney and Derek Boshier study at the R.C.A.
● The poster for Louis Malle's *Les Amants* (Rodin's *The Kiss*) is banned by London Transport.

**Other films**
*Peeping Tom* (Michael Powell)
*Running, Jumping, Standing Still Film* (Richard Lester, Peter Sellers, Spike Milligan)
*A bout de souffle* (Jean-Luc Godard, Fr)
*Look Back in Anger* (Tony Richardson)

**Deaths**
Jacob Epstein
Stanley Spencer

# 1960

● January
Richard Hamilton delivers the lecture 'Glorious Technicolor, Breathtaking Cinemascope and Stereophonic Sound' at the I.C.A.
● March
R.B. Kitaj paintings are exhibited in the *Young Contemporaries* exhibition.
● 10 March
Gustav Metzger's 'Manifesto of Auto-Destructive Art'.
● August
Alfred Hitchcock's *Psycho* opens in Britain and provokes a storm of indignation amongst reviewers.
● November
The National Advisory Council on Art Education produces the 'Coldstream Report', recommending the creation of a Diploma in Art and Design. William Coldstream makes his recommendations to the Summerson committee (chaired by Sir John Summerson) for the restructuring of British art education.
● Picasso retrospective is held at the Tate Gallery, London.
● John Latham makes *Unclassified Material* and *Unedited Material from the Star*, two films featuring book reliefs.
● Jeff Keen begins making films, starting with 8mm photoplays and collage movie-mixes and combining animation with live action.

**Other films**
*La dolce vita* (Federico Fellini, It)

**Publications**
● *Theory and Design in the First Machine Age* by Reyner Banham.
● First issue of *The New Left Review*.

**Births**
Kenneth Branagh
Isaac Julien
Tilda Swinton

TONY HANCOCK IN 'THE REBEL'

TOWARDS A DEFINITIVE STATEMENT ON THE COMING TRENDS IN MENSWEAR AND ACCESSORIES BY RICHARD HAMILTON

# 1961

● January
*The Rebel* (Robert Day), starring Tony Hancock as a London white-collar worker turned French artist, is released. The film contains parodies of William Green's bicycle action painting.
● April
Bridget Riley's first one-person exhibition opens at Gallery One.
● September
R.B. Kitaj, Bernard Cohen, Anthony Benjamin and Brian Wall begin teaching the 'Ground Course' (a prototype 'Pre-diploma course') at Ealing Art School.
● *The Damned* (Joseph Losey)
A science-fiction film, centred on the discovery of a group of radioactive children, that features the sculpture of Elizabeth Frink.
● *Talk* (John Latham)
Abstract film using coloured paper discs.
● Malcolm Le Grice studies at the Slade School of Fine Art.
● Lawrence Alloway resigns as Programme Director at the I.C.A..
● Mark Rothko's solo exhibition is held at the Whitechapel Art Gallery, organised by Bryan Robertson (who was also responsible for the 'Young Contemporaries' series in the early 1960s).
● The comedy revue *Beyond the Fringe* (opened at the Edinburgh Festival, 1960) with Jonathan Miller, Alan Bennett, Peter Cook and Dudley Moore, is a popular success.

## Other films
*A Taste of Honey*
(Tony Richardson)
*Victim* (Basil Dearden)
*Saturday Night and Sunday Morning* (Karel Reisz)

## Deaths
Augustus John

# 1962

● 4 February
*The Sunday Times Colour Magazine* is launched with an article by John Russell on Peter Blake, 'Pioneer of Pop Art'.
● 25 March
Ken Russell's *Pop Goes the Easel* is broadcast on B.B.C. television as part of the arts programme, *Monitor*. It includes 'ground control/capsule conversations' with Peter Blake, Peter Phillips, Derek Boshier and Pauline Boty.
● May
The first issue of *Movie* magazine, edited by Ian Cameron, is published.
● 15 August
*Image in Progress*, the first anthology exhibition of Pop painting, is held at the Grabowski gallery.
● 28 October
*Dr. No*, the first of Ian Fleming's James Bond films, is premièred. Maurice Binder designs the titles.

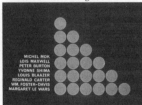

MAURICE BINDER'S TITLE SEQUENCE FOR 'DR. NO'

● 19 November
Robert Freeman and Richard Smith show their film *Trailer* at the I.C.A.
● December
Gustav Metzger gives a lecture at Ealing School of Art on Auto-Destructive Art.
● Coventry Cathedral is opened. It includes a tapestry altarpiece by Graham Sutherland and stained glass by John Piper.
● The Beatles single *Love Me Do* reaches number 17 in the charts.

## Other films
*Lawrence of Arabia* (David Lean)
*The Loneliness of the Long Distance Runner* (Tony Richardson)
*It's Trad Dad* (Richard Lester)

## Deaths
Robert Colquhon
Marilyn Monroe (US)

# 1963

● 7 February
Première of *This Sporting Life* (Lindsay Anderson)
Screenplay by David Storey (a former Slade School student)
● 17 February
R.B. Kitaj's *Pictures with Commentaries/Pictures without Commentaries* is held at the Marlborough New London Gallery.
● June
Bruce Lacey's *First Exhibition of Automata and Humanoids* is held at Gallery One.
● 9 August
*Ready Steady Go!* is first screened on I.T.V. Derek Boshier and Pauline Boty are dancers.
● 7 September
Mark Boyle, Joan Hills and Carol Baker collaborate on a nude 'Happening' at the Edinburgh Festival.
● 23 October
*From Russia With Love* (Terence Young) is premièred.
● Ken Russell's Monitor film *Watch the Birdie* provides a prototype for the myth of the 'Swinging' photographer.
● Eduardo Paolozzi makes the film *History of Nothing* with Denis Postle.
● *Graphics RCA* is held at the Royal College of Art. The accompanying catalogue includes a cookery strip by Len Deighton, images of the set for the B.B.C.'s *Quatermass* and a still from Ridley Scott's student film *Boy on a Bicycle*.
● The first episode of *Dr Who* is broadcast on British television .
● Derek Jarman studies at the Slade School of Art.

## Other films
*Tom Jones* (Tony Richardson)

## Births
Gillian Wearing
Rachel Whiteread

## Deaths
Frank Dobson

# 1964

● 18 May
*New Generation* exhibition is held at the Whitechapel Art Gallery. The first of a series of annual exhibitions, which will include the works of David Hockney, Bridget Riley, Allen Jones, Phillip King and others.
● Spring
*International Exposition of the New American Cinema* at the I.C.A., organised by P. Adams Sitney.
● June
The art magazine *The Studio* is incorporated in the new magazine *Studio International*.
● July
*A Hard Day's Night* (Richard Lester) is premièred in Liverpool. The film is a semi-documentary version of life on the road with the Beatles.
● October
Richard Hamilton's *Paintings, 1955–64* exhibition, including *Hugh Gaitskell as a Famous Monster of Filmland*.
● John Latham begins making his *Skoob Towers*, constructed from discarded art books, encyclopaedias etc.
● Peter Greenaway first shows his paintings in a group exhibition called *Eisenstein at the Winter Palace* at the Lord's Gallery.
● Jeff Keen produces his first twin-screen film, *The Pink Auto*.
● Steve Dwoskin (US) begins lecturing in Graphic Design, Drawing Film and Video at the London College of Printing.

## Other films
*Carry On Spying* (Gerald Thomas)
*The Red Desert* (Michelangelo Antonioni, It)
*Goldfinger* (Guy Hamilton)

## Deaths
Peter Lanyon

# 1965

● 13 June
Bridget Riley's light projections are used as a backdrop to the production of *Sweeney Agonistes* at the Globe theatre.
● 19 June
Gathering of Beat and experimental poets at the Royal Albert Hall signifies the birth of the literary 'Underground'.
● August
The first Notting Hill Carnival takes place as part of an International Community Festival.
● September
The *Commonwealth Arts Festival* includes a central art exhibition, *Treasures of the Commonwealth*, at the Royal Academy, and various dance, music and performance events.
● David Bailey publishes *A Box of Pin-Ups*, a collection of portraits of London celebrities including the Beatles.
● *New Generation* exhibition at the Whitechapel Gallery includes works by William Turnbull, Phillip King, Tim Scott and others.
● Eastman Kodak introduces Super 8mm film.
● *The War Game* (Peter Watkins) is banned by the B.B.C. but shown at cinemas.
● *Boy on a Bicycle* (Ridley Scott) Made while Scott was at the Royal College of Art.
● *Help!* (Richard Lester) Robert Freeman was colour consultant and worked on the titles for this Beatles film.

## Other films
*Repulsion* (Roman Polanski)
*Dracula, Prince of Darkness* (Terence Fisher)
*The Knack* (Richard Lester)

## Publications
*Auto-Destructive Art* by Gustav Metzger.

## Births
Damien Hirst

## 1966

● 16 June
Stuart Brisley directs the publicity shoot for *Paperback Writer*, which is photographed by Robert Whittaker, and involves the Beatles destroying polystyrene sheets.
● 23, 30 September
John Latham's *Film*, a theatrical event, is performed at the Mercury Theatre as part of the Destruction in Art Symposium (D.I.A.S.)
● 13 October
The London Film-makers' Co-op announces its formation.
● October
Bob Cobbing starts 'Cinema 65' screenings at Better Books.
● November
Mark Boyle, Joan Hills and John Claxton form the light-show group 'The Sensual Laboratory'.
● B.F.I. Experimental Film Fund is restructured as B.F.I. Production, under the chairmanship of Michael Balcon.
● The Indica Gallery is opened by John Dunbar with Paul McCartney's patronage. Through 1966 it exhibits the works of the kinetic artists *Groupe Recherches de l'Art Visuel* (G.R.A.V.).
● Terry Atkinson and Michael Baldwin (who will later form Art & Language) meet at Lancaster Polytechnic.

**Other films**
*Modesty Blaise* (Joseph Losey)

**Births**
Douglas Gordon
Sam Taylor-Wood
Jane and Louise Wilson

**Deaths**
Pauline Boty

## 1967

● September
The Drury Lane Arts Laboratory opens with Peter Goldman's *Echoes of Silence*.
● 9 March
The American artist Lilian Lijn's exhibition of light and kinetic works is held at the Indica Gallery.
● 30 March
Peter Blake and the photographer Michael Cooper make the tableau for the cover of the Beatles' *Sergeant Pepper's Lonely Hearts Club Band*.
● Yoko Ono's *No. 4 (365 bottoms ... 365 saints of our time)*, a film of consecutive famous bottoms, is screened. Yoko Ono hires The Continental hotel for the event.
● October
Better Books closes.
● December
Peter Kubelka's films are screened for first time in Britain at the I.C.A.
● Formation of 'Acme Generating Co.', an expanded cinema group that uses film projection, sound and performance (including Jeff Keen, Jim Duke and Tony Sinden).
● *Tonite Let's All Make Love in London* (Peter Whitehead) Film of 'Swinging London' featuring interviews with Michael Caine, David Hockney, Mick Jagger and others.
● Gilbert & George meet while at St. Martin's School of Art. William Raban studies painting at St. Martin's School of Art.

**Other films**
*Dante's Inferno: The Private Life of Dante Gabriel Rossetti* (Ken Russell)
*You Only Live Twice* (Lewis Gilbert)
*Magical Mystery Tour* (The Beatles)

**Deaths**
Joe Orton

## 1968

● April
The P. Adams Sitney *New American Cinema* exhibition tours 12 British universities and the National Film Theatre.
● July
Peter Gidal arrives in Britain and shows his films.
● August
Jeff Keen films are screened at the Arts Lab.
● First Malcolm Le Grice one-man show of paintings and sculpture is held at the Drury Lane Arts Lab. It includes works such as the 'light bulb' film, *Castle 1*.
● British artist Anthony Donaldson makes the film *Soft Orange in LA* with Robert Graham.
● *Darling, Do You love Me?* (Martin Sharp and Robert Whittaker). Short film made by the Oz group and starring Germaine Greer.
● Jean-Luc Godard films *One Plus One* (aka *Sympathy for the Devil*) in London. This film of the Rolling Stones is shown at the London Film Festival with the addition of a recording of the Stones performance, resulting in a skirmish between Godard and the producer Ian Quarrier.
● David Hall (previously a sculptor) begins working in photography and film. His first film is *Vertical*, an experiment with the documentary nature of the medium.
● *Yellow Submarine* (George Dunning). Animated cartoon designed by various animators including Diane Jackson, Edric Radage, Mike Stuart and Heinz Edelman. With a Beatles soundtrack, it includes Surrealist, Op, Pop and Art Nouveau features, from Daliesque distorted clock faces to Op art.

**Other films**
*Barbarella* (Roger Vadim)
*Witchfinder General* (Michael Reeves)
*If ....* (Lindsay Anderson)

## 1969

● February/March
Films from the Sitney tour are donated to the London Film-makers' Co-op. These films form the core of the Co-op collection.
● 30 May
Mark Boyle's *Journey to the Surface of the Earth* is held at the I.C.A. It is a trans-media environment of film, sound, light 'painting' and sculpture.
● September
The exhibition *When Attitudes Become Form* opens at the I.C.A.
● October
Debut of *Monty Python's Flying Circus* on British television.
● *Fluorescent Chrysanthemums*, the first show of contemporary Japanese art, takes place at the I.C.A. and features work ranging from sculpture to music and film.
● *The Art of the Real* exhibition at the Tate Gallery presents American Minimalists such as Don Judd, Carl Andre and Robert Morris.
● Stephen and Timothy Quay come to London to attend drawing courses at the R.C.A.
● Malcolm McLaren attends Goldsmith's College and begins a documentary on the history of Oxford Street.
● The first 'artists films' are financed by the Arts Council's Art Film Committee.
● James Scott makes the film *Richard Hamilton* featuring the artist and his work.
● *The Image* (Michael Armstrong). Film about a haunted artist, starring David Bowie.

**Other films**
*Jerk* (Sally Potter)
*Intervals* (Peter Greenaway)
*The Wild Bunch* (Sam Peckinpah, US)
*Zabriskie Point* (Michelangelo Antonioni, US)

**Births**
Steve McQueen

## 1970

● 3 February
London police seize copy of Andy Warhol's film *Flesh* along with the projector and the records of the theatre screening it. There are no prosecutions.
● April
First issue of *Afterimage*, a publication focusing on avant-garde film, European film and New American Cinema, edited by Simon Field and Peter Sainsbury.
● *First International Underground Film Festival* is held at the National Film Theatre (N.F.T.). It is organised by the Robert Street Arts Lab, the London Film-makers Co-op and the Other Cinema.
● The Arts Council opens the Serpentine Gallery as a venue for young artists.
● Derek Jarman designs sets for Ken Russell's *The Devils*.
● Derek Boshier receives an Arts Council grant for film-making and makes *Link*.
● Peter Gidal joins executive committee of the London Film-makers' Co-op.
● Jeff Keen's *RayDayFilm* is first performed at the London Underground Film Festival.
● Other Cinema's Festival of British Independents includes films by members of the Co-op.
● Artist Barry Flanagan makes films including *The Works I*, *Atlantic Flight* and *Bus Ride*.
● *Performance* (Nicolas Roeg and Donald Cammell)
Made in 1968 and starring Mick Jagger, *Performance* features the first use of Super 8 within a feature film.

**Other films**
*The Go-Between* (Joseph Losey)

**Publications**
*Expanded Cinema* by Gene Youngblood

**Deaths**
Robert Brownjohn
Hein Heckroth

STUART BRISLEY PERFORMS '10 DAYS'

BARRY LYNDON (STANLEY KUBRICK)

# 1971

● February–March
*Warhol* exhibition at the Tate Gallery.
● Spring
N.F.T. begins weekly series, *A Development of New Cinema.*
● September
The London Film-makers' Co-op cinema opens under Peter Gidal and John Du Cane.
● December
The B.B.F.C. passes Stanley Kubrick's *A Clockwork Orange* without any cuts. Kubrick later (1973) withdraws the film from circulation.
● Derek Jarman is asked to design sets for Ken Russell's *The Savage Messiah*, an account of the life of the sculptor Gaudier-Brzeska.
● 17 December
Thirteen film critics write to *The Times* challenging BBFC's decision to pass *Straw Dogs* (Sam Peckinpah) but refuse a certificate for *Flesh.*
● *The Great Ice-Cream Robbery* (James Scott). A two-screen documentary on Claes Oldenburg, filmed while the artist was in London for his retrospective exhibition.
● Exhibition of Tantric art is held at the Hayward Gallery. This is one of many events during the 1970s and 1980s that demonstrate the growing interest in the arts of cultures outside Europe and America.
● National Film and Television School is established in Britain.
● Derek Jarman begins making Super 8 films, including *Studio Bankside* and *Miss Gaby.*

**Other films**
*The Devils* (Ken Russell)
*Get Carter* (Mike Hodges)

**Publications**
*Experimental Cinema* by David Curtis

**Deaths**
Roger Furse
Ezra Pound

# 1972

● Gallery House, an exhibition venue in South Kensington opens with *Three Life Situations*, an exhibition of performance art.
● April
Tony Rayns publishes the first issue of *Cinema Rising*. It includes a directory of British avant-garde and independent film.
● June
Peter Gidal organises *English Independent Cinema* at the N.F.T., the first festival to be devoted entirely to the English avant-garde. It is one of many film seasons and exhibitions that reflect the growth of British avant-garde and underground film-making in the 1970s.
● Autumn
*Afterimage* No. 4 features an article by Malcolm Le Grice on 'Thoughts on Recent Underground Film'.
● Malcolm McLaren opens the boutique Let it Rock and persuades Vivienne Westwood to become his partner. McLaren and Westwood design costumes for Ken Russell's film *Mahler* and *That'll Be The Day* (starring David Essex and Ringo Starr).
● The Collective Women's Film Group is formed.
● Edinburgh Festival Women's Event is organised by Laura Mulvey, Claire Johnston and Lynda Myles.
● The Women's Workshop of the Artist's Union is formed.
● The *New Art* exhibition, organised by Anne Seymour and including works by David Dye (*Unsigning: for eight projectors*) is held at the Hayward Gallery.

**Other films**
*The Boy Friend* (Ken Russell)
*Macbeth* (Roman Polanski)
*Deliverance* (John Boorman, US)
*Frenzy* (Alfred Hitchcock)

**Deaths**
John Grierson

# 1973

● March
Malcolm Le Grice's exhibition *Film Action and Installation* is held at Gallery House. It includes works by Gill Eatherley, Annabel Nicolson, William Raban and Dave Crosswaite.
● May
Peter Gidal organises *Films from the London Film-makers' Co-op* at the NFT.
● May
The second N.F.T Season of English Avant-Garde films is organised by Peter Gidal.
● June
*FILMAKTION* week is held at the Walker Art Gallery, Liverpool – 11 film-makers take part, and it is considered the first major exhibition of expanded cinema.
● July–October
*Magic & Strong Medicine* exhibition is held at the Walker Art Gallery, Liverpool, and includes a programme of performance art.
● The Festival of Independent British Cinema is held in Bristol.
● Bruce Lacey and Jill Bruce make *The Lacey Rituals* – films for 'The Electric Element'.
● Stuart Brisley makes *Arbeit Macht Frei*, a film of a man vomiting, intercut with a desperate face. Production assistant is Ken McMullen (who will later make feature films).
● Stuart Brisley performs *10 Days* at Edition Paramedia in West Berlin.
● Jarman begins editing *In the Shadow of the Sun*, made from material from the films *A Journey to Avebury, Tarot* and *Fire Island*, and footage from *The Devils.*
● Peter Gidal and Steve Dwoskin begin teaching at the R.C.A.

**Other films**
*Don't Look Now* (Nicolas Roeg)

**Deaths**
Pablo Picasso (Fr)

# 1974

● The Independent Film-Maker's Association is formed.
● Terry Gilliam's television animation show, *The Do-It Yourself Film Animation Show*, is broadcast.
● Artist Phillip King makes the film *Open Led Blue Bound* with Antony Parker and Peter Day.
● Vivienne Westwood and Malcolm McLaren change the name of their shop to Sex. They sell black rubber and leather fetish clothing and exhibit in their windows paintings of life on the Left Bank in fifties Paris.
● An exhibition devoted to women artists, with the works of 26 conceptual artists selected by Lucy Lippard, is staged at 48 Earlham Street, Covent Garden. The venue is later transformed into an artists' meeting place.
● Bruce Lacey and Jill Bruce form the Galactic Theatre and begin to work on multi-media performances. They perform *Stella Superstar and Her Amazing Galactic Adventures* using projection and film.
● *Pressure* (Horace Ove) is the first film by a black director to be financed by the B.F.I.
● *A Bigger Splash* (Jack Hazan) David Hockney features in this docu-drama about his work, life and friends.
● Derek Jarman makes *The Devils at the Elgin, Ula's Fete, Fire Island* and *Duggie Fields* (a portrait of the artist Duggie Fields, and a document of his work).

**Other films**
*Penthesilea* (Laura Mulvey and Peter Wollen)
*Monty Python and the Holy Grail* (Terry Gilliam and Terry Jones)

**Deaths**
David Jones

# 1975

● March
*Avant-garde British Landscape Films* are screened in the Tate Gallery film theatre. Organised by Deke Dusinberre the season includes works by Chris Welsby, William Raban, Renny Croft and Jane Clark.
● November
Publication of a *Studio International* edition entitled 'Avant-Garde Film in England & Europe'.
● The London Film-makers' Co-op moves to Fitzroy road. Annabel Nicolson and Lis Rhodes run the programme of screenings
● First major exhibition of Independent Video, *The Video Show*, is held at the Serpentine Gallery, London.
● Rose English (performance artist), performs *Death and the Maiden* with Sally Potter.
● Mona Hatoum (b. Beirut) arrives in London to study at the Byam Shaw School of art.
● *Nightcleaners* (Berwick Street Film Collective)
Film account of the 1971–72 campaign to unionise London's women cleaners.
● Derek Jarman makes *Picnic at Ray's* and *Sebastiane Wrap.*
● Tony Hill's *Floor Film* is shown at the Tate Gallery (in 1977 it is purchased by the Centre Georges Pompidou in Paris).

**Other films**
*Lisztomania* (Ken Russell)
*Tommy* (Ken Russell)
*Barry Lyndon* (Stanley Kubrick)

**Publications**
● *Visual Pleasure and Narrative Cinema* by Laura Mulvey.
● *Film Is ...* by Steve Dwoskin (a book about the International Free Cinema).

**Deaths**
Michael Ayrton
Barbara Hepworth
Roger Hilton

# 1976

● January
The *Festival of Expanded Cinema* is held at the I.C.A., London.
● May/June
*Studio International* publishes an issue on Video Art.
● Summer
An *Afterimage* special issue is entitled 'Perspectives on English Independent Cinema'.
● October
*Sacred Circles: Two Thousand Years of North American Indian Art* is held at the Hayward Gallery.
● 1 December
The Sex Pistols (managed by Malcolm McLaren) appear in Bill Grundy's *Today* show.
● The Arts Council of Great Britain's Artists' Films Committee launches its 'Film-makers on Tour' scheme. Participants include David Dye, Marilyn Halford and Derek Jarman
● Derek Jarman works as set designer for *Nescore*, an advertising film directed by Ken Russell.
● The Acme Gallery opens in Shelton Street, Covent Garden.
● The Tate Gallery *Video Show* includes works by Tamara Krikorian, Brain Hoey, Stuart Marshall and David Hall.
● The London Video Arts Group is formed.
● Rose English's performance work, *Berlin*, made with Sally Potter, is shown at the Roundhouse Theatre.
● Peter Greenaway makes *H is for House* (using country settings to Vivaldi's *Four Seasons*) and *Dear Phone* (a series of red telephone boxes in every imaginable setting).

### Other films
*Sebastiane* (Derek Jarman)
*Bugsy Malone* (Alan Parker)
*The Man Who Fell to Earth* (Nicolas Roeg)

### Deaths
Carol Reed

# 1977

● William Raban first publishes *A Film-maker's Europe*, an informational broadsheet.
● Laura Mulvey and Peter Wollen make *Riddles of the Sphinx*.
● *Perspectives on British Avant-Garde Film* is held at the Hayward Gallery. It includes programmes of Landscape film, Structural film, Expanded cinema and Surrealism, and is funded by the Arts Council throught the Artists' Films Committee.
● Kerry Tringo works on *Passage*, a live art/performance work in which he digs himself out of the Acme Gallery in London, communicating with the outside world only by television and radio. The Acme Gallery is an important venue in Covent Garden for video installation and performance work
● The first of the *Hayward Annuals* takes place, with the aim of presenting a display of British contemporary art.

### Other films
*The Duellists* (Ridley Scott)
*Jabberwocky* (Terry Gilliam)
*Star Wars* (George Lucas, US)

### Deaths
Michael Balcon
Charles Chaplin

# 1978

● *Jubilee* (Derek Jarman) Punk film in which Queen Elizabeth I is transported by an angel into the future; featuring Jenny Runacre, Toyah Willcox and Adam Ant; costumes designed by Christopher Hobbs, production designed by Kenny Morris (from Siouxsie and the Banshees) and John Maybury. *Jubilee* is one of many films and artworks that reflect the renewed interest in 'Britishness' and its heritage, occurring throughout the late 1970s and 1980s.
● Annabel Janckel joins Cucumber Studios. She will make video promos for Elvis Costello and create *Max Headroom*.
● Peter Greenaway makes *Vertical Features Remake*. With soundtrack by Michael Nyman and Brian Eno, it is an absurdist fictional documentary about the Institute of Reclamation and Restoration. It was composed of an imaginary remake of the fictional Tulse Luper film *Vertical Features* (an architectural investigation).
● *A Perspective on English Avant-Garde Film* tours England. Based on the 1977 Hayward exhibition (*Perspectives on British Avant-Garde Film*).
● *A Walk Through H* (Peter Greenaway) Narrative about an ornithologist following a trail blazed by the legendary Tulse Luper.
● Exhibition of Peter Greenaway paintings at the Riverside Studios, London.

### Other films
*Superman* (Richard Donner)

### Publications
*Animations of Mortality* by Terry Gilliam.

### Deaths
Duncan Grant
Keith Vaughan

# 1979

● Sally Potter makes *Thriller*, a feminist revision of the opera *La Bohème*. It includes performance work by Rose English.
● *Film as Film* exhibition is held at the Hayward Gallery, including the film work of many European and American avant-garde artists.
● As a result of the masculine orientation of *Film as Film*, Peter Gidal, Jill Eatherley, Annabel Nicholson and Liz Rhodes pull out of the exhibition and the London Film-makers Co-op and set up Circles, which is responsible for distributing women's work.
● The Quay Brothers make *Nocturna Artificialia,* an animated film featuring a man who imagines himself driving a tram late at night.
● The Festival of Independent and Avant-Garde Film (F.I.A.F.) takes place at Lausanne. British films screened at the festival include Adrian Brunel's *Crossing the Great Sagrada* (1924) and *The Typical Budget* (1925), and Ivor Montagu's *Bluebottles* (1928).
● Derek Jarman makes *Broken English*, featuring Marianne Faithfull singing *Broken English*, *Witches' Song* and *The Ballad of Lucy Jordan*.
● Peter Greenaway makes the documentary *Zandra Rhodes*, featuring the fashion designer.
● *The Great Rock n' Roll Swindle* (Julien Temple). Film of the rise of Malcolm McLaren. McLaren was originally involved in its direction.

### Other films
*Radio On* (Chris Petit)
*Alien* (Ridley Scott, US)
*Monty Python's Life of Brian* (Terry Jones)
*Quadrophenia* (Franc Roddam)
*The Tempest* (Derek Jarman)

### Deaths
Ivon Hitchens
Vincent Korda

# 1980

● *The Falls* (Peter Greenaway) is the first British film to win the BFI award for Best Film for 30 years. It is produced by Peter Sainsbury and includes a soundtrack by Michael Nyman, Brian Eno and others.
● *The Alternative Miss World* (Richard Gayor). Documentary record of Andrew Logan's Alternative beauty contest, staged on Clapham Common in 1978. The film features among the contestants John Maybury and Jenny Runacre, and among the judges Lionel Bart, Zandra Rhodes and Michael Fish.
● Richard Hamilton makes a television commercial for 'The critic laughs', part of the B.B.C series *Shock of the New*.
● Tina Keane's *Shadow of a Journey* is premiered at the Edinburgh Film Festival.
● First publication of *Undercut*, film magazine of the London Film-makers' Co-op.
● Peter Greenaway makes *Act of God* for Thames television.
● *Artist and Camera*, an Arts Council touring exhibition, travels to Sunderland, Liverpool, Llandudno, Southampton, Bristol (Arnolfini) and London (I.C.A.). It includes works by Boyd Webb.

### Other films
*Rude Boy* (Jack Hazan, David Mingay)
*The Shining* (Stanley Kubrick)
*In the Shadow of the Sun* (Derek Jarman)

### Deaths
Terence Fisher
Alfred Hitchcock
John Lennon
Len Lye
George Pal
Graham Sutherland

THE JEWISH SCHOOL BY R.B. KITAJ: A NEW SPIRIT IN PAINTING.

### 1981

● Cerith Wyn Evans, John Maybury and others show their films at the I.C.A. under the title *A Certain Sensibility: The Super 8 Films of John Maybury and Cerith Wyn Evans.*
● January
*The New Spirit in Painting* opens at the Royal Academy, and includes a survey of three generations of artists from Europe and the United States (eg. R.B. Kitaj, Andy Warhol, Francis Bacon).
● Sept 22
*Performance, Video, Installation* opens at the Tate Gallery. The exhibition includes works by Vito Acconci, Robert Morris, Bruce Naumann, Stuart Brisley and video work by David Hall, Ian Baum, Tina Keane and others.
● *TG Psychic Rally in Heaven* (Derek Jarman). Jarman's first production with James MacKay is this 8mm film of Genesis P. Orridge's band Throbbing Gristle's Psychic Rally in Heaven.
● The documentary *The World of Gilbert and George* is produced by Philip Haas for the Arts Council.

**Other films**
*Chariots of Fire* (Hugh Hudson)
*The French Lieutenant's Woman* (Karel Reisz)
*Time Bandits* (Terry Gilliam)

### 1982

● Channel 4 first broadcasts.
● Channel 4 theatrically releases its first low-budget films, including Neil Jordan's *Angel* and Peter Greenaway's *The Draughtsman's Contract.*
● The *Festival of India in Britain* opens. It includes the art exhibitions *In the Image of Man* at the Hayward Gallery, *Between Two Cultures* at the Barbican, *Six Modern Indian Painters* at the Tate Gallery and *India: Myth and Reality* at the Museum of Modern Art, Oxford. The NFT also screens a season of Indian films, including retrospectives of the film-makers Satyajit Ray and Ritwik Ghatak.
● *Pink Floyd The Wall* (Alan Parker)
A live action feature film with animated sequences designed by Gerald Scarfe.
● *Waiting for Waiting for Godot* (Derek Jarman)
Film from a RADA production of Beckett's play designed by John Maybury.
● *The Snowman* (Dianne Jackson) Animated film adapted from the book by Raymond Briggs.
● *Ziggy Stardust and the Spiders from Mars* (D.A. Pennebaker) Film record of David Bowie's 1973 concert at London's Hammersmith Odeon.
● Russell Mulcahy makes a video for Duran Duran's *Is There Something I Should Know.*
● *The Pirate Tape (W.S.B. Film)* (Derek Jarman). This Super 8 film is made from footage of William Burroughs (at the Final Academy Event in September 1982).

**Other films**
*Local Hero* (Bill Forsyth)
*Gandhi* (Richard Attenborough)
*Blade Runner* (Ridley Scott, US)

**Deaths**
Alberto Cavalcanti
Ben Nicholson

### 1983

● Sankofa film workshop is started in London, and is part of the new wave of Black Cinema in Britain (members would include Isaac Julien and Maureen Blackwood).
● The Black Audio Film Collective is founded.
● The Film and Video Umbrella Touring Scheme is set up.
● *New Art* exhibition at the Tate Gallery incorporates audio-visual works by Cerith Wyn Evans, and works by Gilbert and George, Anish Kapoor, Richard Long, Cindy Sherman and others.
● *Frida Kahlo and Tina Modotti* (Laura Mulvey, Peter Wollen) Documentary about the lives and works of the painter Frida Kahlo and the photographer Tina Modotti, made in conjunction with the exhibition *Frida Kahlo and Tina Modotti* at the Whitechapel gallery.
● *Four American Composers* (Peter Greenaway). Channel 4 documentary about the composers John Cage, Robert Ashley, Philip Glass and Meredith Monk.
● Lesley Keen (animator from Glasgow) directs *Taking a Line for a Walk*, a homage to Paul Klee.
● *The Dream Machine* (John Maybury, Cerith Wyn Evans, Michael Kostiff and Derek Jarman).
● *The Gold Diggers* (Sally Potter) Rose English worked on the script and art direction.
● Julien Temple directs a video for *Come Dancing* by The Kinks, which begins with a dance along the aisles of a supermarket.
● Malcolm Morley retrospective is held at the Whitechapel Art Gallery.

**Deaths**
Anthony Blunt
Bill Brandt
Kenneth Clark
Tristram Hillier

### 1984

● September
Palace Productions' début feature *The Company of Wolves* (Neil Jordan) is released.
●The Turner Prize is founded. For the first few years the prize is awarded for the greatest contribution to art in Britain and is open to collectors, writers, curators and administrators. The first winner is Malcolm Morley.
● *British Art Show – Old Allegiances and New Directions 1979–84*, includes film works by Paul Bush, Jayne Parker and John Smith, and art works by Boyd Webb, Paula Rego and others.
● *The Hard-Won Image: Traditional Method and Subject in Recent British Art* ia held at the Tate Gallery and includes works by Francis Bacon and Lucian Freud.
● *Imagining October* (Derek Jarman). Jarman, Richard Heslop, Cerith Wyn Evans, Carl Johnson and Sally Potter work on photography for the film. Jarman centres the film on the painter John Watkiss.
● *Scenes and Songs from Boyd Webb* (Philip Haas). With photography by Wolfgang Suschitzky, this film shows the artist designing and creating eight new pieces for the film.
● First national festival of Super 8 film held in Leicester
● Derek Jarman retrospective is held at I.C.A. (paintings, installations and film screenings).

**Other films**
*A Passage to India* (David Lean)
*Making a Splash* (Peter Greenaway)
*Signs of Empire* (Black Audio Film Collective)

**Publications**
*Dancing Ledge* by Derek Jarman

**Deaths**
Thorold Dickinson
Ivor Montagu
Anne Rees Mogg
Paul Rotha

### 1985

● *Lost Magic Kingdoms and Six Paper Moons*, an exhibition by Eduardo Paolozzi is held at the Museum of Mankind, London.
● *The New Pluralism – British Film and Video*, is held at the Tate Gallery.
● *Rocks and Flesh: An Argument for British Drawing* at Norwich School of Art Gallery. Curated by Peter Fuller and drawing attention to the British Romantic tradition.
● *German Art in the 20th Century* is held at the Royal Academy. The first of a series of exhibitions surveying art in the twentieth century.
● *The Angelic Conversation* (Derek Jarman)
This multi-partite film is set in the English countryside to Shakespeare's Sonnets.
● *The Child of the Saw* (Dan Landin and Richard Heslop) Heslop graduated from Malcolm Le Grice's department at St. Martin's School of Art, and made aggressive 'scratch' films, brutally edited using imagery from war newsreels.
● Tony Hill (experimental film-maker) makes *Downside Up*, a film in which the camera revolves about an axis, moving through various scenes of British life.
● Nick Park joins Aardman Animation.
● Howard Hodgkin wins the Turner Prize.
● *Synchronisation of the Senses*, retrospective of New Romantic Super 8 film is held at the I.C.A.
● Derek Jarman film retrospective at the Edinburgh Festival.

**Other films**
*Territories* (Isaac Julien)
*Brazil* (Terry Gilliam)
*My Beautiful Laundrette* (Stephen Frears)
*A Zed and Two Noughts* (Peter Greenaway)

**Publications**
*Images of God* by Peter Fuller.

FIRST ISSUE OF 'MODERN PAINTERS'

MONA HATOUM'S 'MEASURE OF DISTANCE' (VIDEO)

# 1986

# 1987

# 1988

# 1989

# 1990

## 1986

● The Limelight club opens; its crypts are decorated with a John Maybury photo-montage of Leigh Bowery images.
● *Caravaggio* (Derek Jarman) Film about the life of the Italian painter Caravaggio with Tilda Swinton, Nigel Terry, Sean Bean and Gary Cooper

'CARAVAGGIO' (DEREK JARMAN)

● Jarman makes pop videos for The Smiths (*Ask*) Easterhouse (*1969*), Bob Geldof (*I Cry Too* and *Pouring Rain*).
● Derek Jarman is the first film-maker to be nominated for the Turner Prize, and he exhibits a series of paintings associated with *Caravaggio*. Gilbert and George win the prize.
● Stephen Johnson of Aardman Animation makes the video promo *Sledgehammer* for Peter Gabriel.
● The Quay Brothers make the animation *Street of Crocodiles*.
● Black Audio Film Collective makes the film *Handsworth Songs*.
● To celebrate the 50th anniversary of Surrealism *British Surrealism Fifty Years On* is held at the Mayor Gallery. *L'Amour Fou*, an exhibition of Surrealist photographs, is held at the Hayward Gallery.
● Damien Hirst studies at Goldsmiths' College of Art.

**Other films**
*Sid and Nancy* (Alex Cox)
*A Room With a View* (James Ivory)
*Absolute Beginners* (Julien Temple)
*Passion of Remembrance* (Isaac Julien)

**Deaths**
Henry Moore

## 1987

● Griffin Productions makes the group of films 'Painting with Light' for the B.B.C, in which artists experiment with Quantel TV Paintbox. Richard Hamilton participates.
● Philip Haas makes *Stones and Flies*, a documentary about Richard Long, following his walk through the desert.
● *The Belly of an Architect* (Peter Greenaway). Greenaway relates the confrontation between two architects in Rome, one a historical figure, the other a fictional character.
● The Arts Council and British Council touring exhibition, *The Elusive Sign: British Avant-Garde Film and Video 1977–87*, is selected by Catherine Lacey, Tamara Krikorian and Michael O'Pray.
● *British Art in the 20th Century* at the Royal Academy.
● *The Last of England* (Derek Jarman). Photography (particularly riot sections) is by Richard Heslop (graduate of St. Martin's School of Art).
● Jarman makes pop videos for The Pet Shop Boys' *It's a Sin* and *Rent*.
● *Handsworth Songs* (Black Audio Film Collective) wins the BFI John Grierson Award.
● Richard Deacon wins the Turner Prize.
● Gillian Wearing studies at Goldsmith's College (1987–90).

**Other films**
*Hope and Glory* (John Boorman)
*Maurice* (James Ivory)

**Publications**
Peter Fuller sets up the magazine *Modern Painters*, orientated towards British art.

**Deaths**
Norman McLaren
Andy Warhol (US)
Basil Wright

## 1988

● 17 July
*Eisenstein: His Life and Work* opens at the Museum of Modern Art, Oxford. The exhibition includes works by Sergei Eisenstein, and audio-visual installations. A season of Eisenstein films also runs at the N.F.T.
● The Museum of the Moving Image (M.O.M.I.) opens on London's South Bank.
● The Tate Gallery Liverpool opens, occupying part of the converted Albert Dock complex of warehouses, and designed by James Stirling, Michael Wilford and Associates.
● *Late Picasso* exhibition is held at the Tate Gallery. A reassessment of Picasso's violent and sexually explicit late works (1953–72), it includes those works based on the paintings of Manet and Velazquez.
● *The Essential Black Art* is held at the Chisenhale Gallery. The exhibition, organised by Rasheed Aareen later goes on tour.
● Damien Hirst organises *Freeze*, an exhibition of work by fellow Goldsmith graduates Ian Davenport, Gary Hume, Sarah Lucas, Simon Patterson, and Fiona Rae. The exhibition is held in a docklands warehouse and accompanied by a sponsored catalogue.
● Ridley Scott directs *The Lock*, an advertisement for Löwenbrau.
● Tony Cragg wins the Turner Prize.

**Other films**
*Drowning by Numbers* (Peter Greenaway)
*Distant Voices Still Lives* (Terence Davies)
*Guilt* (Peter Gidal)

**Publications**
*Materialist Film* by Peter Gidal.

**Deaths**
Emeric Pressburger

## 1989

● 29 November
*The Other Story*, an exhibition of the work of Afro-Asian artists in post-war Britain, is held at the Hayward Gallery (later touring to Wolverhampton and Manchester). It includes works by Frank Bowling, Francis Newton Souza, Mona Hatoum and others.
● The Hayward Gallery holds a retrospective of the works of Andy Warhol.
● *The Brooch Pin and the Sinful Clasp* (Joanna Woodward) Animated film featuring the performance artist Rose English.
● *Italian Art in the 20th Century* is held at the Royal Academy, London.
● Nam June Paik exhibition is held at the Hayward Gallery.
● *The Cook The Thief His Wife & Her Lover* (Peter Greenaway) Costumes designed by Jean-Paul Gaultier
● *Serpent River* (Sandra Lahire) Lis Rhodes is ssistant editor on this film (produced by the Arts Council and Channel 4 and distributed by Circles).
● *The Art of Photography* exhibition is held at The Royal Academy, London.
● Tony Kaye directs *Relax*, a television advertisement for British Rail and the Quay Brothers direct *Mr & Mrs Crisp* for K.P. Skips.
● Richard Long wins the Turner Prize.

**Other films**
*War Requiem* (Derek Jarman)
*Henry V* (Kenneth Branagh)
*Looking for Langston* (Isaac Julien)

**Deaths**
Laurence Olivier

## 1990

● May
Jay Jopling opens a project room for contempoary art on the 1st floor of 44 Duke St., London. This later becomes known as the White Cube Gallery, and its first exhibition is of work by Itai Doron. The space is refurbished by the minimalist architect Claudio Silvestrin.
● Tilda Swinton curates the first I.C.A. Biennial of Independent Film and Video.
● Anish Kapoor is selected to represent Britain at the Venice Biennale.
● *Signs of the Times*, a video and film installation exhibition at the Museum of Modern Art, Oxford, curated by Chrissie Iles and including works by Judith Goddard, Paul Bush, David Hall and Susan Hiller.
● Tony Kaye directs *God Bless The Child*, an advert for Volkswagen cars.
● Steve McQueen at Goldsmiths' College, with Jane and Louise Wilson.
● John Maybury makes the music video for Sinead O'Connor's *You Do Something to Me*.
● Damien Hirst curates the warehouse exhibition *Modern Medicine*.

**Other films**
*The Garden* (Derek Jarman)
*Strapless* (David Hare)

**Deaths**
Peter Fuller
Angus McBean
Michael Powell

BBC 2 IDENT BY THE BROTHERS QUAY

# 1991

● September
A season of Derek Jarman films is screened at the National Film Theatre.
● *Pop Art: An International Perspective* is held at the Royal Academy and includes works by Andy Warhol, Roy Lichenstein, Allen Jones, Richard Hamilton and others.
● *Garden of Earthly Delights* (Judith Goddard)
A video version of Bosch's paintings which turns the 90s into a nightmarish world of monstrous creatures. Made using high-tech computer animation effect and live footage, the work takes the form of a triptych installation.
● After having been suspended for a year, the Turner Prize is reinstated. Anish Kapoor wins the prize.
● The first issue of *Frieze*, a magazine of contemporary art and culture, is published. It is founded and co-edited by Matthew Slotover, Thomas Gridley and Amanda Sharp.
● Nick Park wins an Academy Award for his plasticine animation *Creature Comforts*.
● *The Physical Self*, Peter Greenaway exhibition (installation) is held at Boymans van Beuningen museum, Rotterdam.

### Other films
*Edward II* (Derek Jarman)
*Prospero's Books* (Peter Greenaway)
*Young Soul Rebels* (Isaac Julien)
*Thelma & Louise* (Ridley Scott, US)

### Deaths
Joy Batchelor
Bill Douglas
David Lean
Tony Richardson

# 1992

● June
*Film and the Visual Arts*, a short season of films commissioned by the Program for Art on Film's Production Laboratory (USA), includes films by Philip Haas, The Brothers Quay and Ken McMullen. It is held at the N.F.T.
● 20 November
*Sister Wendy's Odyssey*, a series of ten minute art appreciation programmes, begins on B.B.C.2.
● 18 Sept
An international conference on New Queer Cinema begins at the I.C.A.
● Second I.C.A. Biennial of Independent Film and Video, curated by Peter Wollen.
● Grenville Davey wins the Turner Prize.

### Other films
*Orlando* (Sally Potter)
*Peter's Friends* (Kenneth Branagh)
*The Long Day Closes* (Terence Davies)
*Basic Instinct* (Paul Verhoeven, US)
*The Player* (Robert Altman, US)

### Deaths
Francis Bacon

# 1993

● The Tate Gallery St. Ives opens. Designed by Eldred Evans and David Shalev, it displays works by artists associated with St. Ives.
● *Gravity and Grace: The Changing Condition of Sculpture 1965–75* at the Hayward Gallery. An exhibition including sculptural work by Joseph Beuys, Marcel Broodthaers, Barry Flanagan, Richard Long, Bruce Nauman and others.
● Rachel Whiteread wins the Turner Prize. The K Foundation advertise on television during the broadcast of the ceremony, and award an alternative prize to Whiteread as the worst artist.
● *Some Organising Principles*, Greenaway exhibition (installation) at the Glynn Vivian Gallery, Swansea.
● *The Audience of Mâcon*, Greenaway exhibition at the Ffoto Gallery, Cardiff.
● *Blue* (Derek Jarman) Monochromatic film influenced by the work of Yves Klein. A blue screen is accompanied by a lyrical soundtrack.
● *The Wrong Trousers* (Nick Park) Oscar-winning animation.

### Other films
*Wittgenstein* (Derek Jarman)
*The Baby of Mâcon* (Peter Greenaway)
*Much Ado About Nothing* (Kenneth Branagh)
*Bhaji on the Beach* (Gurinder Chadha)

### Deaths
Elisabeth Frink

# 1994

● Video works by Willie Doherty are nominated for the Turner Prize. Anthony Gormley wins the prize.
● R.B. Kitaj retrospective is held at the Tate Gallery. The Arts Council/*Sight and Sound* 'Art into Film' project is linked with it.
● *Some Went Mad, Some Ran Away* is held at the Serpentine Gallery. An exhibition curated by Damien Hirst, with works by 25 international artists including Hirst, Ashley Bickerton, Abigail Lane and Kiki Smith. Hirst's own work *Away From the Flock* is vandalised during the exhibition (ink is poured into the tank containing a sheep).
● *Picasso: Sculptor/Painter* exhibition is held at the Tate Gallery.
● *American Art in the Twentieth Century* is held at the Royal Academy.
● 3rd I.C.A. Biennial of Film and Video is curated by John Wyver. It includes a screening of films by the Themersons.
● *Designs of the Times: Thirty Years of British Art Direction*, season of films at the NFT including *The French Lieutenant's Woman*, *The Man Who Fell to Earth* and *Dr. Strangelove*.
● Vivienne Westwood designs the Cort Romney collection for the film *Prêt-à-Porter* (Robert Altman, US).

### Other films
*Pulp Fiction* (Quentin Tarantino, US)
*Four Weddings and a Funeral* (Mike Newell)
*Shallow Grave* (Danny Boyle)
*Carrington* (Christopher Hampton)

### Deaths
Lindsay Anderson
Leigh Bowery
Peter Cushing
Derek Jarman

# 1995

● 2 May
The 'Art Now' room is set up at the Tate Gallery, to display and promote contemporary art.
● June
The *Rites of Passage* exhibition at the Tate Gallery, includes video work by Susan Hiller, Bill Viola and Mona Hatoum.
● 12 November
*The British Art Show 4*, a touring exhibition, opens in Manchester. It includes video works by Douglas Gordon, Georgina Starr, Mark Wallinger, Jane and Louise Wilson and Gillian Wearing, and film works by Tacita Dean, Ceal Foyer and Steve McQueen.
● *Minky Manky* is held at the South London Gallery.
● *Mirage: Enigmas of Race, Difference and Desire I*, is held at the I.C.A. It includes films, performances and an exhibition which charts the influence on black artists of Frantz Fanon. The exhibition features a film work by Steve McQueen, *Five Easy Pieces*.
● The *Africa 95* season includes the exhibitions *Seven Stories of Modern Art in Africa* at the Whitechapel Gallery and *Africa: The Art of a Continent* at the R.A. The N.F.T. screens a season of films entitled *Screen Griots*.
● Damien Hirst makes the pop video for Blur's single, *Country House*.
● Tilda Swinton becomes a living art work, lying in a glass case in *The Maybe* at the Serpentine Gallery.
● Bruce McLean makes *Urban Turban: A Moving Picture*, a three-screen film.
● Damien Hirst wins the Turner Prize, exhibiting *Mother and Child*.
● Tony Hill makes the advert *Arc* for Natwest, based on his earlier experimental film *Downside Up* (1985).

### Other films
*Institute Benjamenta* (Brothers Quay)

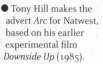

VIVIENNE WESTWOOD'S FALL/WINTER 1995–96 COLLECTION, 'LES FEMMES': WESTWOOD DESIGNED COSTUMES FOR 'PRET-A-PORTER' (ROBERT ALTMAN)

WCAD Library

100101730